CORPORATE SOCIAL RESPONSIBILITY AND ALCOHOL

INTERNATIONAL CENTER FOR ALCOHOL POLICIES

Series on Alcohol in Society

CORPORATE
SOCIAL RESPONSIBILITY
AND ALCOHOL
THE NEED AND POTENTIAL FOR PARTNERSHIP

EDITED BY

MARCUS GRANT
and
JOYCE O'CONNOR

Routledge
Taylor & Francis Group

NEW YORK AND HOVE

Published in 2005 by
Routledge
Taylor & Francis Group
270 Madison Avenue
New York, NY 10016

Published in Great Britain by
Routledge
Taylor & Francis Group
27 Church Road
Hove, East Sussex BN3 2FA

Printed in the United States of America on acid-free paper
10 9 8 7 6 5 4 3 2 1

International Standard Book Number-10: 0-415-94948-3 (Hardcover)
International Standard Book Number-13: 978-0-415-94948-4 (Hardcover)
Library of Congress Card Number 2004023793

Library of Congress Cataloging-in-Publication Data

Corporate social responsibility and alcohol : the need and potential for partnership / edited by Marcus Grant and Joyce O'Connor.
    p. cm. -- (ICAP series on alcohol in society)
    Includes presentations delivered at a conference held in Oct. 2002 in Dublin, Ireland.
    Includes bibliographical references and index.
    ISBN 0-415-94948-3 (hardback)
    1. Social responsibility of business--Congresses. 2. Alcoholism--Congresses. 3. Alcoholic beverage industry--Congresses. I. Grant, Marcus. II. O'Connor, Joyce. III. Title. IV. Series on alcohol in society.

HD60.C692 2005
663'.1'0684--dc22
    2004023793

Taylor & Francis Group
is the Academic Division of T&F Informa plc.

Visit the Taylor & Francis Web site at
http://www.taylorandfrancis.com

and the Routledge Web site at
http://www.routledge-ny.com

Contents

Editors

Marcus Grant is president of the International Center for Alcohol Policies (ICAP), a not-for-profit international organization funded by 10 international beverage alcohol companies. ICAP's mission is to promote understanding of the role of alcohol in society, to help reduce the abuse of alcohol worldwide, and to encourage dialogue and pursue partnerships with the alcoholic beverage industry, the public health community, and others interested in alcohol policy. He served as the director of the Alcohol Education Center, London, where he was responsible for the national coordination of postqualification training on alcohol problems for health and social service staff. During this period, he also served as chairman of the Alcohol Education Section of the International Council on Alcohol and Addictions and honorary tutor in education at the Institute of Psychiatry, University of London. He joined the headquarters staff of the World Health Organization in Geneva in 1984, where he was responsible for global activities on the prevention of alcohol and drug abuse in the Division of Mental Health. He was appointed chief of Prevention, Advocacy and Health Promotion within the Global Program on Substance Abuse, which was established in 1990. He has published extensively on alcohol education and training, on prevention, and on social policy.

Joyce O'Connor is president of the National College of Ireland. She is chair of the Further Education and Training Awards Council (FETAC) and a member of the National Qualifications Authority of Ireland. She also chairs Dublin Inner City Partnership, is a council member of the Dublin Chamber of Commerce, and executive director of the Cement Roadstone Holdings PLC. She has served as the Irish representative to the World Health Organization and chaired the WHO expert committee on Alcohol and the Workplace. Professor O'Connor is an Eisenhower Fellow. She has published widely and has received a number of prestigious awards, including recognition by the International Institute for Alcohol and Addiction for her research on drinking behavior.

Contributors

Adrian Botha
SABMiller, plc
London, UK

Chris Britton
Diageo, plc
London, UK

Hugh Burkitt
Burkitt DDB
London, UK

Peter H. Coors
Coors Brewing Company
Golden, Colorado, USA

Peter Cressy
The Distilled Spirits Council of the
    United States
Washington, DC, USA

Monica Gourovitch
The Distilled Spirits Council of the
    United States
Washington, DC, USA

Marcus Grant
International Center for Alcohol
    Policies
Washington, DC, USA

Hurst Hannum
Tufts University
Medford, Massachusetts, USA

Eleni Houghton
Consultant
Pittsburgh, Pennsylvania, USA

David Logan
The Corporate Citizenship Company
London, UK

Meg Mackenzie
Alcohol Advisory Council of
    New Zealand
Wellington, New Zealand

Mike MacAvoy
Alcohol Advisory Council of
    New Zealand
Wellington, New Zealand

Marjana Martinic
International Center for Alcohol
    Policies
Washington, DC, USA

Joyce O'Connor
National College of Ireland
Dublin, Ireland

John Orley
Consultant
Guernsey, Channel
  Islands

Gaye Pedlow
Diageo, plc
London, UK

Stanton Peele
Psychologist and
  Consultant
Morristown, New Jersey, USA

Leanne Riley
World Health Organization
Geneva, Switzerland

Ann Roche
National Centre for Education and
  Training on Addiction
Adelaide, South Australia, Australia

Daniya Tamendarova
International Center for Alcohol
  Policies
Washington, DC, USA

Acknowledgments

The editors wish to acknowledge the participation of all the presenters at the Alcohol, Ethics and Society international conference on rights and responsibilities held in Dublin in October 2002. The National College of Ireland (NCI), as host of the conference, and the staffs at NCI's Centre for Corporate Responsibility and the International Center for Alcohol Policies are to be thanked for their significant efforts that led to the success of the conference and the realization of this volume.

Many of the conference presentations are included in this volume in a form that reflects its focus on corporate social responsibility (CSR). Other material was commissioned afterward to complement the conference discussions. John Orley merits specific recognition for his valuable contribution, which provides a framework of CSR and role for public-private partnerships, especially as these relate to the beverage alcohol industry. David Thompson, Daniya Tamendarova, and Brett Bivans provided indispensable editorial assistance, which effectively brought together these several sources in a coherent volume. Our heartfelt thanks to them as well as Gaye Pedlow, Barton Alexander, and Sietze Montijn, who helped guide this process.

DISCLAIMER

Chapter 1

Introduction

Marcus Grant and Joyce O'Connor

Corporate Social Responsibility and Alcohol: The Need and Potential for Partnership is the eighth book in the ICAP Series on Alcohol in Society. It advances the debate on the rights and responsibilities of those involved in developing alcohol policies by exploring the relationship between alcohol, ethics, and corporate social responsibility (CSR).

In October 2002 in Dublin, the National College of Ireland (NCI) and the International Center for Alcohol Policies (ICAP)[1] held an international conference on "Alcohol, Ethics and Society." It consisted of three thematically separate but linked sessions, addressing Government Regulation, Industry Self-Regulation and Personal Pleasure; Research and Education; and Advertising, Marketing and Sales; there were also opening and closing plenary sessions. Much of the work at the conference took place in multidisciplinary discussion groups. The conference coincided with the opening of the Centre for Corporate Responsibility within the National College of Ireland, which is located at the International Financial Services Centre in Dublin.

This volume on corporate social responsibility draws on and expands some of the presentations made during the Dublin conference. The summaries of

---

[1] ICAP is dedicated to promoting the understanding of the role of alcohol in society through dialogue and partnerships involving the beverage alcohol industry, the public health community, and others interested in alcohol policy, and to helping to reduce the abuse of alcohol worldwide. ICAP is a not-for-profit organization supported by 10 major international beverage alcohol companies. This book was commissioned by ICAP. For more information on ICAP and its Cooperation Guidelines, visit www.icap.org.

all the presentations made in Dublin are available on the ICAP website (www.icap.org). The views expressed in this book and in the papers on the website are those of the authors alone and do not necessarily reflect the position of NCI, ICAP, or its sponsors. As is clear from these papers, the debates that took place in Dublin in October 2002 were lively and wide ranging. It was, indeed, the quality of the debates that led us to the conclusion that we should use the conference as a stimulus to create the current volume, rather than taking the more conventional route of using the volume to report on the conference.

At least a third of the material included in this volume was commissioned after the conference, and many of the papers included were significantly rewritten to reflect our focus on the theme of corporate social responsibility. We are convinced that the time is right for a volume that addresses both CSR in general and, more specifically, its relationship to alcohol policy and the place of alcohol in society.

This volume also focuses on the need and potential for partnerships, both as part of an overall CSR strategy and specifically in relation to alcohol. It includes a 5-year report on CSR activities by ICAP sponsor companies following the ICAP Framework for Responsibility (originally published in the ICAP publication *Alcohol and Emerging Markets: Patterns, Problems and Responses*; see Pedlow, 1998). The framework is a simple guideline for beverage alcohol companies on how to give appropriate attention to social and health issues when conducting their business in developing countries and emerging markets. The reporting on the period 1999–2003 (see chapter 16) assesses the progress of industry efforts against these guidelines, including areas of CSR activities that are not related to alcohol.

The issue of corporate social responsibility is a complex theme for any industry, especially so for the beverage alcohol industry. The chapters that follow examine the strengths and weaknesses of CSR and seek to define ways in which an industry that produces a product such as alcohol beverages (having the potential for good and for harm) can learn from the lessons of other industries.

ICAP certainly acknowledges that CSR does not represent a universal panacea for the ills of society, including corporate excesses and alcohol abuse. Many critics, for instance, take the view that CSR amounts to little more than better public relations. They hold that a company that has a poor track record, for example in the environmental area, can publish a new mission statement, adopt a new slogan, or commission a new advertising campaign. The result may be a new, greener image that may be quite satisfactory to shareholders for a time. That image may well be sustained until the next environmental incident. But by then the real damage to the reputation of the company will only be deepened by the shallow nature of its commitment in the first place.

Corporate social responsibility is about values and putting values into practice. It represents a serious and sustained commitment by a company to behave as a good corporate citizen and to demonstrate the requisite good behavior across the widest possible range of corporate operations, including environmental, human rights, and employment issues. The first key phrase arising from the definition of CSR is *operational change*. This volume is conceived on the assumption that CSR is seen by corporations as a positive social force.

A company that outlines a new set of values for itself, but does nothing about applying those values in daily practice, is not engaged in corporate social responsibility. CSR involves making a real commitment to putting values into practice. And where do those values come from? Operational values involve a lot of soul-searching for many organizations. They also involve a commitment from both corporate shareholders and stakeholders, including government, regulators, employees, suppliers, advocacy groups, and consumers. Most corporations that embark on the CSR process do so believing that it is necessary and that it makes economic sense. The corresponding values are then integrated into the core business strategy.

When it recognizes that its customers have a legitimate stake in the behavior of the company and that it is under scrutiny, business—and especially global business—has to adapt to the awareness that its customers are increasingly demanding responsibility.

In all cases where meaningful change has been the result, dialogue and interaction have been part of the process. The most significant interaction a company may undertake in this process is with its critics. The process of voluntary change resulting from such interaction often involves painful realizations, and an openness to respond is critical.

This volume examines the case for the beverage alcohol industry to recognize a significant need and potential for corporate social responsibility in the industry. The key influences on the relationship between alcohol and society, and particularly on how young people learn to use alcohol, include ethnic and cultural influences, parental influences, peer group influences, and social and personal influences. Some of these influences are stronger than others, but they all interact—there is no single factor that can be said to be dominant in the development of drinking patterns. For that reason, it is clear that no single prescription can be offered to society—any society—on how to address the harms associated with alcohol abuse and to find ways to promote the right role for alcohol in that society.

None of this suggests that the challenges in relation to alcohol are insurmountable. On the contrary, a responsible industry has an important role to play in facing the challenge of a society marked by its product. Rather than an approach that assigns blame to the consumption of alcohol, it is surely possible to move the debate forward through partnerships. This requires that the parties respect one another's positions, believe in one another's integrity, and show a duty of care so that, in working through the issues, an honesty and directness will emerge. Here perhaps—in keeping with the volume's subtitle—is where the *need and potential for partnership* will be most evident.

REFERENCE

Pedlow, G. (1998). Alcohol in emerging markets: Identifying the most appropriate role for the alcohol beverage industry. In M. Grant (Ed.), *Alcohol and emerging markets: Patterns, problems, and responses* (pp. 333–351). Philadelphia, PA: Brunner/Mazel.

Chapter 2

Corporate Social Responsibility and Corporate Citizenship: Definitions, History, and Issues

David Logan and Joyce O'Connor

INTRODUCTION

Corporate social responsibility (CSR) and corporate citizenship are terms describing corporate activities beyond profit-making, but the terms are being increasingly used to describe the role of business in society. They can include such topics as being ethical in trading and encouraging the safe use and disposal of products. CSR involves a broad commitment by companies to social welfare and the common good and to the policies that support them. It involves not just the products that a company manufactures, but also being a good corporate citizen in terms of the employees that it hires and the way it looks after them. It is also about protecting the environment and getting involved in the local community and the wider culture in which the company engages in business.

There are three key components:

- the basic values, ethics, policies, and practices of a company's business;
- the voluntary contributions made by a company to community development;
- the management of environmental and social issues within the value chain by the company and its business partners, from the acquisition and production of raw materials, through the welfare of staff, to product sale, use, or disposal.

These three areas will be dealt with in this volume, largely focusing on the third. Within that third area, particular attention will be paid to the beverage alcohol industry and within that again to the issue of responsible marketing, including advertising and promotional strategies.

Recent changes in the socioeconomic and political climate are creating growing expectations that corporations will behave responsibly. The driving forces behind these changes are wide-ranging, from consumers, governments, and employees to civil society organizations and investors. In recent years, the antiglobalization movement has grown stronger and more effective. As part of a broader process of globalization, companies are being called upon to adopt higher standards of governance and accountability and accept greater responsibility for the communities in which they operate and in the wider world. Businesses are perceived to be benefiting from and perpetuating the low labor and environmental standards that are prevalent in developing countries. The civil society movement, grouping different nongovernmental organizations (NGOs) from all over the world, made itself apparent at the demonstrations against the World Trade Organization (WTO) Seattle Round in 1999 and has continued to make itself felt. Among other things, it is asking corporations for more transparency and accountability. Media organizations are also taking an interest in these issues, often seeking to expose instances of perceived corporate malpractice.

Furthermore, national governments are encouraging corporations to embrace their wider responsibilities to society. In Denmark, for example, the minister for social affairs launched a campaign in 1994 titled "Our Common Concern: The Social Responsibility of the Corporate Sector." This was an initiative inspired and animated by the notion that social welfare is not solely the concern of the public sector, but also a task for business and the citizen, both in the workplace and in the local community. In 1998, the ministry was instrumental in setting up the Copenhagen Centre, which promotes public and private partnerships (Copenhagen Centre, 1998). In the United Kingdom, a minister for corporate social responsibility was appointed in March 2000 within the Department of Trade and Industry. An interdepartmental group has been established to improve coordination of activities to promote CSR across the whole government (Department of Trade and Industry, 2001). In the Netherlands, social responsibility is high on the political agenda. In 2000, the official governmental advisory body on social and economic policy published its advice to the cabinet on strategies for CSR.

From another direction, some investors are now expressing concern about where and how their money is used. Socially responsible investment (SRI) has recently experienced a surge in popularity among mainstream investors. According to the Social Investment Forum (SIF), a U.S. national nonprofit organization promoting the integration of social responsibility with investment, more than $1 out of every $9 under management in the United States is now invested in ethically screened funds (Social Investment Forum, 2003). In Europe, a recent survey by an Italian think tank, Avanzi, indicated that on June 30, 2003, there were 313 green, social, and ethical funds operating. This was a 12% increase over 18 months (since the end of 2001) and a 97% increase since the end of 1999 (Bartolomeo, Daga, Familiari, Hinderer, & Bennett, 2003).

A recent paper by Stewart Lewis (2003), managing director of Market and Opinion Research International (MORI) polling company, pointed out that 80% of the public tend to believe that large companies have a moral responsibility to society and that this tendency has been increasing. The extent of the trend is clear from a question MORI has asked consumers for a number of years: In their behavior and decisions as consumers, how important is the social responsibility of the company whose products and services are being offered? The proportion of consumers who say it is *very* important to them nearly doubled in the period 1998–2002. The majority of the public, however, also believes that large companies "don't really care" about the long-term environmental and social impact of their actions. In other words, the public feels a dissonance with business. In its perception, big business lacks interest in exactly those issues of increasing interest and priority to the public (Lewis, 2003).

In another poll, conducted on behalf of CSR Europe in September 2000, MORI interviewed 12,000 consumers in 12 European countries on their attitudes toward the role of businesses in today's society. Seventy percent of European consumers said that a company's commitment to social responsibility is important when buying a product or service, and one in five would be very willing to pay more for products that are socially and environmentally responsible. The poll found that the majority of European citizens believe that industry and commerce do not pay enough attention to their responsibilities. Agreement with this proposition was found to be highest (over 70%) in Finland and Great Britain. With globalization, the boundaries of power and influence in society of both business and government are shifting, expanding, and coming closer together. This is reflected in the public's view: according to MORI, "The responsibility for addressing social issues lies increasingly with large companies, as well as the government." Two thirds of European citizens subscribe to this view, with greatest support in Switzerland, Spain, and the Netherlands, where more than 80% of consumers agreed (Market and Opinion Research International/CSR Europe, 2000).

HISTORICAL PERSPECTIVE

Although there are no universally agreed-upon definitions of the terms "corporate citizenship" and "corporate social responsibility," the historical meaning, now seen as somewhat restricting but still very current in the United

States, refers to the voluntary philanthropic contributions that businesses make over and above their mainstream activities. As large industrial corporations developed in the 19th century, many of their owners assumed an active and, indeed, a leading role in the development of the local communities and society where they were based. Business leaders helped get schools and universities built and made financial contributions over and above their taxes to support infrastructure projects, museums, sports, and recreation facilities. Great cities like Manchester, Bombay, New York, and Sydney were given many of their public assets such as libraries and concert halls by the business leaders of the time. These business leaders—such as Carnegie, Rockefeller, and Wellcome—went on to endow great foundations to carry on the community work that they saw as their "social responsibility" or good citizenship.

This tradition seems to have been based on two complementary motives. First, the ethical imperative—often articulated by religious groups—was that those who have wealth and power should help those who do not, and so charitable giving was expected of wealthy industrialists. Second, there was an element of social investment in which businesses would gain long-term benefits from having first-class schools, technical institutes, and universities in their cities. U.S. business schools, for example, were often started by business leaders and still receive extensive support from companies.

However, these wider contributions to 19th-century society did not dispel a deep dissatisfaction with capitalism on the part of workers and others. Some of the early exercises in corporate power, coupled with the excesses of laissez-faire capitalism in the industrial revolution, with its mass dislocation of people to squalid cities, provoked the rise of communism and socialism. There were moves to abolish the combination of the economic power and charity of rich capitalists and replace it with public ownership of the means of production and a rational system of entitlements and social services managed by the state. From 1917 onward, in both the developed and developing world, this approach sought to bring private economic power under the control of the state

With the exception of the United States, governments worldwide came to dominate social provision in developed and developing countries alike. Business paid its taxes, while national and local governments provided the services and took care of social and cultural affairs. The 19th-century tradition, however, did not completely disappear in the developed countries with the advent of large welfare states. In recent years, George Soros, Ted Turner, and Bill Gates in the United States organized their personal philanthropies like earlier generations of business leaders. Even in the 1950s and 1960s, companies in the United States, Europe, and beyond continued to make charitable gifts, but the word "social" more or less dropped out of the discussion of corporate responsibility because of the role of the state in the provision of education and welfare. Corporate responsibility became focused on issues much more internal to the management of the business, such as how a company treated its employees and customers. Consumer power, emerging in the 1950s, grew to be a force to shape corporate behavior, as did environmental concerns in the 1970s and beyond. The various degrees of state control over economic, social, and cultural life have, meanwhile, been found wanting. Global society began the movement back to giving private enterprise a greater role, not only in the economic, but also in social and cultural spheres. The definition of corporate citizenship, going beyond charitable contributions, was becoming established.

The 1980s then saw the ending of the post-World War II consensus about the dominant role of the state in Western society, with an expansion of the role of the market and a cutting back in the role of the state. Subsequently, the command economies in Russia and China collapsed, and the protectionist and socialist policies of many governments in the developing countries soon followed suit. Some 3 billion people have thus recently made the transition from command and state-controlled to market economies, which has opened vast new markets and bases of production for the rest of the world. Private investment has flooded into developing countries, and whereas it accounted for less than half of the resource inflow into developing countries in 1990, this proportion had risen to 88% by 1997 (World Bank Group, 1999). Private firms gained the benefits of much greater commercial freedom at home, while at the same time critical global trends were developing and opening up vast new opportunities for these reinvigorated private companies of the United States, Western Europe, Asia, and the rest of the world.

These factors have all led to a significant transfer of power to the private business sector and a relative decline in the power of government. Many of the world's multinational companies are now much larger in terms of revenue and the estimated job-dependent population than most small countries (see Table 2.1). Private business has thus moved into the vacuum created by the contraction of the state and plays a major role in all aspects of our global economy, society, and culture. The market economy is, with very few exceptions, increasingly at the heart of our global society, and the debate about corporate citizenship and social responsibility is about the type of behavior the world wants from its global, national, and local companies. It is a debate of great importance to the future of all countries, rich and poor alike; each in different ways is affected by the gathering trend toward global economic integration.

Leading companies themselves are tending to prefer the term "citizenship" because of its implied balance between rights and responsibilities. NGOs, the media, and religious groups on the other hand tend to stress "corporate responsibilities" and want to expand the scope of those responsibilities. They are still suspicious of the power of business but are increasingly recognizing its important role in shaping our global society and its great potential as a partner in addressing social and other issues.

TABLE 2.1. Countries and Multinational Companies Compared

Countries	GDP (billion $US)*	Population (millions)	Companies	Annual revenues (billion $US)*	Direct employees	Population dependent (millions)**
Denmark	156	5.2	General Motors	168	647,000	9.7
Hong Kong	142	6	Ford	146	371,702	5.5
South Africa	131	42	Toyota	108	130,736	2.4
Malaysia	80	20	Hitachi	75	330,152	4.9
Pakistan	60	136	Siemens	63	379,000	5.6
New Zealand	n/a	5	Philips	41	262,500	3.9
Ireland	53	3.5	PepsiCo	31	486,000	7.2
Bangladesh	29	118	Pemex	28	120,945	1.8
Sri Lanka	13	18	McDonald's	11	237,000	3.5

Sources: Logan, 1998. GDP and population figures from World in Figures 1998 (The Economist, 1998); company revenues and employees from Fortune Global 500: The world's largest corporations (1997).

*GDP and annual revenues are not directly comparable in a technical sense; corporate value added would be a more accurate figure but is rarely available, yet the comparison helps make a general point about the relative size of major companies and smaller countries.

**"Dependent population" is an estimate, calculated by including, in addition to direct employees, three supplier jobs in the company's backward linkages; one supplier job in the forward linkages, and the assumption that all these workers in the supply chain have a spouse and two children.

RESPONSIBLE BUSINESS PRACTICE

The capitalist position is that companies benefit society by just going about their everyday business. If they do nothing more than just pursue this honestly, then they are fulfilling much of their corporate social responsibility. It is the everyday activity of business that has a profound social impact, rather than any relatively small voluntary community contributions that it may make, however valuable these may be. The real power of a business to affect society lies in the vast amounts of money turning over in its revenues and expenditure and not in its philanthropic giving.

The realization of this connection between the everyday activity of companies and the well-being of society is driving a new, more comprehensive approach to corporate citizenship and places a new emphasis on the need for businesses to operate ethically. Companies are society's great wealth creators.

They collect and pay huge sums in taxes, making government possible. They also create jobs, train employees, provide health care for workers and their families, transfer technology around the world, and produce a vast array of goods and services that enhance and even save people's lives. As Vijay Mallya (2002) pointed out to the Conference on Alcohol, Ethics, and Society, held in Dublin in October 2002, 65% of the price of every bottle of alcohol that is sold in India represents government revenue. Next to sales tax, it is the highest revenue earner for state governments (India operates a federal system in which each state has its own government raising its own taxation).

Alcohol prohibition, it must be noted, is a popular policy with significant sections of the Indian population and thus forms part of the platform for many state politicians. The chief minister of the Indian state Andhra Pradesh introduced prohibition, which had been part of his political platform, but soon had to repeal it because it drove the state to bankruptcy. In fact, Andhra Pradesh has introduced prohibition four times since independence in 1947, and all four times it has been repealed. Governments, therefore, need to be mindful of their symbiotic relationship with companies, recognizing that they should be treated fairly and as partners. Companies, on the other hand, have to recognize that with their enormous influence and power comes the responsibility to conduct business ethically for the sake of the societies in which they operate.

It is an accepted fact in the world of business that the primary obligation of large profit-driven companies is to their shareholders. Nevertheless, those companies also have obligations to their employees, customers, suppliers, and the community: "Loyalty is half of business ethics, but social responsibility is the other half" (Solomon, 1994, p. 71). The idea that the measure of the overall performance of a company should be based on its combined contribution to economic prosperity, environmental quality, and social capital has come to be called "the triple bottom line." Companies, therefore, should be deemed to be accountable for their actions, not just formally to their owners but also in less well-defined ways to a much wider group of stakeholders. This view has become central to the management of corporate citizenship and social responsibility issues. Businesses need to act honestly and ethically with regard to their internal management and auditing, but corporate social responsibility also requires them to focus on their wider responsibilities.

THE RIGHTS AND RESPONSIBILITIES OF CORPORATIONS AND THE ROLE OF DIRECTORS

The traditional assumption is that shareholders are out to maximize their financial returns from their holdings, and the directors of a company, being the agents of the shareholders, should do their utmost to maximize those returns.

Indeed, directors have been in the position where they could be sued by shareholders if they pursued other objectives for the company. There is, however, a trend in some jurisdictions to allow directors to consider the interest of other stakeholders (e.g., workers, customers, suppliers) in their decision making. One might indeed ask whether it is wise for society to create and perpetuate organizations whose only responsibility is to maximize shareholder value. Corporations have been given rights (similar to individual rights) such as the ownership of property (including patents, copyrights, and brand names), and these rights have been defined through the historical development of conventions and laws, usually within a democratic political process. Corporations are, however, social artifacts, and the modern market economy is played out according to certain socially constructed rules and laws. Within that framework, society imposes responsibilities on corporations—they must, after all, operate safe workplaces, uphold the quality of their products, control pollution, and so forth.

There might be those who argue that other things in life matter besides economic efficiency, and that some efficiency loss might be acceptable to pay for a more equitable society with a somewhat better quality of life for many, rather than maximizing these benefits for a few. However, this might not be a position that the majority of shareholders in a company would be prepared to endorse, and it would be better to use an economic argument to persuade them to sacrifice some immediate profit for the possibility of some improved long-term returns. The conventional argument for the maximization of shareholder value as the prime company objective comes from the idea that competition maximizes efficiency and there can be a general economic equilibrium in the presence of perfect competition. Imposing social responsibility on corporations will lead them away from profit maximization, which in turn undermines economic efficiency and the benefits of a free market. Yet the real world is far from being a perfectly competitive economy (for example, patents create temporary monopolistic situations, albeit for the ultimate good of society). Some balance is required between allowing complete freedom for corporations and placing controls on them. The benefits of freedom are great, but the costs to society can also be great. Corporations therefore need to exercise social responsibility; shareholders are more likely to agree to this if such responsibility can be seen to add value to the companies' shares. The trend now is to provide a framework that fosters CSR and favors economic benefits from CSR activities. This goes with the knowledge that some degree of coercion is possible (providing it does not distort the market excessively), knowing that corporations thrive because the state provides them with certain beneficial rights to which they must respond by fulfilling certain responsibilities (Roberts, Breitenstein, & Roberts, 2000).

There are those who argue that corporations, by their very nature, can only operate to increase the returns on shares and are virtually incapable of exercising responsibility where this might decrease returns. It has to be borne in mind that the maximization of returns on shares is not the only efficient way of running an economy—many other factors are involved. There will always of course be some tension between the maximization of profit and the fulfillment of social responsibilities, but both regulatory and social pressure, coupled with dialogue and partnership, can lead to a situation where all parties can feel satisfied with the outcome.

VOLUNTARY CONTRIBUTIONS TO SOCIETY

Philanthropic giving to the surrounding communities is one of the ways in which businesses can respond to their wider responsibilities. The giving is often toward activities that are directly related to the commercial activities of the company, or to the benefit of the society in which the employees live and work. In some cases this is because the contribution includes "in-kind" services using the expertise that is available within the company or products that it can supply free or at cost. However, there are also companies that give to causes they deem worthy but are outside their fields.

One aspect of corporate social responsibility, thus, is the voluntary contributions that companies make to the community. Companies are expected to play a role as good citizens in making a contribution to the maintenance of the fabric of society that sustains the framework of law and civilization within which they do business. It is in this arena that most NGOs interact with companies. It is a small but valuable part of the overall picture of corporate citizenship because of both the practical help and the symbolic value of the engagement with the wider society.

There are three basic types of voluntary contributions that companies can make to society. These are:

- Charitable gifts aimed at promoting the common good. These rarely have measurable benefits to the business itself, but they help to establish a reputation of a caring company.
- "Community investment" aimed at a few areas of interest to the company and designed to protect and promote its long-term interests. This could include support for local anticrime initiatives by retail businesses, or the improvement of education and training, or local health provision to benefit employees and their families. The returns to the business are measurable in some degree by an improved physical or social environment in which to do business.

- Commercial initiatives to achieve a wide range of business goals and promote brands. These can include support for research in universities or for supplier development. Returns to the business are measurable in terms of increased sales and market share or access to new ideas. (London Benchmarking Group, 2002)

It is vital to understand these corporate motives if more companies are to be engaged in projects. Some companies around the world have made a major commitment to philanthropy. Many in the developing world are engaged in community investment on issues such as health because they need to protect employees. All companies, wherever they are, respond to an argument of direct commercial self-interest. The second and third types of contribution mentioned above are, therefore, more appealing to shareholders.

THE CORPORATION AND THE NONPROFIT SECTOR

The interaction between business and the societies in which it trades is profound and multifaceted. Companies are both the source of many benefits to society and are deeply involved in many of its most pressing problems. The mechanics for improving the interaction and engaging business in a more effective dialogue with the other key elements of society need to be further examined. We can visualize the social organization of countries being divided into three distinct sectors, each of which operates with its own distinct goals and organizational styles to meet different aspects of society's wants and needs. These sectors are:

- the public sector, representing national, local, and other forms of government;
- the for-profit sector, representing private business;
- the nonprofit sector, representing a wide range of citizen-led, independent organizations providing services and campaigning in the public interest.

The balance of economic significance in a given country varies greatly among these sectors. All countries have well-developed public and for-profit sectors, with varying shares of gross domestic product (GDP), but the level of development of the nonprofit sector varies greatly. In the United States, where the nonprofit sector is most developed and best financed, it accounts for approximately 6% of GDP. In Britain, the nonprofit sector is estimated at about 4.5% of GDP. In postcommunist countries such as Hungary, it is estimated at 1.5%, although the sector is somewhat on the periphery of society in China. The nonprofit sector is very active in such countries as Bangladesh,

India, Jamaica, and South Africa (where it has a very dynamic interface with private business), but little is known of its scale and funding sources.

A key issue to be faced in developing the dialogue between business and the wider society is the need to strengthen the nonprofit sector as a partner in the process. As suggested above, little is known about the size and effectiveness of the nonprofit sector across the world or, more particularly, the role that business takes in supporting it. However, most of the income of the sector comes not from the philanthropic giving of the private sector, but from fees earned for services or from public sector support. The latter is increasingly just another form of fee income as governments contract out national and local services to the nonprofit sector. This is laudable, for to flourish and be truly independent, the nonprofit sector needs multiple streams of income from a variety of sources supplemented by a wide range of volunteer effort. According to the report from the Johns Hopkins University Comparative Nonprofit Sector Project, philanthropy from all sources accounts for only a relatively small proportion of revenue for the nonprofit sector—about 11% (Salamon, Anheier, List, Toepler, & Sokolowski, 1999). Furthermore, in the United States, where there are good data, corporate philanthropy is by far the smallest component of total philanthropic support for the sector (American Association of Fundraising Counsel Trust for Philanthropy, 1997).

However, before we dismiss corporate philanthropy as a factor in sustaining the nonprofit sector, it is important to realize that the complete opposite of the U.S. case is true in the former communist countries and most developing countries (which contain the vast majority of the world's population). In many of these countries there is only the most limited tradition of individual giving (not least because the mass of people are very poor), and there are few, if any, benevolent rich people to set up foundations or leave bequests to fund charities. Consequently, 94% of the philanthropic funding sources taken for granted in the United States do not exist in the countries containing the vast majority of the world's people, so that corporations have a major role to play in helping the emergence of a nonprofit sector. In the 19th century, the United States itself was a developing country. The spirit of self-help that played a great part in its development was greatly fostered by corporations and their wealthy leaders such as Ford, Rockefeller, and J. P. Morgan. In most of the developing countries of the world today, private corporations and governments dominate society and have a critical role to play in helping to kick-start the spirit of voluntary action and self-help among ordinary citizens.

In the developing countries, social conditions are different and some leading businesspeople seek to address the massive social problems that exist, building up educational, social, and physical infrastructure. For example, the city of Jamshedpur in Bihar, India, has been built by the Tata Steel Company, which runs much of its social services. Similarly, the Anglo American

Corporation in South Africa provides a wide range of services and facilities to its employees and the wider community. Just as in the United States in the 19th century, businesses working in the developing world know that they cannot operate effectively if certain basic social conditions do not exist. If government is not capable of providing these conditions, business has often been willing to do so.

There is no lack of further examples of this type of corporate philanthropy in which companies try to improve the wider physical or social environment around their operations. Chevron's Small and Medium Enterprise (SME) Program, for example, was initiated in partnership with the United Nations Development Programme (UNDP), the European Bank for Reconstruction and Development (EBRD), and the U.S. government. This project cultivated the fledgling local credit culture and created a network of advisory resources in Kazakhstan's Caspian basin by fostering access to credits for start-up micro-business (ChevronTexaco, 2003; U.S. Agency for International Development, 2003). Diageo also provides an illustration of such activity with its main environmental and humanitarian project, Water of Life, funding the provision of safe water in communities in 34 countries around the globe. This is done with financial support from the Diageo Foundation and in collaboration with a number of local and international nonprofit organizations (Diageo plc, 2003).

"PURE" PHILANTHROPY AND CSR

Some, on the other hand, would argue that pure philanthropy is not part of corporate social responsibility. Companies (and individuals within an organization) may be motivated to carry out philanthropic acts for moral reasons and not any commercial motive. This approach is described in the literature as discretionary, voluntary, or philanthropic corporate social responsibility. It goes beyond the usual economic confines of social responsibility in contributing to the common good at the possible, probable, or even definite expense of the business (Lantos, 2001). It does more than just prevent and rectify harms that a company may cause, but assumes the responsibility for societal problems that the company has not created. A good example of voluntary CSR can be seen in the activities carried out by the Ben & Jerry's ice cream company through the Ben & Jerry's Foundation (described in its Social Performance Report):

> About half our philanthropic dollars went to the Ben & Jerry's Foundation. Its mission is to support progressive social change in the United States by contributing to grassroots groups that focus on the underlying conditions that create social problems such as

racism, sexism, poverty and environmental destruction. (Ben & Jerry's, 2000)

This approach has been questioned by a number of commentators, notably by Milton Friedman (1970) who argued that "The social responsibility of business is to increase its profits." More recently, the point has also been made by Lantos (2001), who argued that voluntary CSR falls outside the scope of *business* responsibility. Thus, the motivation for voluntary CSR lies in the personal values and principles of some individuals within businesses, who see it as "the right thing to do" (Jenkins & Hines, 2003).

Corporate social responsibility, however, involves much more than philanthropy, if indeed it should be taken to include pure philanthropy at all. It entails taking account of the environment in which companies exist and from which they get their materials, goods, and services as well as assuming some responsibility over all stages of the product lifecycle—from initial manufacture to distribution, sale, recycling, and ultimate disposal.

CSR WITH EXPLICIT COMMERCIAL ADVANTAGE OR IN RESPONSE TO LEGISLATION

Included in our listing of the types of CSR were commercial initiatives to achieve a wide range of business goals and promote brands in which returns to the business are measurable in terms of increased sales and market share or access to new ideas. For instance, social responsibility dictates that car manufacturers should develop and promote low-pollution vehicles. Legislation and regulation can make such vehicles commercially attractive. It might be debatable whether this is CSR or merely filling a market niche, but such a distinction is unnecessary. Many socially responsible activities can make good economic sense, but this does not stop them from being beneficial for the society at large. Similarly, a decision by a licensee to promote low-alcohol and nonalcoholic beverages alongside alcohol could be both responsible and profitable. As already pointed out, just going about business in an honest and ethical way is an aspect of social responsibility. Again, one might question whether an apparently responsible action taken in response to legislation should be included as CSR or whether any act of social responsibility must always be "voluntary." Placing warning labels on packets of cigarettes or on advertisements for tobacco or alcohol beverages, required by law in some countries, can serve as an example. Even in this case, responsibility could be manifest in negotiations between the private sector and legislators on the form the legislation takes.

CAUSE-RELATED MARKETING

Voluntary giving and commercial profits do not, however, have to be mutually exclusive. Philanthropy can be used as a means of improving a company's image (and therefore have a commercial value), as evidenced in the notion of cause-related marketing (CRM). This refers to a commercial activity in which companies and nonprofit organizations form alliances to market an image, product, or service for mutual benefit. Some companies also extend their relationship with an organization or a cause beyond just marketing, by integrating it with other company activities, such as community involvement, employee volunteerism, or corporate philanthropy. Cause-related marketing campaigns vary in their scope and design, the types of nonprofit partners, and the nature of the relationships between companies and their marketing partners. In the most common type of relationship, a company might donate a portion of each purchase made by its customers during a specific period of time to the nonprofit entity. However, there are several variations on this theme and not all CRM campaigns channel money to nonprofits. Some engage principally in educational or awareness-building activities.

One reason for the growth of cause-related marketing is that publicly owned companies in particular are taking a more strategic approach to their community involvement efforts, seeking ways of benefiting community organizations while also furthering their business goals. Another reason for the growth is that public opinion research has shown that effective CRM programs can enhance a company's reputation and brand image and increase the credibility of its marketing effort while giving customers a convenient way to contribute to nonprofit organizations through their purchasing decisions. Companies that have engaged in CRM report that it attracts and builds long-term relationships with customers. For example, affinity credit cards, in which a nonprofit organization benefits each time a consumer uses the card to make a purchase, help credit card companies to develop long-term relationships with consumers. For many companies, CRM has created an alternative and distinctive approach to brand advertising. In a crowded marketplace, it allows companies to distinguish themselves from their peers by offering the consumer an opportunity to contribute to something more than the company's bottom line (Business for Social Responsibility, 2003; Business in the Community, 2004).

CSR CAN MAKE ECONOMIC SENSE

Corporate social responsibility involves making a real commitment to putting values into practice; these new operational values may involve a lot of soul-searching for many organizations and can involve costs. There are companies for whom the adoption of CSR has meant an end to exploitation. Businesses have had to examine their own positions, and often their consciences, in relation to human rights issues, to the environment from which they have been profiting for decades, and to the community around them that has been seen in the past as little more than a market to be exploited (see Figure 2.1).

However, as in the case of cause-related marketing, many companies find that it is possible to operate on the basis of principle and at the same time be profitable. Indeed, there has been a great deal of experience to suggest that companies that place a premium on employee health and safety, environmentally friendly work practices and nonabusive work methods, and exhibit concern for honesty and fairness in the treatment of customers do very well. A British government publication promoting corporate social responsibility goes to great lengths to explain that activities in this field have led to financial gain for the companies concerned (Department of Trade and Industry, 2001).

We live in a world of intelligent consumers. Marketing experts realize it and advertisers realize it, although some companies still hold back. It is nevertheless the case that consumers ask questions about the products they buy, not just questions about ingredients, or colorings, or genetically modified substances, but questions like:

- Were all concerned in the manufacture of the product treated fairly?
- Was the environment damaged?
- Are we being told the whole truth?

FIGURE 2.1. Roger Beale Cartoon
Source: Cause Related Marketing Who Cares Wins, Sue Adkins.

Whether we like it or not, business—and especially global business—has to adapt to the awareness that its customers are increasingly demanding responsibility. Corporations of all sizes are recognizing the importance of their role in society and the "bottom line" benefits of adopting a positive approach to CSR. They are seeing that by taking account of social and environmental as well as economic impacts, they can strengthen their brand, enhance their corporate reputation with customers and suppliers, and attract and retain a committed and skilled workforce. For a business, demonstrating corporate citizenship offers an opportunity for competitive edge and to become a company with whom consumers are happier and more comfortable doing business (CSR Europe/Corporate Citizenship Company, 2001).

CONTINUED VIGILANCE AMONG STAKEHOLDERS

One of the most profound realities about corporate social responsibility, however, is that it seldom springs from within. Exceptions include long established values-based companies like Johnson & Johnson, Cadbury Schweppes, Unilever, Guinness, Volvo, Tata, and Sony. But there are many instances where it has slowly dawned on leaders of large conglomerates and former state-owned firms that there is a lot being said about them in the outside world, and while some of it may be too harsh, a great deal of it is true. Leaders of business who come to that realization almost always embark on the CSR process, believing that it is necessary, while realizing that there are some costs involved. The notion that all CSR is voluntary to the point of being altruistic would be a naive one. That does not make CSR less valid. If business recognizes its customers as having a legitimate stake in the behavior of the company, and if it recognizes that it is under scrutiny, it is healthy. In all cases where meaningful change has occurred, it has been through dialogue and interaction, along with the recognition that shareholders are not the only stakeholders. The most meaningful interaction a company may have in this process is with its critics. The process of voluntary change resulting from such interaction often involves painful realizations and an openness to respond.

The European Commission (2001), in its green paper, has defined corporate social responsibility as "essentially a concept whereby companies decide voluntarily to contribute to a better society and a cleaner environment" (p. 5). One of the additional ingredients of CSR, and one perhaps not entirely encompassed in the European Commission's definition, is the need for continued vigilance among stakeholders. Vigilance needs emphasis for a number of reasons. First of all, it is abundantly clear that there are companies capable of having a large influence on the world we live in, but for some of these organizations CSR is still a distant reality. Indeed, there are some to which we would be grateful if they would just report their accounts scrupulously. But even for those many companies that now take their responsibilities in the world seriously, there are many and varied pressures on them to step back. Corporate social responsibility is easier for business in a time of rapid economic growth, but, when there is pressure on the bottom line, investment in community activity, safety, or better work practices can look a lot less desirable.

Pressures are therefore needed to encourage businesses to follow and develop the path of CSR. Governments can provide the legislative framework that facilitates it and may even provide certain financial incentives (such as tax breaks). The intergovernmental organizations, such as the European Union and the United Nations, can promote a climate that fosters CSR.

UNITED NATIONS GLOBAL COMPACT

The idea of governments embracing partnership with the private sector is a new one in many countries and is still resisted by many in the public sector who remain suspicious of the motives of corporations. The UN system, as part of the public sector, has always had reservations about dealing with corporations. As can be seen in the section on developments in the pharmaceutical sector in chapter 3, attitudes are changing. This change was made explicit in January 1999 at the World Economic Forum, when the secretary-general of the United Nations, Kofi Annan, challenged business leaders to join an international initiative—the Global Compact—that would bring companies together with UN agencies, labor, and civil society to support 10 principles in the areas of human rights, labor, the environment, and corruption. The Global Compact's operational phase was launched at UN headquarters in New York on July 26, 2000.

Through the power of collective action, the Global Compact seeks to advance responsible corporate citizenship so that business can be part of the solution to the challenges of globalization. In this way, the private sector, in partnership with other social actors, can help realize the secretary-general's vision of a more sustainable and inclusive global economy (United Nations Global Compact Office, 2003).

The Global Compact is a voluntary corporate citizenship initiative with two objectives:

- to make the Global Compact and its principles part of business strategy and operations;
- to facilitate cooperation among key stakeholders and promoting partnerships in support of UN goals.

The United Nations Global Compact's 10 principles in the areas of human rights, labor, the environment and corruption enjoy widespread consensus, being derived from:

- the Universal Declaration of Human Rights;
- the International Labour Organization's Declaration on Fundamental Principles and Rights at Work; and
- the Rio Declaration on Environment and Development.

The 10 principles are:

Human Rights

1. Businesses should support and respect the protection of internationally proclaimed human rights within their sphere of influence.
2. Businesses should make sure that they are not complicit in human rights abuses.

Labor Standards

3. Businesses should uphold the freedom of association and the effective recognition of the right to collective bargaining.
4. Businesses should eliminate all forms of forced and compulsory labor.
5. Child labor should be effectively abolished.
6. Businesses should eliminate discrimination in respect of employment and occupation.

Environment

7. Businesses should support a precautionary approach to environmental challenges.
8. Businesses should undertake initiatives to promote greater environmental responsibility.
9. Businesses should encourage the development and diffusion of environmentally friendly technologies.

Corruption

10. Businesses should work against all forms of corruption, including extortion and bribery.

It must be emphasized that the Global Compact is not a regulatory instrument. In other words, it does not "police," enforce, or measure the behavior or actions of companies. Rather, the Global Compact relies on public accountability, transparency, and the enlightened self-interest of companies, labor, and civil society to pursue the principles upon which the Global Compact is based, initiating and sharing substantive action in partnerships.

PARTNERSHIP

Many significant activities by business in society involving corporate social responsibility require collaboration and partnership with others, and particularly with the public sector. Hence partnership has come to be seen as a necessary condition with the various partners having different roles. These partners include governments, intergovernmental organizations such as the United Nations, the private sector, voluntary and advocacy organizations, and academic communities. This process has come to be called public-private partnership, but it is increasingly recognized that there is a need for both *bipartite* and *tripartite* collaboration between the public, private, and nonprofit sectors. It is true that some degree of CSR can be manifest by a company carrying out unilateral internal benevolent acts, such as providing its employees with amenities, but this is a very limited interpretation.

As discussed above, CSR involves much more than philanthropy. It entails taking account of factors throughout the value chain. This includes the environment in which companies exist and from which they get their materials, goods, and services, as well as assuming some responsibility over all stages of the product lifecycle, from initial manufacture to distribution, sale, recycling, and ultimate disposal. To do this requires partnerships and a certain understanding between all parties as to their respective motives and objectives. Having a well-defined goal on which all partners agree is vital, but is not enough in itself. There also needs to be an appreciation by each partner as to why it is involved, what it hopes for, and what are the comparable motivations and expectations of the other partners. Often, these will not be identical. Nor do they need to be for success, provided that each party understands the others and can accept their aims (Mitchell, 1998).

Some of the most interesting developments in partnership theory in recent years have come from the field of business strategy in which partnerships, even between what at one level might be competitors, are seen as vital to long-term success. More important, several of the crucial components of partnership theory—the idea of collaboration as opposed to compromise and the idea of the value of conflict—are drawn directly from negotiation, games, and innovation theory. The reason for this profusion of partnerships within the cor-porate sector is because it has been realized that different interests, and even competing interests, are not the same as irreconcilable interests.

CORPORATE RESPONSIBILITY IN THE VALUE CHAIN

As part of their ethical responsibilities to their wider constituency of stakeholders, companies are expected to take responsibility for what happens all along the value chain. This is a particular area in which differing interests between stakeholders become apparent and need resolution. Companies should be monitoring environmental issues such as how their raw materials are being acquired, as well as looking at all levels of manufacturing and the distribution and sale of their products. They are being asked to provide similar accounts on social issues. In addition to their own behavior, they are also being asked to answer for the behavior of business partners and those to whom they outsource work in the forward and backward linkages of the value chain.

The questioning of *backward linkages* includes large retailers (such as Marks and Spencer and Sainsburys in the United Kingdom) being asked about the conditions of employment and wages of their suppliers in Africa or Asia. Business linkages to the developing world where food and products like clothing are being sourced, from societies where low wages, poor conditions, child labor, and environmental problems are endemic, are a cause for concern to consumers in Europe. As part of this accountability in backward linkages, companies also need to be able to trace environmental impacts from the acquisition of raw materials.

The growing commitment of many companies to environmental stewardship is a testimony to the power of partnership to change the nature of the partners' perception of both their core interests of profit on the one hand and care of the environment on the other. In the case of industries such as oil and mining, it was thought that there could be little common ground between the environmentalists and the industry. What began with a wary if not adversarial approach has moved to genuine partnership between environmentalists and the industry. This partnership between the mining industry and the environmental movement is one of the most remarkable instances of partnership at work. Whereas throughout the 1980s and early 1990s the two groups saw each other only as hostile threats, with starkly incompatible core interests, the two have now established the International Council on Mining and Metals, a joint body that manages the industry's Global Mining Initiative on environmentally responsible mining. Most remarkably, both partners have noted how the partnership has changed each other's notion of core interests. For the mining industry, there has been a growing recognition that responsible environmental

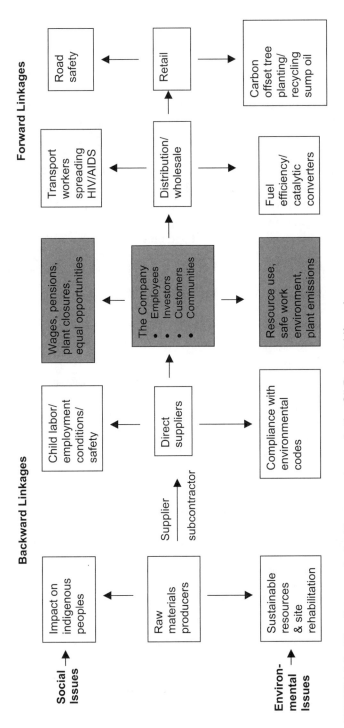

FIGURE 2.2. The Company in the Economy: Issues in the Oil Product Lifecycle

practices are part of its core interests, and for environmentalists, there is an acceptance of the industry's continued profitability as part of their core interests (Luik, 2002).

Examples of *forward linkages* include concerns about the misuse of products and their safe disposal. Environmentalists have long asked questions about what responsibility the manufacturer or retailer has for safely disposing of or recycling products once used. Those involved in road safety want vehicle manufacturers to take some responsibility for influencing the ways their cars are used. Similarly in the social sphere, questions are asked about the responsibility of beverage alcohol companies to help control drink driving and underage consumption of their products. The misuse of prescription pharmaceuticals raises similar issues of social responsibility, and major pharmaceutical companies are also working on issues such as creating access for the poor to high-priced life-saving drugs. A diagrammatic depiction of forward and backward linkages seen in the oil product lifecycle is shown in Figure 2.2. These linkages, particularly the forward linkages, and the possible harms that can be associated with them, is the subject of the next chapter.

REFERENCES

American Association of Fundraising Counsel (AAFRC) Trust for Philanthropy. (1997). *Giving USA 1997.* New York: Author.

Bartolomeo, M., Daga, T., Familiari, G., Hinderer, A., & Bennett, N. (2003, September). *Green, social and ethical funds in Europe 2003.* Milan, Italy: Avanzi SRI Research/ Sustainable Investment Research International (SiRi) Group.

Ben & Jerry's. (2000). *Social audit 2000: Social mission and philanthropy.* Retrieved June 21, 2004, from http://www.benjerry.com/our_company/about_us/social_mission/ social_audits/2000/socialmission00.cfm.

Business for Social Responsibility (BSR). (2003). *Cause-related marketing.* Issue Brief. Retrieved June 21, 2004, from http://www.bsr.org/CSRResources/IssueBrief Detail.cfm?DocumentID=215.

Business in the Community (BITC). (2004). *Cause-related marketing campaign.* Retrieved June 21, 2004, from http://www2.bitc.org.uk/programmes/programme_directory/ cause_related_marketing/index.html.

ChevronTexaco. (2003, April). *Case studies in international community engagement.* ChevronTexaco International Relations/Public and Government Affairs. Retrieved June 10, 2004, from http://www.chevrontexaco.com/social_responsibility/community/ docs/intl_case_studies.pdf.

Copenhagen Centre. (1998). *Copenhagen Centre: New partnerships for social responsibility.* Retrieved June 10, 2004, from http://www.copenhagencentre.org/sw219.asp.

CSR Europe/Corporate Citizenship Company. (2001). *European postal services and social responsibilities.* Retrieved June 10, 2004, from http://www.csreurope.org/upload-store/cms/docs/CSRE_pub_Post-english.pdf.

Department of Trade and Industry (DTI). (2001, March). *Business and society: Developing corporate social responsibility in the UK.* London: Author.

Diageo plc. (2003, February). *Corporate citizenship case study: Water of life.* Retrieved June 21, 2004, from http://www.diageo.co.uk/pageengine.asp?menu_id=0&site_id=0 &section_id=0&page_id=660.

The Economist. (1998). *The Economist pocket world in figures, 1998.* New York: John Wiley.

European Commission. (2001, July). *Promoting a European framework for corporate social responsibility.* Green Paper. Luxembourg: Office for Official Publications of the European Communities.

Fortune Global 500. (1997, August 4). The world's largest corporations. *Fortune, 136*(3), F1–12.

Friedman, M. (1970, September 13). The social responsibility of business is to increase its profits. *New York Times Magazine,* 32–33.

Jenkins, H., & Hines, F. (2003). *Shouldering the burden of corporate social responsibility: What makes business get committed?* Working Paper Series No. 4. Cardiff, United Kingdom: Centre for Business Relationships, Accountability, Sustainability and Society (BRASS), Cardiff University.

Lantos, G. P. (2001). The boundaries of strategic corporate social responsibility. *Journal of Consumer Marketing, 18*(7), 595–630.

Lewis, S. (2003, January). *Corporate brand and corporate responsibility.* London: Market and Opinion Research International (MORI).

Logan, D. (1998, Summer). *Global power brings global social responsibility: The challenge to business.* Corporate Citizenship Company. Retrieved on June 10, 2004, from http://www.corporate-citizenship.co.uk/resources/show_article.asp?ArticleID=11.

Logan, D. (1999, June). *Corporate citizenship: Defining terms and scoping key issues.* London: Corporate Citizenship Company.

London Benchmarking Group. (2002). *Best practices in community capacity building through corporate philanthropy. Research methodology: LBG model.* Retrieved October 29, 2003, from http://www.corporate-philanthropy.com/methodology_lbg.asp.

Luik, J. (2002, October 17). *The promise of partnership for research, education, and public policy.* Unpublished paper presented at the Alcohol, Ethic, and Society Conference, Dublin, Ireland.

Mallya, V. (2002, October 16). *God, country and the spirit of man.* Unpublished paper presented at the Alcohol, Ethic, and Society Conference, Dublin, Ireland.

Market and Opinion Research International (MORI)/CSR Europe. (2000). *Public attitudes to corporate social responsibility: The first ever European survey of consumers' attitudes towards corporate social responsibility.* Brussels, Belgium: CSR Europe.

Mitchell, P. (1998). Public and private partnerships in prevention and research: II. Effective partnerships between the public and private sectors. In M. Grant & J. Litvak (Eds.), *Drinking patterns and their consequences* (pp. 272–276). Washington, DC: Taylor & Francis.

Roberts, M. J., Breitenstein, A. G., & Roberts, C. S. (2000, April 7–8). *The ethics of public-private partnerships.* Paper presented at the workshop on Public-Private Partnerships in Public Health, Endicott House, Dedham, MA.

Salamon, L. M., Anheier, H. K., List, R., Toepler, S., & Sokolowski, S. W. (1999). *Global civil society: Dimensions of the nonprofit sector.* Baltimore: Johns Hopkins Center for Civil Society Studies.

Social Investment Forum (SIF). (2003, December). *2003 report on socially responsible investing trends in the United States.* Washington, DC: Author.

Solomon, R. C. (1994). *The new world of business: Ethics and free enterprise in the global 1990s.* Lanham, MD: Rowman & Littlefield.

The Economist. (1998). *The Economist pocket world in figures, 1998.* New York: John Wiley.

United Nations Global Compact Office. (2003, January). *Global Compact: Corporate citizenship in the world economy.* New York: Author.

U.S. Agency for International Development (USAID). (2003). *Development alliances: Chevron partnerships.* Retrieved June 21, 2004, from http://www.usaid.gov/locations/europe_eurasia/car/briefers/dev_alliances.html.

World Bank Group. (1999). *Global development finance.* Washington, DC: Author.

Chapter 3

Corporate Social Responsibility and Product Safety: A Role for Public-Private Partnership

John Orley

Chapter 2 dealt primarily with the issue of corporate social responsibility (CSR) and its importance in improving society, either through general good works or purely by trading honestly and adhering to ethical principles in going about business. This chapter looks at areas where a company's products have the potential to do harm and where the health and safety of the consumer, or indeed the public at large, can be an issue. The discussion focuses only on goods other than alcohol, which will be dealt with in chapter 4.

Philanthropic support for good works in the community may seem far removed from corporate activities relating to product safety and lessening possible risks associated with product use. The differences, however, are ones of degree: real similarities do exist. The distance between, say, a beverage alcohol company sponsoring a sports tournament and the same company sponsoring an alcohol misuse project is not so great that experience from one cannot be valuably transferred to the other, particularly in the way that partnerships can be used in the process. As already discussed in chapter 2, companies' CSR with regard to their products extends both backward and forward in the value chain. The possible environmental or social harm that the manufacture of a product can entail lies within the "backward linkages." The harms that can arise from the use of a product belong to the "forward linkages." Even within the forward linkages, we need to consider aspects of product use that could bring harm to society through, for example, environmental damage, as well as aspects of use that can cause personal harm to individuals through misuse (e.g., pharmaceuticals, alcohol, or automobiles). There are, of course, some products that span both aspects, such as chemicals or automobiles, which can damage the environment through, say, pollution and also harm the consumer if used irresponsibly. There are certainly lessons to be learned from all these areas, lessons that help us to understand how partnerships can be used to minimize the possible harms.

This chapter focuses on the forward linkages, looking at the issue of how companies deal with the safety of their products, how they try to target the risky use of those products, and how their sales and distribution policies might minimize harm. There are indeed many products that, when used irresponsibly, can lead to harm. It behooves the companies who manufacture those products, as part of their CSR, to be involved in efforts to ensure that what they produce is made available in appropriate ways and is used responsibly. The extent of that involvement and the manner in which it takes place will of course vary greatly according to the culture and traditions of the sector. The chapter starts with a discussion of the concepts of risk and harm, as they are relevant to commercial products, and then continues with a review of issues across a few products, including pharmaceuticals and automobiles. Chapter 4 focuses on the issue of alcohol beverages.

RISK AND HARM

If an available product has the potential to cause harm to those who use it, there is then a responsibility (on somebody) to inform those who use the product about the harms. In the case of cars, drivers take it upon themselves to learn to drive well since they have to pass a test to get their drivers' licenses. In the case of sports equipment (e.g., skis), people often take lessons so they can enjoy their sport more and lessen the risks to themselves and others. In this case, however, there is no obligation to take lessons or pass a test, and there is little or no obligation on the manufacturers of sports equipment to provide information about risks. In the case of scuba divers in the United States, for example, no government agency is involved in supervising certification of divers, but many scuba-diving retail stores see it as their responsibility to provide good-quality scuba-diving training for their customers (Dive Sports, Inc., 2003; Professional Association of Diving Instructors, 2003).

So it is with many activities and products, including drinking alcohol. Those participating are expected to know the risks and are expected to learn to use the product responsibly, so they can both enjoy it and avoid harm to themselves or others. The question arises as to who should have the responsibility for ensuring that consumers learn to "optimize" their use of the product. Traditionally, this has been left to the consumers, but pressures can be exerted by making it necessary to get, say, a driver's license or by putting in place sanctions against those who misuse the product (e.g., not wearing seat belts, disregarding speed limits, or drinking and driving). Learning to drive well, to drink well, or to ski well requires knowledge, guided practice, and a responsible attitude.

As to how information should be provided or attitudes formed and the extent to which companies should take responsibility for the free choices made by its customers will depend on many factors. This was highlighted in 2002 with the first lawsuit against McDonald's on the charge that its products cause obesity and that the company's promotions encourage excessive consumption but fail to give consumers sufficient information to warn them of the dangers. The case was eventually dismissed by the U.S. Federal Court in 2003.

The provision of such knowledge and the formation of constructive attitudes are unlikely to be seen as directly increasing the profitability of the manufacturing or distributing companies and in some instances might actually diminish sales. However, such activities may be undertaken as part of the companies' CSR. In the case of breast-milk substitutes, it is claimed that the way they are promoted and advertised influences their consumption. In this case, therefore, responsibility can be exercised by producers who advertise or by distributors and retailers who run promotions to ensure that the strategies adopted do not lead to the product's inappropriate use. In the case of automobiles, there is a need to ensure that drivers have the skills to drive well, although typically the support of such education has not usually been considered to fall within the CSR of the automobile industry or others commercially involved in selling vehicles.

Together with examining the role of the corporate sector, one can look at how much responsibility the state or society should take (by introducing controls or conducting public education) and how much should be left to the choice of consumers. There are two divergent views on this question. The conservative position is generally associated with a greater emphasis on individual freedoms and individual responsibility for managing risks and for any harm suffered. The politically liberal view contends that the responsibility lies with society in general and emphasizes government action. Whatever one thinks, there is no doubt that individual choice will play a large part, so the factors that influence choice need to be addressed (provision of knowledge, advertising, and promotions). It would be naive, however, to think that behavior depends purely on rational choices, which are based on knowledge. Attitudes, societal norms, and peer pressure are among other potent factors that influence the way products are used, such as the way cars are driven.

Although information can be provided through educational programs, much information is also contained in advertisements and is implied and obviously geared toward encouraging sales. It is, therefore, important to ensure that the messages are put in such a way as to promote responsible use of the product once bought. Advertising in general is usually covered by generic codes, but these broad codes can be supplemented by codes specific to certain industries and products. Certainly, some sort of regulatory framework covering advertisements and education is desirable; this can range from active government intervention to self-regulation and voluntary compliance by the industry.

Self-regulation and government regulation, however, are not mutually exclusive. The effectiveness of these approaches relies on finding the right balance between government regulation and an industry that is accountable for its own actions. How far the scale is tipped in favor of one over the other depends on the political climate, culture, prevailing views within a particular society, and the nature of the risk. Crucially, regulation, however it is structured, should take place in a spirit of partnership rather than confrontation. The current trend toward more deregulation has highlighted the need for self-regulation to be effective and backed by some degree of independent oversight. Self-regulation should not give companies an easy way of avoiding controls, nor be taken to mean that there would be any less rigor in the process of regulation. A more detailed description of self-regulation of advertising in general, but with a particular focus on alcohol beverages, is available in two ICAP reports (International Center for Alcohol Policies, 2001, 2002).

A FOCUS ON PARTICULAR INDUSTRIES

There is a wide range of possible products that could be dealt with in this chapter, including infant formula/breast-milk substitutes, nuclear materials, fuel oil, and sports equipment (particularly for the more extreme and risky sports), which, although beneficial or at least relatively risk-free when used as directed, can have damaging or polluting effects when misused. There are also products that, even when used as recommended, have damaging effects (e.g., armaments, tobacco), but whose manufacturers can still exercise CSR in many aspects of how they run their businesses (e.g., complying with codes and regulations, providing employee welfare). The point to be made is that a significant number of potentially harmful products and processes are legally traded, but in most cases collaboration and goodwill between the industries concerned and the other sectors have mitigated the harms.

Chemicals

The growing public concern about the safety and proper use of chemical products has spurred the industry into providing more information on potential health and environmental effects of its product. This is done partly through the International Council of Chemical Associations (ICCA), "a world-wide voice of the chemical industry," and its research, information, and educational initiatives aimed at making health, safety, and environmental protection an integral part of the designing, manufacturing, marketing, distributing, using, recycling, and disposing of chemical products (International Council of Chemical Associations, 2002).

The Responsible Care program of ICCA is a voluntary initiative that now embraces 46 countries and includes 85% of chemical manufacturing in the world (International Council of Chemical Associations, 2002). Responsible Care is managed by the industry itself. It aims to improve performance by identifying and spreading good management practices through the publication of codes or guidance documents; it also promotes mutual support and the sharing of experience, relying on peer pressure to influence its members. The aim is to replace the competitive approach of the past in matters of health, safety, and environmental concerns. Responsible Care promotes cooperation with governments and other organizations in the development and implementation of regulations and standards, helping companies to meet or exceed these requirements.

In addition, individual chemical manufacturers have become involved in a number of product stewardship initiatives. For example:

- An ICCA member company, NOVA Chemicals contributes significantly to postconsumer polystyrene recycling efforts (NOVA Chemicals, 2003). Apart from recycling plastics directly from its facilities, NOVA Chemicals became one of the founders of the Canadian Polystyrene Recycling Association (CPRA), an organization that has tripled public awareness about polystyrene recycling in Ontario (Canadian Polystyrene Recycling Association, 1999).
- Syngenta Ltd., a leading agrochemicals manufacturer, helps train farmers around the globe in proper use of its crop protection chemicals and technology. The company broke new ground with the use of standardized pictograms to ensure that those with limited literacy can understand how pesticides should be prepared and used (Syngenta Ltd., 2003).
- One of the actions undertaken by the BASF Group under the umbrella of product stewardship is the distribution of three brochures to all its customers in 170 countries, putting together the product safety information on colorants for paints, plastics, and printing inks. These brochures explain the toxic characteristics of colorants. The statutory requirements

linked to the use of these products are also tackled: food contact legislation, approval for dyes used in toys, compliance with other regulations,
and presence in various inventories. These brochures make a contribution to the BASF's dialogue with its customers on questions relating to
product safety (BASF Group, 2003).

Tobacco

Tobacco is distinct in that, even when consumed in moderation, it still has
adverse effects on health. Even so, no government has banned the sale or
smoking of tobacco, and as long as this is true, there will be companies pro-
ducing to meet the demand. Research shows that society would prefer that
demand be met by companies that manage their environmental impact, treat
their suppliers and employees well, and invest in their communities. Assuming that cigarette manufacturers want their customers to continue smoking, the
features of a socially responsible tobacco company would include:

- seeking to reduce the harm inflicted by its product;
- having an active program to reduce its environmental impact;
- managing human rights issues along its supply chain;
- developing and supporting its employees; and
- reporting its CSR performance to the public.

British American Tobacco has recently become the first tobacco company
to produce such a public CSR report. It has, thus, mounted a challenge to those
who believe there cannot be a socially responsible tobacco company by rigor-
ously following best practices on how stakeholders should be consulted and
outcomes reported (British American Tobacco, 2002).

Breast-Milk Substitutes

Breast-milk substitutes are another product that can be harmful in unskilled
hands. The World Health Organization (WHO) estimates that 1.5 million
infants die around the world every year because they are not breastfed. Where
water is unsafe, a bottle-fed child is up to 25 times more likely to die from
diarrhea than a breastfed child. In 1981, the World Health Assembly adopted
the International Code of Marketing of Breast-milk Substitutes, which was
aimed at ensuring that mothers were not misled about the benefits of breast-
milk substitutes versus breast-feeding (World Health Organization, 1981).
Ever since, a battle has been waged between activists and international agri-
business which campaigners accuse of undermining child health in poor countries by aggressively peddling infant formula. Although the global health-care

community maintains that "the burden of compliance" rests with the manufacturers themselves, governments also have a duty under the code to set up monitoring systems and provide information and training to support the code's recommendations.

A nonprofit organization, Baby Milk Action, works within a global network to monitor the marketing of the baby food industry and reduce the extent of inappropriate infant feeding. One of the things the organization has criticized over the years has been the indiscriminate giving of free samples of substitutes to mothers of newborn babies, which is banned under the code. Another has been the placing of tins of whole milk powder (cheaper than formula, but inappropriate for infants) next to tins of formula on the shelves of shops. Poor mothers, probably less educated in these matters, will be tempted to buy the cheaper product. The milk substitutes issue has been made more complicated by the advent of the AIDS epidemic over the past two decades. Some health workers believe that bottle-feeding is the best way to help reduce the risk of mother-to-child HIV transmission through breast milk.

Unfortunately, dialogue does not seem to have been established between the parties, although the area cries out for constructive partnership. Instead, what we see is open hostility, with Baby Milk Action leading a campaign to boycott the leading world producer, Nestlé (Baby Milk Action, 2003), while other manufacturers, such as Mead Johnson and Danone, are not beyond its criticism for allegedly violating the provisions of the code.

Automobiles

As pointed out at the start of this section, automobiles provide an example of a product that can cause both environmental damage (through pollution) and damage to the individual user through accidents (often associated with irresponsible use).

An example of an effort to tackle pollution may be found in the quest for more efficient use of resources as well as pollution prevention, the two goals that bring together, among others, the automobile industry, governments, retailers, and consumers. Examples of such partnerships and other efforts include the ReinCARnate Vehicle Recycling Program in Canada, the work of the United States Council for Automotive Research (USCAR), and the Consortium for Automotive Recycling (CARE) in the United Kingdom. These organizations promote safer old car recycling; most operate through private-private partnerships (automobile manufacturers and vehicle dismantlers and recyclers). As another example, USCAR (an umbrella organization of DaimlerChrysler, Ford, and General Motors) participates in the Partnership for a New Generation of Vehicles. This is a nonprofit organization established in 1992 as a joint effort between the U.S. government and automobile manufacturers for research into and development of new vehicle technologies that are safer, stronger, and more fuel-efficient. These partnerships are complemented by individual automobile companies' initiatives focused on resource conservation and pollution prevention among suppliers and within their own manufacturing facilities and distribution systems—all part of product stewardship, also known as "extended product responsibility."

Voluntary agreements between industrial sectors and governments also exist, including those dealing with pollution prevention. The Motor Vehicle Manufacturers' Agreement, the Metal Finishers' Agreement, and the Automotive Parts Manufacturers' Agreement are examples of such undertakings in the United States. Under these agreements, the companies pledge to reduce specific pollutant emissions by signing on to a specific action plan developed together with local or federal governments (Swenarchuk & Muldoon, 1996).

Cars, however, are also products with the potential for causing harm to individuals when driven or used irresponsibly. According to the U.S. National Safety Council (NSC) and its Safety Agenda for the Nation, in 1999 an average of 112 people were killed on the U.S. highways *every day* of the year. Motor vehicle crashes accounted for 43% of all unintentional injury fatalities in that year and resulted in 2.2 million disabling injuries. In addition, the financial cost of highway crashes in the United States was significant: an estimated US$192.2 billion in 1999, including US$20.7 billion in medical expenses, US$66.4 billion in lost wages and reduced productivity, and US$45.8 billion in vehicle damage (U.S. National Safety Council, 2000).

Safer cars, roadway improvements, enhanced emergency medical services, increased seat belt use, and other factors have cut the rate of highway deaths per 100,000 population by nearly a half since 1972—to 15 deaths per 100,000 currently, the NSC reports. To continue and accelerate this trend, the Safety Agenda for the Nation proposes action on several key traffic-related issues: occupant protection, young driver safety, drink driving, large truck safety, and pedestrian safety. NSC's website indicates that the strategy to be used for implementing the agenda is through partnerships with a broad range of non-profit organizations, as well as corporations, including car manufacturers. Part of their effort will go toward encouraging the enforcement of existing legislation on, for instance, seat belts and drink driving and to promote the introduction of such legislation where it does not already exist (U.S. National Safety Council, 2000).

The safety of young drivers is a particular concern. Teenage drivers make up almost 7% of the licensed drivers in the United States, but they are involved in 16% of all police-reported crashes. In 2000, the estimated economic impact of police-reported crashes involving drivers between 15 and 20 years old was US$32.8 billion. One key to solving this problem is to gradually introduce young drivers to the responsibility of driving, allowing them to gain experience under low-risk conditions. Currently, 25 states and the District of Columbia provide this kind of graduated driver licensing (GDL), and the NSC advocates the adoption of GDL programs in the remaining states and the strengthening of the programs in states that already offer them.

Another active U.S. effort directed at the safety of young drivers is the Air Bag and Seat Belt Safety Campaign, also initiated by the NSC. The National Transportation Safety Board (NTSB) has pointed out that around 9,000 people are killed in traffic crashes each year because they do not wear safety belts, which is equivalent to a Boeing 737 plane crash every week for a year. Although national seat belt use stands at 75%, research shows that the remaining 25% who do not wear seat belts are disproportionately teenagers and young men aged from 18 to 34. At 66%, teenage seat belt use is far behind the rest of the population. The Air Bag and Seat Belt Safety Campaign is an intensive education and action campaign by a public-private partnership of automobile manufacturers, insurance companies, child safety seat manufacturers, occupant restraint manufacturers, government agencies, health professionals, and child health and safety organizations (U.S. National Safety Council, 2003).

Importantly, insurance companies have also shown CSR in this field. The Insurance Institute for Highway Safety, for example, is a nonprofit research and communications organization funded by automobile insurers. The institute's research focuses on countermeasures aimed at all three factors in motor vehicle crashes—human, vehicular, and environmental—and on interventions that can occur before, during, and after crashes to minimize losses. In 1992, the Vehicle Research Center (VRC) was opened. The VRC, equipped with a state-of-the-art crash test facility, is the focus of most of the institute's vehicle-related research. The institute's affiliate organization, the Highway Loss Data Institute, gathers, processes, and publishes data on the ways in which insurance losses vary among different kinds of vehicles. The institutes are uniquely positioned to influence highway safety issues because the best interest of insurers in reducing highway losses inherently coincides with the public's best interest (Insurance Institute for Highway Safety/Highway Loss Data Institute, 2003).

Another example of insurance companies taking charge in an effort to diminish risks associated with driving is the Advocates for Highway and Auto Safety, an alliance of consumer, health, and safety groups and insurance companies and agents cooperating "to make America's roads safer" (Advocates for Highway and Auto Safety, 2002). Involvement of insurance companies in these endeavors is a good example of how CSR can work. With data that can inform appropriate action, companies can reduce the number of claims. Working together, the insurance companies and their partners from other industries, as well as from the nonprofit and public sectors, can all achieve their various aims.

At the global level there is the Global Road Safety Partnership (GRSP), a joint initiative of the World Bank and International Federation of Red Cross and Red Crescent Societies. The mission of this partnership is to reduce the number of lives lost unnecessarily in traffic accidents. Developing and transitional countries are a special priority; 10 focus countries are currently implementing GRSP programs (Global Road Safety Partnership, 2003).

Pharmaceuticals

The potentially harmful nature of many pharmaceutical products is generally recognized, and for this reason their sale is often restricted. This is done by limiting the outlets that can sell pharmaceuticals, by requiring a doctor's prescription for their sale, and by requiring the staffing of the outlets to be under the supervision of a trained pharmacist. In addition to these constraints, efforts are made to inform the public about the potential harms that can come from the misuse of medicines. Despite all this, of course, medicines are misused; for example, people may give (or sell) their prescription drugs to others or take overdoses with the deliberate intention of self-harm.

There is, of course, also the issue of product safety and the need to find drugs that have minimal adverse side effects. It is certainly part of a pharmaceutical company's responsibility to be transparent and honest about any adverse effects when they are found. Many criticisms have been voiced about companies that have been slow to reveal their suspicions about a particular product or have concealed such information in order not to jeopardize sales.

Thus, pharmaceutical companies are fulfilling some of their social responsibilities by just improving the information they provide to their customers beyond their statutory obligations. For example, under the umbrella of product stewardship and its Responsible Care program, Solvay France has trained its marketing managers on the handling of its products at storage facilities where there have been concerns about product quality controls. Specialists make recommendations about product handling, and Solvay provides customers with CD-ROMs describing its products in detail, descriptive stickers along with the user's guide, and access to a toll-free telephone number for immediate information. Furthering the direct dialogue between the company and consumers is aimed at complementing the product safety information available through the Internet, enhancing benefits and safety for all.

The harms associated with the pharmaceutical industry have been spotlighted as a result of inactivity as much as harmful product use or the concealment of possible adverse effects. By its commercial nature, the industry is geared to maximizing profits, and hence its research and development efforts have been concentrated on treatments for the diseases of the relatively wealthy at the expense of the poor in the developing world. The latter would not be able to afford the sort of money that is usually required for new treatments on their introduction, money that would normally be justified on the grounds of financing the research and development of the treatment. Traditionally, there has been a spirit of suspicion between the public health community and the pharmaceutical industry. There may also be some underlying feeling that private companies should not be making profits out of the sufferings of the poorest people. Supplying such people at a discount may mean setting higher prices for the richer customers. Nevertheless, it should be possible to come to some kind of compromise among the industry, the representatives of the consumers in the poorest countries (governments and health-focused NGOs), and donor agencies.

In recent years, this atmosphere of suspicion has been breaking down, and a Geneva-based Initiative on Public–Private Partnerships for Health has been established, which formed the theme for an issue of the *Bulletin of the World Health Organization*:

> The global burden of disease, especially the part attributable to infectious diseases, disproportionately affects populations in developing countries. Inadequate access to pharmaceuticals plays a role in perpetuating this disparity. Drugs and vaccines may not be accessible because of weak distribution infrastructures or because development of the desired products has been neglected. This situation can be tackled with push interventions to lower the costs and risks of product development for industry, with pull interventions providing economic and market incentives, and with the creation of infrastructures allowing products to be put into use. If appropriately motivated, pharmaceutical companies can bring to partnerships expertise in product development, production process development, manufacturing, marketing, and distribution—all of which are lacking in the public sector. A large variety of public-private partnerships, combining the skills and resources of a wide range of collaborators, have arisen for product development, disease control through product donation and distribution, or the general strengthening or coordination of health services. Administratively, such partnerships may either involve affiliation with international organizations, i.e., they are essentially public-sector programs with private-sector participation, or they may be legally independent not-for-profit bodies. These partnerships should be regarded as social experiments; they show promise but are not a panacea. (Widdus, 2001, p. 713)

Elsewhere in the *Bulletin* article, the author states:

> Commercial pharmaceutical and other health-related companies have entered into a remarkable number of collaborations with public

sector and civil society organizations in order to improve access to health products for poor populations. An initial inventory of over 70 collaborative relationships, mostly at the international level, has been established under the Geneva-based Initiative on Public–Private Partnerships for Health. These ventures involve a diversity of arrangements, varying with regard to participants, legal status, governance, management, policy-setting prerogatives, participants, contributions, and operational roles. (p. 717)

Apart from the harms that arise from the lack of medications where they are needed, there are also harms that can come from the misuse of pharmaceuticals, and it is incumbent on the industry to respond to these as well. There have been some partnerships involving the pharmaceutical industry where the focus has been on preventing products causing harm. In the United Kingdom, statutory bodies such as the National Institute of Mental Health in England (NIMHE) and the Medicines Control Agency have worked with the manufacturers of pharmaceuticals to help prevent overdoses by reducing the count per package for aspirin and paracetamol. They are also planning to print warning labels on packages together with a national helpline number. Collaboration on other possible safety measures is also taking place, for example, efforts to ensure that when a doctor changes a patient's prescription medicine, any unused stocks of the former medicine are brought back to the pharmacy before the new one is dispensed.

At a more local level, Boots Healthcare International (BHI), a leading retail company in the global self-medication market in the United Kingdom, helped in staging an event to improve children's safety. Around 1,200 10- and 11-year-old children participated in the Police Safety Zone campaign in April 2000. The event focused on alerting children to the hazards around them, such as electricity, water, railways, and strangers. BHI staged a trailer containing potentially hazardous chemicals and medicines commonly found in the home and taught the children how to deal with them. Over 50 BHI staff were involved in the program run by the Nottinghamshire Police (International Business Leaders Forum, 2000).

REFERENCES

Advocates for Highway and Auto Safety. (2002). *About advocates for highway and auto safety*. Retrieved June 21, 2004, from http://www.saferoads.org/sec_about.htm.
Baby Milk Action. (2003, January–March). *Campaign for ethical marketing*. Cambridge, United Kingdom: Author.
BASF Group. (2003). *The social dimension of sustainability*. Retrieved October 29, 2003, from http://www.basf.de/en/corporate/sustainability/gesellschaft/.
British American Tobacco. (2002, June). *Social report 2001/2002*. London: Author.

Canadian Polystyrene Recycling Association (CPRA). (1999). *History of CPRA*. Retrieved October 30, 2003, from http://www.cpra-canada.com/all.html.

Dive Sports, Inc. (2003). *Scuba training at dive sports*. Retrieved June 21, 2004, from http://www.divesports.com/training.htm.

Global Road Safety Partnership. (2003, June). *Annual report*. Retrieved June 21, 2004, from http://www.grsproadsafety.org.

Insurance Institute for Highway Safety/Highway Loss Data Institute. (2003). *About the institutes*. Retrieved June 21, 2004, from http://www.hwysafety.org/about.htm.

International Business Leaders Forum (IBLF). (2000). *Boots Healthcare International*. Retrieved June 21, 2004, from http://www.iblf.org/csr/CSRWebAssist.nsf/content/f1b2a3v4.html.

International Center for Alcohol Policies (ICAP). (2001, January). *Self-regulation of beverage alcohol advertising*. ICAP Report 9. Washington, DC: Author.

International Center for Alcohol Policies (ICAP). (2002, December). *Self-regulation and alcohol: A toolkit for emerging markets and the developing world*. Washington, DC: Author.

International Council of Chemical Associations (ICCA). (2002). *Responsible care status report 2002*. Brussels: Author.

NOVA Chemicals. (2003). *2002 responsible care annual report*. Retrieved June 21, 2004, from http://www.novachemicals.com/06_community/rc_annual_03/01_whatis_1.htm.

Professional Association of Diving Instructors (PADI). (2003). *PADI: The way the world learns to dive. Mission statement*. Retrieved October 30, 2003, from http://www.padi.com/english/common/padi/mission.asp.

Swenarchuk, M., & Muldoon, P. (1996, March). *Deregulation and self-regulation in administrative law: A public interest perspective*. Canadian Environmental Law Association (CELA) Publication No. 285. Retrieved October 30, 2003, from http://www.cela.ca/law&dereg/deregfulltext.pdf.

Syngenta Ltd. (2003). *Social responsibility*. Retrieved October 30, 2003, from http://www.zeneca.com/en/social_responsibility/index.aspx.

U.S. National Safety Council. (2000). *Safety agenda for the nation*. Itasca, IL: Author.

U.S. National Safety Council. (2003). *Air bag and seat belt safety campaign*. Retrieved October 30, 2003, from http://www.nsc.org/airbag.htm.

Widdus, R. (2001). Public–private partnerships for health: Their main targets, their diversity, and their future directions. *Bulletin of the World Health Organization, 79*(8), 713–720.

World Health Organization (WHO). (1981). *International Code of Marketing of Breastmilk Substitutes*. Geneva: Author.

Chapter 4

Perspectives on Partnerships for Corporate Social Responsibility in the Beverage Alcohol Industry

John Orley and David Logan

THE POTENTIAL FOR PARTNERSHIPS

We have seen in the previous chapters how corporate social responsibility is best exercised through commercial enterprises working in partnership with the other sectors. The potential partners for the beverage alcohol industry are little different from those for other industries, and include governments, the intergovernmental organizations, the nongovernmental voluntary and advocacy organizations, and the public health and research communities.

These various partners have different roles. Governments are responsible for setting the rules for policy operation, and the process can be as important as the outcome. The intergovernmental organizations search for a degree of international (global or regional) consensus in policy and strategies for action within their mandates. The private sector operates largely with the expectation of providing profit for its shareholders, but with responsibilities to other stakeholders. Voluntary and advocacy organizations are typically problem oriented, with an emphasis on a narrower agenda in which partnership seems less virtuous than working to change the system. The academic research community is highly focused on the inquiry process itself and on the charge of pursuing the truth; for them, working with other parties may appear to be an intrusion on their independence. The working of partnerships drawn from these different perspectives requires an attitude of compromise and cooperation.

Governments

Governments have a clear role to play in the development of alcohol policies. One of their primary responsibilities is to ensure the safety of their citizens. They have the responsibility for formulating, implementing, and enforcing legislation and regulations about alcohol. To be both effective and acceptable, the policies must reflect the views of the other sectors and take them into account. In recent years the concept of public-private partnership has gained a strong foothold in the development of government policy, and a growing role has emerged for the commercial sector as an active participant in the formulation and implementation of socially responsible policies. Governments, however, have a responsibility to ensure that a balance is struck between pursuing the safety and welfare of society as a whole and protecting the rights of the individual. For individuals to be allowed freedom of choice requires that they be provided with clear and balanced information. The provision of such information through alcohol education becomes a responsibility for the many actors involved, and not just government.

Intergovernmental Organizations

The intergovernmental organizations (IGOs) have responsibility for trying to achieve some degree of consensus among the governments of the world (e.g., the United Nations) or a region (e.g., the European Union) that they serve. Primarily, they provide a vehicle for communication; they may have more or less authority in the implementation process, but more often than not they have an advisory role, their recommendations requiring national (or local) government action for implementation.

The Private Sector

Beyond its responsibilities to its shareholders, the beverage alcohol industry has responsibilities to its consumers and the public at large, recognizing that alcohol, if consumed responsibly, can enhance pleasure and quality of life and, if misused, can bring about considerable harm. The alcohol industry, like any commercial enterprise, has social responsibilities to its employees, to its suppliers, and to the wider communities in which it operates. These are similar to those any company might have, but in addition the beverage alcohol industry needs to ensure that the risks and harms associated with alcohol misuse are minimized and that the health and psychosocial benefits associated with responsible consumption are maximized. Examples of the more general forms of corporate social responsibility exercised by the beverage alcohol industry, as well as some of the ways that it has responded to the risks, are contained in subsequent chapters of this book.

Nongovernmental Organizations

Nongovernmental organizations (NGOs), at times referred to as "private voluntary organizations," "civil society organizations," and "citizen associations," can also play a significant role in the formulation of alcohol policies. Consumer groups can be particularly important at the community level. The main strengths of these organizations, in fact, lie in their local expertise and links with local actors and networks that can be mobilized quickly. NGOs, especially in the developing countries, often have the best access to poorly served constituencies that are hard to reach through official government channels. Some NGOs perceive health and social well-being policies as inherently at odds with the industry's interests to promote free trade, sales, and consumption of its product, and a number of them, implicitly at least, are against any form of alcohol consumption. Others differentiate between moderate alcohol use and its misuse, focusing on preventing such problems as drink driving, alcohol-related violence, and underage drinking, without embarking on a crusade against drinking alcohol. Still others aim to facilitate a constructive dialogue among professionals in the field, aiming to "build capacity globally for the benefit of individuals, families, communities, businesses and the future social and economic health of the world" (International Council on Alcohol and Addictions, 2003).

The Research Community

Research scientists are responsible for providing the best possible evidence for the development of approaches that encourage responsible drinking and for evaluating their success. The research should be conducted in ways that are free from any ideological or political influences. Funding for research comes from a variety of sources, and funders can in one way or another have some influence on the questions asked and on the way the results are presented. For this reason, it is important that sources of funding are declared when results are published. Certain principles have been set out that should govern the implementation of research on alcohol consumption when that research involves cooperation among the industry, governments, and the scientific and academic communities. These have been published as the Dublin Principles (International Center for Alcohol Policies and National College of Ireland, 1997).

PARTNERSHIPS IN PRACTICE

Various examples exist of collaboration between the different parties set out above, although in the field of policy development it may involve little more than the lead agency obtaining views from a wider constituency.

- *Partnership in policy development—led by government.* For example, the United Kingdom's Government Strategy Unit Alcohol Project has consulted widely on the National Alcohol Harm Reduction Strategy (Department of Health and Prime Minister's Strategy Unit, 2002).
- *Partnership in regional or global consensus building—led by an IGO.* For example, in 2002, the World Health Organization (WHO) developed a statement on the marketing and promotion of alcohol to young people. Among others, the alcohol industry was consulted in the process (Global Alcohol Policy Alliance, 2002). In response to a request from WHO, the International Center for Alcohol Policies (ICAP, 2002) prepared a background paper at a technical meeting convened to develop the statement. The paper reflects the ethical position of ICAP's beverage alcohol industry sponsors regarding the effect of alcohol advertising on youths and suggests collaboration between ICAP and the international organizations, including UN bodies such as WHO. This paper is to be included in the official WHO monograph on alcohol marketing and young people. Following this technical meeting and further informal discussions with a number of alcohol companies, representatives of WHO met with representatives from the industry (World Health Organization, 2003). This reflects the determination of WHO to engage with all interested stakeholders in formulating a policy to address the public health consequences of alcohol consumption worldwide.
- *Partnership in harm prevention programs.* As is the case with the intergovernmental organizations, the NGOs are generally regarded as impartial humanitarian benefactors and this can make them effective as operating partners in alcohol harm prevention initiatives. The choice of method used to prevent harm caused by alcohol, as well as the attitudes toward the industry and alcohol consumption itself, varies widely within the international NGO community. Some NGOs see alcohol in the same light as illegal drugs and tobacco, harmful under any circumstances and in any quantity, whereas others regard its consumption in moderation as perfectly acceptable. Examples of partnership are described in chapter 10, particularly in the section on social aspects organizations (SAOs).
- *Partnership in research.* The research institutions rely on external sources of funding to support their work. This may come from government-funded

research councils or institutes (such as the National Institute on Alcohol Abuse and Alcoholism in the United States) or from the beverage alcohol industry. For example, the Alcoholic Beverage Medical Research Foundation (ABMRF) represents a collaboration between academia and industry. It is a nonprofit research foundation that focuses on examining the health and behavioral effects of alcohol, including the effects of moderate alcohol consumption. The foundation provides grants for a number of academic investigators from universities and research institutions in Canada and the United States, and supports conferences and workshops aimed at encouraging scientific studies on alcohol use and the prevention of its misuse. (Alcoholic Beverage Medical Research Foundation, 2003)

THE ROLE OF THE INDUSTRY

Many different kinds of partnership can exist, combining the skills and resources of a wide range of collaborators. Administratively, such partnerships may be led by government bodies, that is, they are essentially public-sector programs with private-sector participation, or they may be led by independent nonprofit bodies implementing strategies on behalf of governments, or at least with their approval. Some may be industry led, but with government and NGO involvement or approval. Some industry programs are summarized in chapter 10. A fuller description of the actual efforts by the ICAP sponsors (which are representative of large companies within the beverage alcohol industry) to exercise their corporate social responsibility in emerging markets and developing countries is provided in chapter 16. First, however, there are some general points that can be made.

In some of the examples cited earlier in this book, related to pharmaceuticals for instance, the companies for the most part have not been asked to collaborate in ventures that affect the profitability of their regular products in already existing markets. The involvement of the insurance companies in efforts to improve road safety and driving skills might actually improve their profitability. The promotion of responsible drinking, however, might be seen as something that could reduce the profitability of the beverage alcohol industry in existing lucrative markets, at least in the short term.

The argument is that if those who do drink consumed no more than the recommended daily maximum, overall consumption would fall dramatically. Because of this perception (whether true or false), there are those who feel that the industry can never put its heart into partnerships created to formulate policy and implement programs for responsible drinking. These perceived conflicts of interest make some commentators from the public health and nonprofit sectors shy away from collaboration with the industry. Although there may indeed be some who consider that public and private interests with regard to beverage alcohol are incompatible, experience has also shown that partnership in this field can be an effective and viable approach. Those who are committed to the partnership concept recognize that, although the goals of the public and private sectors may not always be identical and perhaps not even fully compatible, this does not rule out dialogue and joint action on a wide range of issues.

The alternative to such a partnership is an exclusionary model, which creates an adversarial relationship between the beverage alcohol industry and the public health community. This polarization leads to competing research agendas and claims, where science becomes politicized and where policy is made without the involvement of the industry (Luik, 2002). The lessons from other sectors, as is evident in the case of breast-milk substitutes described in chapter 3, are that such a process serves no one's interests, and least of all those interested in the public good. Experience has shown that even though the involved parties may start out as seemingly opposed, partnerships can develop from an adversarial relationship to one of trust and, eventually, of productive collaboration. As Grant points out in chapter 5, partnership does not have to involve consensus and can exist despite differences between the partners. For it to work, however, the partnership process needs to be founded on mutual respect, trust, transparency, and shared beliefs. In that way, one can arrive at benefits for all the parties involved.

The stereotypical views held in each sector manifest themselves in the polarities brought to light in discussions. For example, the industry may be seen as a volume-driven, profit-maximizing entity, so much so that any reference to responsibility and self-restraint must, by definition, be against its interests and therefore unacceptable to it. According to such a view, the drinks industry suffers from two problems. First, it produces a product that can have serious negative social and health consequences for some; and, second, it does so for profit. This second aspect of the industry's perceived identity is almost as controversial as the first. However, there is clear evidence that leading companies are willing to listen to concerns and in many cases act on them. Indeed, private industry cannot be entirely blamed: governments own many of the world's largest drinks companies, as in Poland and Russia, two countries where the social problems of alcohol misuse are serious.

As one of the consequences of polarization between the industry and the public health community, one often hears a call for harsh measures to limit the availability of alcohol. Yet, in those societies where drinking of alcohol is part of everyday life, there are dangers in introducing such strict measures, as was seen during prohibition in the United States. Even in India, where a significant proportion of the population disapproves of drinking alcohol, prohibition creates problems. As Mallya (2002) has pointed out, in India not only does the loss of tax revenue for the state concerned make government impossible, but the illicit and unhealthy trade that prohibition encourages becomes unacceptable. The claim that irreconcilable interests preclude any sort of partnership between the public health community and the industry appears, for instance, in Barry's paper presented at the Dublin conference (Barry, 2002). Barry states that "The Government in Ireland has a choice to make: protect the health of the people or allow the drinks industry to satisfy its shareholders at the expense of the health of the population." This sounds good in rhetoric but it is not necessarily the case that an interest in sales and profit places one in opposition to harm reduction. If it were, then any business that produces a product or offers a service that carries a risk to the user could be criticized on these grounds. As has been demonstrated earlier in this book, the evolution of the idea of corporate social responsibility over recent decades has moved on from the notion that there has to be a simple opposition between profits and the public good. Not only does the public expect corporations to live up to quite high standards of social responsibility, but investors are increasingly recognizing that the rights given by society to corporations, which enable them to improve their business performance, have to be balanced by the exercise of responsibility that might, in the short term at least, adversely affect profits. This balance is best achieved through the process of partnership and dialogue, which should be about the great potential of "and," as in health *and* profits, rather than the limitations of "or," as in health *or* profits. If we are to have dialogue about policy, then some kind of framework for dialogue is needed, with some agreement about the issues to be discussed. The Geneva Partnership document provides such a framework, dealing as it does with the following issues (International Center on Alcohol Policies, 2000):

- The need for public policies that balance benefits against risks, providing some degree of control over the sale of alcohol without "punishing" legitimate moderate drinkers;
- The enforcement of laws and regulations regarding the sale and consumption of alcohol;
- Reasonable taxation;
- The control of access and availability;
- The regulation of advertising and promotion;
- The provision of information and education, especially for young people;
- Health care responsibility for prevention and rehabilitation for those with problems;
- Ensuring responsible serving of alcohol and promoting positive drinking environments;
- The need for research and the dissemination of results.

THE INFLUENCE OF CONFLICTING AGENDAS

The beverage alcohol industry is sometimes portrayed as the great impediment to responsible drinking with an agenda of maximizing consumption regardless of harm. On the other hand, it should not be assumed that all members of the public health community are necessarily motivated only by a desire for the public good, with no other agenda. For instance, running throughout an article by McCreanor, Casswell, and Hill (2000) and several supporting comments, which all take a position against the beverage alcohol industry, there is a distinctly antibusiness, antiglobalization, antimarketing, as well as antidrink perspective that colors the authors' premises, arguments, and empirical claims. Whether or not one agrees with this ideological position, it is clear that their position goes beyond one of pure concern for public health and that a certain agenda determines their argument. The fact is that most protagonists have some kind of agenda from which they work, and one cannot assume that all public health experts have purely "health" motivations simply because they are part of the public health community.

   Just as the alcohol industry does not have to be in opposition to a public health position, so the use of industry money for research does not automatically invalidate that research (although it should of course be declared). Even state funding of public health research is not free from interests that might be considered biased. The public health research community is almost entirely supported by a state that accepts and attempts to control the risks associated with alcohol on the one hand, while the state happily accepts a share of the profit through taxation. As Fillmore and Roizen (2000) note in their comment on McCreanor, Casswell, and Hill:

> The editorial suggests a naïve objectivism—contrasting a putatively purely disinterested, well-meaning public health camp with a distorting, profit-driven industry-sponsored camp. The largest patron of mainstream alcohol-related public health research is the state, with its own strongly competing interests with respect to alcohol. Hence, state-funded alcohol research is by no means immune from the influences of extra-scientific cultural-political factors and the fruits of such research are subject to the state's selective and self-serving use. (pp. 188–189)

   Bias can manifest itself in various ways. For instance, it was evident in the reaction to the report by Seltzer (1997) on the findings of the Framingham Heart Study—a longitudinal project on coronary heart disease (CHD) run by the National Heart, Lung, and Blood Institute since 1948–1949—showing the positive effects of moderate drinking on preventing CHD:

conflicts of interest and pressures on investigators need not arise exclusively from commercial organizations. A nonprofit governmental agency that funds research can also suppress some of its findings, and can alter definitions and analyses to make results that originally contradict a governmental policy emerge as supportive. (p. 628)

Seltzer's work was denied publication by the National Heart, Lung, and Blood Institute on the grounds that an article linking moderate drinking and prevention of CHD would be "socially undesirable in view of the major health problem of alcoholism that already exists in the country" (Seltzer, 1997, p. 628). It has only been in more recent years that the health benefits of moderate drinking have become a topic that can be discussed openly, without hiding that knowledge from the "naïve public," whose informed decisions were deemed to be likely to lead to harm.

THE IMPORTANCE OF PARTNERSHIP

Partnership is the way forward in dealing with the issues concerning social aspects of alcohol. It has already been shown to work and is in line with what is happening across a wide spectrum of businesses and society. Above all, partnership is necessary because none of the individual players in the debate has the capacity to deliver a total solution to the problems of alcohol and society. In particular, the formal sectors of government, the industry itself, and the nonprofit sector, including academia, need to be brought into partnership in various ways if the issues are to be successfully addressed. These three operate in the context of a wider informal sector of society, consisting of families, friends, and wider peer groups, as well as the media conveying messages from the formal sectors (such as advertising and health messages) and the wider world. Partnership, however, is not universally accepted as a necessary strategy: as pointed out above, the health community in particular has serious reservations about engaging in partnership with the industry. This is a matter of concern because it will thwart progress.

Certainly the public needs to be made aware of the various harms that can arise from alcohol consumption. Equally, apart from those advocating complete abstention, there is general agreement that it is possible to drink responsibly. Every effort, therefore, must be made to promote the kinds of environments in which alcohol is drunk responsibly. The existing controls in many countries go as far as is possible to minimize the potential harms. However, proper enforcement of the laws and regulations is often lacking. The industry has shown itself to be very ready to collaborate in the regulation of marketing and advertising. The industry's preference lies with self-regulation, of course, but it is willing to ensure that self-regulation is not seen to be a way of covering up wrongdoing.

There is a wide range of factors that influence alcohol consumption, and the diversity of these factors means that any attempt to change hazardous patterns of drinking and promote beneficial ones must involve many different partners. The strategies needed for alcohol abuse prevention, health promotion, and the promotion only of sensible drinking require the cooperation of governments, health advocacy organizations, the academic community, and commercial interests. Participants from each sector bring with them values and norms that are based on their individual experiences and that influence their expectations of how such partnerships should function. The implementation of strategies responding to these concerns requires a number of factors to operate. There needs to be good role models available who can help to encourage or set appropriate societal norms. Above all, there needs to be strong leadership, which in turn requires a shared vision between all parties involved, and this can only come about through open, sharp, and truthful dialogue.

As pointed out already, it is not logically necessary that the profit imperative for shareholders place the beverage alcohol industry in opposition to the public health goal of harm reduction. It is true that at times the industry may be opposed to particular strategies purporting to lead to harm reduction, but it must be allowed to question whether the public health community's policies for harm reduction are in fact sound. The industry would of course particularly question those strategies for which there is no (or only equivocal) evidence that they prevent misuse but which might interfere with the legitimate marketing of their products. To be opposed to certain strategies does not mean that the industry is fundamentally opposed to the notion of public health or to that of harm reduction.

UNDERSTANDING SECTOR STRENGTHS

One of the problems of promoting a partnership approach is that the three formal sectors are in themselves very diverse. For example, the government sector has within it the law enforcement, health, local regulation, planning, and taxation authorities. All these can have conflicting, rather than complementary, agendas. Similarly, in the industrial sector, the big manufacturers have limited links with the retailers, while some of the worst problems in the industry come from small opportunistic marketing companies. Within the big companies, where the pressures toward good citizenship are most real, the social responsibility specialist may not communicate effectively with the marketing department. In the nonprofit sector there are constant tensions between the research community and the frontline care providers.

Consequently, when the three formal sectors come together, there is no common position on the issues from within each sector. More needs to be done to develop a common position, particularly within the government and industry sectors, both of which have very complex systems for engaging with other partners and the informal sector on the issues. Simple partnerships across two sectors may be more straightforward to manage, but tripartite partnerships across the formal sectors might well be the most productive on the key issues.

When addressing the social aspects of alcohol in society, each of the three formal sectors has distinct strengths that can be deployed. They also have clear weaknesses in their ability to address some problems or aspects of problems. For example, corporate marketers are great communicators, but the corporate sector has little or no idea about how to deal with long-term problem drinkers. The public sector can set a framework of law for the sale of alcohol, but it cannot supervise activities in every aspect of the trade. Bar staff, for instance, need training and support to manage customer behavior, and this is difficult within a multitude of small outlets. Academics can do valuable research, but it is useless unless their findings can be implemented in practice.

Each sector needs to be clear about its strengths and weaknesses in its ability to address the issues at hand. The key is for each sector (and even subsector) to understand the social problems being confronted and the capacity of each sector to influence change. The manufacturers are able to control images in advertising but have only moderate influence on retailer behavior and virtually no influence at all on chronic drinkers. On the other hand, health professionals and the nonprofit community know how to help chronic drinkers with their problems but have real difficulty in scaling up their approach and communicating with those at risk.

If each sector could prepare an analysis of its own strengths and weaknesses in addressing social problems, it would be possible to map where the responsibility to lead key interventions might lie. Playing to the strengths of each sector, rather than dwelling on their relative weaknesses, is most likely to produce the best results. Clearly no one sector can do it all. Together, their resources can be more effective.

TOWARD COHERENT CROSS-SECTOR STRATEGIES

Despite all that has been achieved in engagement between the alcohol industry and other sectors so far, there are still problems of understanding and communication. These will limit future success in facing important issues. If companies can clearly show elements of concern for social responsibility, there can be debate about whether this is enough or of the right sort. The companies should not be excluded from the dialogue purely on the grounds of being part of the industry sector. Similarly, despite their good works, public health practitioners are stereotyped by some as paternalistic "killjoys," prone to inefficiency and didactic communications. These simplistic labels are not helpful, and, in order to overcome them, much more—not less—interchange between the sectors is necessary. Such interchange might be helped, for example, by young marketing people spending time with at-risk underage drinkers, while health communicators might learn a lot from working alongside successful marketers. These kinds of cross-sector "seeing is believing" experiences need to be organized in a systematic way if greater understanding and the potential for partnerships are to be developed.

Once the framework of a cross-sector approach has been mapped out, there is a range of mutually supportive strategies that can be deployed. They may vary for the general adult population and for vulnerable groups, such as the young, where demand creation is contained through the responsible targeting of advertising and supply is restricted by licensing laws and retailer good practice. Attitudes toward alcohol and its use are the products of both rationality and emotion as shaped by the culture in which the individual lives. A creative response needs to take these different components into account. Providing facts alone may not be enough, but emotional appeals for and against alcohol without facts are equally suspect from the point of view of a true educator. One of the polarities in this field is between the tendency for those concerned about alcohol to stress the facts about the problems alcohol can produce, and the propensity of modern brand marketing to focus largely on an appeal to pleasure, with little reference to the utility of the product and its potential effects on the individual. It should, however, be possible to support the sensible drinking message of the health community with the creative flair of the advertisers. This would be an excellent way of playing to the relative strengths of each sector.

It can be hypothesized that a partnership model is the best. Indeed, in some cases it is the only way to handle key issues of alcohol in society. The prima facie evidence is strong, although the practical problems of making partnerships work may seriously militate against success. It cannot just be assumed that partnerships will work. Research is needed into the effectiveness of the partnership approach in addition to researching the issues themselves. Examples and case studies exist, but they need to be properly evaluated in terms of their contribution relative to other means of intervention. What is learned from both failed and successful partnerships then needs to be fed back into the debate in constructive ways. Such a strategy would allow for the feedback of good practice to support the growing discipline of cross-sector approaches to addressing the role of alcohol in society. This is a sound management approach to the issues, one that is becoming increasingly prevalent in the public and nonprofit sectors, as well as in the private sector.

REFERENCES

Alcoholic Beverage Medical Research Foundation (ABMRF). (2003). *About ABMRF. A unique partnership: Industry and academia.* Retrieved June 21, 2004, from http://www.abmrf.org/about.htm.

Barry, J. (2002, October 16). *Alcohol in Ireland: A lot of damage done, more to do.* Unpublished paper presented at the Alcohol, Ethics, and Society Conference, Dublin, Ireland.

Department of Health and Prime Minister's Strategy Unit. (2002). *National alcohol harm reduction strategy: Consultation document.* London: Author.

Fillmore, K. M., & Roizen, R. (2000, February). The new Manichaeism in alcohol science. *Addiction, 95*(2), 188–189.

Global Alcohol Policy Alliance (GAPA). (2002). Declaration of the technical consultation to the WHO on the marketing and promotion of alcohol to young people [online version]. *The globe: Drinking it in. WHO targets alcohol marketing.* Retrieved June 21, 2004, from http://www.ias.org.uk/publications/theglobe/02issue2/globe0202_p5.html.

International Center for Alcohol Policies (ICAP). (2000). *The Geneva partnership on alcohol: Towards a global charter.* Washington, DC: Author.

International Center for Alcohol Policies (ICAP). (2002). *Industry views on beverage alcohol advertising and marketing, with special reference to young people.* Washington, DC: Author.

International Center for Alcohol Policies (ICAP) and National College of Ireland. (1997). *The Dublin Principles of cooperation among the beverage alcohol industry, governments, scientific researchers, and the public health community.* Washington, DC: Author.

International Council on Alcohol and Addictions (ICAA). (2003). *ICAA: Who we are.* Retrieved June 21, 2004, from http://www.icaa.de/.

Luik, J. (2002, October 17). *The promise of partnership for research, education, and public policy.* Unpublished paper presented at the Alcohol, Ethics, and Society Conference, Dublin, Ireland.

Mallya, V. (2002, October 16). *God, country and the spirit of man.* Unpublished paper presented at the Alcohol, Ethics, and Society Conference, Dublin, Ireland.

McCreanor, T. F., Casswell, C., & Hill, L. (2000). ICAP and the perils of partnership. *Addiction, 95*(2), 179–185.

Seltzer, C. C. (1997). "Conflicts of interest" and "political science." *Journal of Clinical Epidemiology, 50*(5), 627–629.

World Health Organization (WHO). (2003, January 31). *WHO to meet beverage company representatives to discuss health-related alcohol issues.* Retrieved June 23, 2004, from http://www.who.int/mediacentre/releases/2003/pr6/en/.

Chapter 5

Alcohol Policy Through Partnership: Is the Glass Half Empty or Half Full?

Marcus Grant

PRINCIPLES OF PARTNERSHIP

In our private lives, many of us have experienced the most common form of partnership: marriage or its equivalent. Two individuals are drawn together by personal and social forces to forge a union that does not negate either party as individuals but creates something that is stronger than the two individuals acting in isolation.

A parallel can be drawn with the development of alcohol policy. Partnership is not a goal but a way to achieve a goal. The goal is to define the role of alcohol in a society so that benefits are maximized and problems are minimized. All those who can agree to that goal are potential members of the partnership to achieve it. How many of these potential partners are actually willing to accept the marriage vow is the subject of this chapter.

Public-private partnerships are especially important for social policy development—a reality that has been recognized by the United Nations and its specialized agencies. For example, the World Health Organization (WHO) has developed guidelines on interaction with commercial enterprises (WHO, 2000). These guidelines characterize the general principles of partnership as mutual respect, trust, transparency, and shared benefits. These four principles can be applied to the area of alcohol policy.

Mutual Respect

No sector of society has exclusive ownership of alcohol policy. Within government, departments of health, trade, justice, treasury, agriculture, and others all have strong interests in alcohol policy. Beyond government, the medical and social service communities have interests, as do religious groups and a wide range of nongovernmental organizations (NGOs). There are, too, the research and scientific institutions that are engaged in studying the effects of alcohol on individuals and society. Finally, there is the private sector, including not just the producers of beverage alcohol, but also the retailers, the hospitality industry, and those involved in many aspects of tourism and the media.

This is an extensive list, but the point to be made is that all these groups have a legitimate interest in alcohol policy development, and all have something relevant to contribute to the process. They are all potential partners, but they all also have their particular interests to promote, so that it is reasonable to expect that there will be conflicts between some of those interests. If all partners, however, demonstrate mutual respect, there should be ample space for legitimate differences.

Trust

Just as there can be mutual respect, even when the interests of the partners conflict, so it is not necessary for them to agree for there to be mutual trust. In the area of alcohol policy, there is a legacy of mistrust that needs to be addressed directly, but that should be a challenge, not an impediment to partnership. Experience at the International Center for Alcohol Policies (ICAP) has shown that, as people from different backgrounds and orientations actually work together, they learn to trust each other more, although some are not willing to work together at all. Not everyone is willing to join a partnership, and no one who is unwilling should be forced to do so. Yet, in absenting themselves, they lose the opportunity to build mutual respect and trust.

Transparency

It is the third principle—transparency—that fosters greater trust. There are of course self-interests, but the partners also have common interests in reducing the problems associated with alcohol abuse. Transparency is crucial in the process of partnership; indeed, full disclosure was one of the key principles identified when developing the Dublin Principles (Dublin Principles:

Principles of Cooperation Among the Beverage Alcohol Industry, Governments, Scientific Researchers, and the Public Health Community, 1997). It is essential, not just for reporting on research findings, but for the whole process of building and sustaining alcohol policy partnerships.

Shared Benefits

It is in everyone's best interest to work for better and more comprehensive alcohol policies. Shared benefits do not mean identical benefits for everybody, and indeed it may be necessary to give up some intermediate benefits for the sake of a larger goal. Thus, for example, the public health community might need to relinquish the "single-distribution" theory and accept that moderate alcohol consumption is associated with possible health benefits, a great deal of pleasure, and levels of risk that are low enough for most to consider them within acceptable limits (Single & Leino, 1998). For its part, the beverage alcohol industry might need to do more to prevent those underage sales, which it already claims it does not want. Partnership calls for a reappraisal of values, but it is always worth the effort in the end.

THE ROLE OF PARTNERSHIPS IN ALCOHOL POLICY DEVELOPMENT: RESULTS FROM AN ICAP SURVEY

In early 2002, ICAP conducted an informal postal survey of ministers of health, directors general of health services, and key policy professionals in national governments, quasi-governmental bodies, and other national entities responsible for developing and implementing alcohol policies around the world. There were responses from 48 countries, representing all geographic areas.

The purpose of this survey was to gather perspectives on various issues relating to alcohol policy development around the world. Because of the informal nature of the survey, it has been criticized for both its methodology and its conclusions (Babor & Xuan, 2004). However, the findings offer an indication of views and roles relevant to the alcohol field. Presented here are the results pertaining to the issue of partnership and, in particular, the role, if any, that governments see for partnership with the beverage alcohol industry in the process of policy development.

The subtitle of this chapter—"Is the glass half empty or half full?"—reflects respondents' evenly split views as to whether the beverage alcohol industry is a relevant and useful partner in alcohol policy development. Globally, 50% of countries viewed the industry as a viable partner and 50% did not. There were, as would be expected, some regional differences within this 50/50 split. In Africa, 60% of respondents saw the beverage alcohol industry as a partner, as did 58% from Latin America. By contrast, none of the Scandinavian countries viewed the industry as a partner. In general, though, the picture is relatively consistent. When developing and developed countries were compared, the similarity was more striking than the difference: 53% of developing countries and 44% of industrialized countries were in favor of partnership.

Of those who responded that partnership between government and industry was desirable, the overwhelming majority (96%) identified public education as a main area for cooperation. The other three areas most frequently cited were drinking and driving (83%), underage drinking (79%), and advertising and marketing (75%). It is interesting to compare this prioritization of areas for partnership action with what *all* respondents identified as the most pressing global challenges, regardless of their position on the partnership question. There, the top challenge was seen as underage drinking (81%), followed by public education on alcohol (73%), drinking and driving (65%), and prevention and treatment (also 65%). When asked to identify the top priority for the future, 85% of *all* survey respondents chose increased public education about alcohol.

Public education about alcohol therefore emerges as the top global priority for action *and* as the most worthwhile area for public–private partnership. It is not possible to determine, on the basis of this survey, exactly what might be included in such public education. As a minimum, people clearly need to have accurate information about the relative alcoholic strengths of different drinks and about common serving sizes, although this information will be of little value in the absence of guidelines on what constitutes appropriate drinking patterns for those who are legally able to drink and choose to do so.

There are also implied challenges here for several of the partnership members. Can the beverage alcohol industry fully commit to promoting only responsible drinking, even if that might result in reduced profits? Can educators and health advocates devise educational strategies that will show better success rates than in the past? Can researchers leave their ivory towers and contribute positively to the overwhelming popular demand for more effective education? Can governments balance the books between the need for better health of their populations and the need for steady tax revenues from alcohol sales? These are, of course, exactly the kinds of questions that can be more productively handled in the context of a working partnership than they ever could be in isolation.

An examination of the responses about what was actually happening in the countries surveyed gives a different picture from the answers about whether they thought that partnership was a good idea. Although 50% of countries that responded to the survey thought partnership was desirable, among those, fewer could point to current partnership arrangements. In fact, 44% of mature markets (or industrialized countries) had experience of actual partnerships, compared to only 25% of developing countries. Here, in other words, differences were more striking than similarities. Even within Europe, 71% of Western European countries could point to activities involving the beverage alcohol industry, but only 17% of Eastern European countries could do so. Only about a third of the countries in Africa and Latin America could cite examples of current partnerships that included the industry.

The full results of the survey are available from ICAP, including examples of the kinds of partnership programs that respondents cited (ICAP, 2002). These range from public education campaigns to server training initiatives, from traffic injury prevention to fetal alcohol syndrome awareness. The point to be emphasized, however, is that the *desire* for public–private partnerships appears to outstrip their actual *occurrence*. The world—or, at least, half the world—seems to view partnerships favorably, but opportunities are being lost to translate these good intentions into practice. An important finding of the survey was that public education about alcohol is the overwhelming global priority and also the top priority for partnership action. This surely indicates a powerful sense of the direction in which to go; although education cannot provide all the answers and is not as effective as it could be, it does seem to command general support. It is worth then making the most of that opportunity and focusing on providing more and better public education about alcohol. This should give stakeholders more opportunities to act together in partnership. The potential is there, and those committed to promoting public-private partnerships on alcohol policy should do their utmost to take up the challenge.

CONFLICTS OF INTEREST

It is worth reflecting on the 50% of countries that remain skeptical about the potential of a partnership approach to alcohol policy—those for whom the glass is decidedly half empty. Not surprisingly, they tended to cite the commercial interests of industry members as the main impediment to cooperation. Comments reflected their view of the industry as being exclusively profit oriented, uninterested in public health, and aggressive in its marketing practices. They see a fundamental conflict of interest between public health and private wealth and conclude that, as a consequence, not only is partnership impossible, but even meaningful dialogue is out of the question.

Just because there is a conflict of interest between two parties, there is no reason to assume that they cannot communicate effectively. After all, politicians of different parties work together daily in most countries in the world. To return the analogy from the start of this chapter, the working together of the partners in a stumbling marriage forms the daily business of most marriage counselors. When dialogue starts, it often turns out that many conflicts of interest are perceived rather than real. Partnership, however, as defined earlier, is about more than dialogue, it is about working together and accepting that not all views need to be identical.

The principles of mutual respect, trust, and transparency can be maintained in the face of a conflict of interest. The only principle that is in doubt, therefore, is that of shared benefits. It is reasonable to ask whether the financial health of the beverage alcohol industry is compatible with the good health of the drinking population. That is a question that can be tested empirically, and it is precisely through partnership arrangements that it can best be tested. There will always be some congenital bachelors and some marriages that fail. But neither of these facts is sufficient to argue against the merit of individuals having the courage to seek out a mate and to try to live together in the hope of living better. Alcohol policy partnerships, in their way, are also about working together in the hope of creating a better world for all.

REFERENCES

Babor, T., & Xuan, Z. (2004). Alcohol policy research and the grey literature. *Nordisk Alcohol- & Narkotikatidskrift*, 21 (English supplement), 125–137.

Dublin Principles: Principles of Cooperation Among the Beverage Alcohol Industry, Governments, Scientific Researchers, and the Public Health Community. (1997). In M. Grant & J. Litvak (Eds.), *Drinking Patterns and Their Consequences* (229–301). Washington, DC: Taylor & Francis.

International Center for Alcohol Policies (ICAP). (2002). *Alcohol policy through partnership: Is the glass half-empty or half-full? A survey of key policy makers.* Washington, DC: Author.

Single, E., & Leino, V. E. (1998). The levels, patterns, and consequences of drinking. In M. Grant & J. Litvak (Eds.), *Drinking patterns and their consequences* (pp. 7–24). Washington, DC: Taylor & Francis.

World Health Organization (WHO). (2000). *Guidelines on working with the private sector to achieve health outcomes: Report by the Secretariat.* Geneva: World Health Organization (unpublished document EB107/20). Retrieved August 13, 2004, from: http://www.who.int/gb/ebwha/pdf_files/EB107/ee20.pdf.

Chapter 6

Drinking Education: Minimizing Negatives or Optimizing Potential?

Stanton Peele

Views of alcohol vary for different individuals, cultures, and epochs. In particular, some people and societies view mild imbibing as a joyous experience, while others view alcohol as evil. That images of alcohol vary, even sometimes in the same place and for the same person, is captured in a popular historical anecdote:

> A Congressman was once asked by a constituent to explain his attitude towards whiskey. "If you mean the demon drink that poisons the mind, pollutes the body, desecrates family life and inflames sinners, then I'm against it," the Congressman said. "But if you mean the elixir of Christmas cheer, the shield against winter chill, the taxable potion that puts needed funds into public coffers to comfort little crippled children, then I'm for it. This is my position, and I will not compromise." (Lender & Martin, 1982, p. 169)

Parts of society in the United States—and, increasingly, the public health bodies worldwide—emphasize exclusively the danger and drawbacks of consuming alcohol, although none suggest prohibiting the substance. Yet, the way in which we conceive of the drinking experience strongly influences the nature of that experience, often in a self-fulfilling way. Thus, ignoring health and pleasure benefits, while referring only to the danger and harm associated with alcohol, may delay—even permanently impair—people's ability to adopt sensible and pleasurable drinking practices. This chapter describes an approach using positive models of drinking, emphasizing the pleasure it can provide.

THE PLEASURE OF ALCOHOL

Some cultures and people seem to view alcohol much more positively than Americans do currently. Throughout history there have been unabashed paeans to beverage alcohol, often in musical form:

> A good wine is to be praised above all other things . . .
> Whoever wants to drink as much as I
> Will also be made happy by this wine.
>
> (Orlando Lassus [1532–1594], *Ein Guter Wein*)

In *Drinking Occasions: Comparative Perspectives on Alcohol and Culture*, Dwight Heath (2000) notes about contemporary Spain, "[Alcoholic beverages] have always been the major social lubricant and a source of conviviality and sociability" (p. 11). Alcohol is consumed throughout the day, virtually every day; it is thought of as an essential pleasure. Yet, drunkenness and misbehavior when drinking are strongly disapproved of. This attitude toward and style of drinking is traditional throughout Mediterranean cultures.

The intense experience of pleasure with alcohol consumption is common, even in English-speaking cultures. Psychologist Geoff Lowe (1999) reviewed data from the Mass-Observation Archive at the University of Sussex, which has assessed the lives, views, and feelings of ordinary British people for 50 years. In 1993, Mass-Observation respondents were asked to write about pleasure and good times. Many discussed their drinking experiences, including the following two respondents. A 35-year-old female wrote:

> Good wine can make me feel orgasmic. The nose, taste, and glow one gets can be overwhelming. I have occasionally had wine so delicious it has almost brought tears to my eyes. The ability to taste different spices, fruits, flowers, herbs within one glass of wine differentiates good wines to bad wines for me, and a good wine requires time and thought to be enjoyed fully. However it is not for me, a thing to be deeply discussed and analysed as to what the definitive taste or nose is, but something to be slowly explored and quietly enjoyed. If I were to be marooned on a desert island I would have a good case of wine as my luxury (plus a corkscrew and a large glass!). (p. 258)

A 42-year-old male stated:

> I am sitting outside a cottage/farmhouse in the evening somewhere
> in France (or maybe anywhere else in southern Europe) on a warm
> evening. It's a rural area—there is no traffic noise, no dogs barking,
> nobody asking me to do things for them. I have a good novel and
> a glass of red wine. In the background the crickets are chirping.
> Perhaps I am sitting with my wife who is reading a book as well,
> or perhaps I am with a group of 6 male friends who I go cycling
> with every other year and we have been for a meal and some drinks
> in the local bar. This for me is probably the ultimate pleasure!
> (pp. 258–259)

Lowe further noted that the pleasures people experienced, whether with or
without drinking, varied according to their place in the life span:

> Respondents aged 50 to 69 years reported significantly more nature-
> based pleasures than those younger than 39 years. Those aged 20
> to 29 years reported more sex pleasures and those younger than
> 20 years more social pleasures than those aged 50 to 59; those
> younger than 30 as a whole reported more active and more self-
> indulgent pleasures than other age groups. And those aged 30 to
> 39 years reported slightly more eating/drinking/smoking pleasures
> than did other groups. Elderly respondents reported more family
> pleasures than did the young (almost three times as many). Com-
> pared with men, women reported significantly more nature, social,
> family, and holiday-based pleasures, but their alcohol consumption
> was lower. (pp. 256–257)

Drinking pleasures were not limited to any one form of alcohol or to any
particular age range of respondents. Worldwide, at least among European cultures, general population surveys uniformly identify pleasure as first among
the effects of drinking. Respondents in surveys in the United States, Canada,
and Sweden predominantly mention positive sensations and experiences associated with drinking (e.g., relaxation and sociability), with little mention of
harm (Pernanen, 1991). In two Australian surveys, most respondents identified relaxation, stress reduction, and improved psychological well-being as
benefits of drinking (Hall, 1995; Hall, Flaherty, & Homel, 1992). In Finland,
both student and general populations reported positive effects more often than
negative (Mäkelä & Mustonen, 1988; Mäkelä & Simpura, 1985; Nyström,
1992). Lowe (1994), analyzing the Mass-Observation Archive data together
with surveys of adolescent drinkers and temporary abstainers, reported that

people usually found drinking enjoyable. Leigh and Stacy (1994) found among several groups of drinkers in the United States that, when asked about the effects of alcohol, drinkers list positive effects first and foremost.

PUBLIC HEALTH GROUPS PLACE DRINKING HARMS FOREMOST

Although historically and cross-culturally drinking is experienced as pleasurable, contemporary public health organizations now focus exclusively on the dangers of alcohol. It is not possible to cite all the examples of this, but recent developments show acceleration in this trend and a particular focus on attacking the alcohol industry. At the 2001 Stockholm conference, organized by the World Health Organization's Regional Office for Europe and focused especially on the young, Gro Harlem Brundtland (2001), then the director-general of WHO, stated:

> Globally, 140 million people are suffering from alcohol dependence. Around the world, alcohol takes a heavy toll—damaging public and private life with countless traffic fatalities and injuries, home fires, drowning, suicides and violent crimes. But also debt problems, ruined careers, divorces, birth defects, and children with permanent emotional damage. … Data from across the world suggests that a culture of sporadic binge drinking among young people may now be increasing also in developing countries. While overall rates of adult per capita consumption are falling in many countries, young people are too often drinking excessive quantities of alcohol to intoxication in single drinking episodes.

WHO has now committed itself to an international fight against drinking with the specific goal of reducing alcohol consumption, particularly among the young.
    The United States is especially noteworthy for its efforts to discourage young people's drinking. In 2002, the National Center on Addiction and Substance Abuse (CASA) at Columbia University published a report titled *Teen Tipplers: America's Underage Drinking Epidemic* (National Center on Addiction and Substance Abuse, 2002a). CASA cited data from a number of sources in alarming terms. In a press release that accompanied the release of the report, CASA's president Joseph Califano, Jr. said that "underage drinking has reached epidemic proportions in America," adding that "this report is a clarion call for national mobilization to curb underage drinking" (National Center on Addiction and Substance Abuse, 2002b). Also in 2002, the American Medical

Association (2002) issued a report titled *Partner or Foe: The Alcohol Industry, Youth Alcohol Policies, and Alcohol Policy Strategies*. The goal of this report was to undercut all efforts to encourage moderate drinking on college campuses (Anheuser-Busch's social norms program was targeted in particular) on the grounds that the industry profits by encouraging drinking of the heaviest consumers and by encouraging youthful drinking.

TRENDS IN YOUTHFUL DRINKING

Clearly there are dangers to consuming alcohol, and these dangers are especially evident in youthful drinkers. Brundtland (2001) cited a worldwide increase in binge drinking among the young. These types of activities have been evident among young drinkers in the United States for decades. For example, the Monitoring the Future (MTF) survey measures high school drinking along with other variables. Among 12th graders, according to MTF, 73% had consumed alcohol over the prior year in 2001, roughly the same percentage as in 1993 (the first year in which this question was assessed in the same way); 50% had drunk alcohol in the past 30 days (slightly more than the 1993 figure). As far as getting drunk was concerned, 53% had done so in 2001, the same as in 1991. The percentage of those getting drunk in the past 30 days was 33%, compared with 32% 10 years before (Johnston, O'Malley, & Bachman, 2002; see Table 6.1).

Binge drinking among American college students has been an area of special concern and monitoring. Henry Wechsler, the director of the College Alcohol Studies Program at the Harvard School of Public Health, and colleagues studied binge drinking on U.S. college campuses between 1993 and 2001 (Wechsler et al., 2002). Although the number of abstainers had increased between these points, the percentage of students who binge drank remained the same, while those who *frequently* binge drank *increased* significantly,

TABLE 6.1. High School Senior Drinking, 1991/3–2001 (% prevalence of use)

Alcohol	1991/3	2001
Any Use		
In past year	73	73
In prior 30 days	49	50
Been drunk		
In past year	53	53
In prior 30 days	32	33

Source: Johnston, O'Malley, and Bachman (2002).

despite active college drinking prevention programs organized in connection with the research (see Table 6.2).

There is one other negative aspect of youthful drinking worth noting: the increase in dependence symptoms among young drinkers in recent decades. Dependence symptoms, like blackouts or uncontrolled drinking, withdrawal, and tolerance, represent the most severe range of drinking problems. Between 1967 and 1984, according to national alcohol surveys sponsored by the U.S. National Institute on Alcohol Abuse and Alcoholism (NIAAA) and conducted by the Alcohol Research Group (ARG), Americans in their 20s who reported at least one such symptom dramatically increased from 15% to 25%, combining men and women (Room, 1989). Looking only at those who reported three or more such symptoms, ARG researchers noted a further increase of 50% between 1984 and 1995, from 10% to 15% (Midanik & Greenfield, 1997, 2000).

DOES DRINKING HAVE BENEFITS IN ADDITION TO PRODUCING PLEASURE?

It seems evident that drinking will persist among young people, as well as among adults. The question is, how problematic will such drinking be for the young? Thus far, we have shown no ability to reduce the harmfulness of drinking among those aged under 30. This continued drinking by the young, often of a high-risk nature, should be viewed in the context where prohibition of alcohol, as a goal, has been rejected by Western (and most other) nations.

Total prohibition of alcohol is not considered a plausible goal in Western countries because consumers in them demand the right to consume alcohol. At the same time, beginning in the 1980s, the health benefits of consuming alcohol became clear. Primarily, moderate drinking reduces the risk, and occurrence, of coronary artery disease (CAD). Since, for most population groups in the United States and elsewhere in the Western world, CAD is the largest cause of death, this translates into lower mortality rates and greater life expectancy for moderate consumers of alcohol compared with abstainers (Klatsky, 1999). In addition to being a political and social impracticality, by the late

TABLE 6.2. College Past-Year Binge Drinking, 1993–2001 (% prevalence in each survey)

Drinking Pattern	1993	2001
Abstained	16	19
Binge drank	44	44
Binge drank frequently	20	23

Source: Wechsler et al. (2002).

1990s, it thus became a dubious public health proposition to try to eliminate drinking in countries with high rates of CAD. In other words, more people would *lose* life years in those countries if alcohol consumption were suddenly to disappear than would gain from such prohibition (Single, Robson, Xie, & Rehm, 1998).

Furthermore, a steady stream of research has begun to identify potential—and in some cases fairly well established—*psychological* benefits from moderate drinking. According to a survey by Peele and Brodsky (2000; see also Chick, 1999), these benefits include, in addition to positive feelings, the following:

> To a greater degree than either abstainers or heavy drinkers, moderate drinkers have been found to experience a sense of psychological, physical, and social well-being; elevated mood; reduced stress (under some circumstances); reduced psychopathology, particularly depression; enhanced sociability and social participation; and higher incomes and less work absence or disability. The elderly often have higher levels of involvement and activity in association with moderate drinking, while often showing better-than-average cognitive functioning following long-term moderate alcohol consumption. (Peele & Brodsky, 2000, p. 241)

One area that has repeatedly shown positive findings in prospective research (that is, research where subjects are identified and then followed up throughout their life spans) is improved cognitive functioning.

TEACHING THE YOUNG TO DRINK

How Do Children Learn About Alcohol?

Children learn how to drink from a range of influences, perhaps primarily from role models, most notably family members and peers (Milgram, 2001). They learn also from cultural influences (Heath, 2000; Weiss, 2001). In more culturally homogenous societies, this applies also to the larger societal culture and ethnic and cultural subgroups (Sanchez-Sosa & Poldrugo, 2001). In both Western, economically advanced nations and in developing ones, education in drinking is influenced by advertising (Stockdale, 2001). Some of this advertising is by industry and some by public health organizations, which generally inculcate antialcohol messages. In U.S. society in particular, but increasingly in the Western world in general, alcohol education is part of the school curriculum (Hanson, 2001). As societies become more diverse and technologically advanced, school and media are becoming relatively more important in socializing drinking styles than are parents and ethnic-cultural groups. Peers, however, remain important—peers, who are subjected to the same societywide media and educational influences (Newman, 2001).

What Do Young People Learn About Alcohol?

At this point, at least in the United States, nearly all young people have been informed repeatedly of the harm that alcohol can cause. Among other forms of harm, they are very familiar with alcohol dependence, and in fact often note symptoms of alcohol dependence in themselves. Very often, however, the only alternative they perceive is not to drink at all: like the alcoholic who alternates between avoiding booze and drinking excessively, young people often drink to excess when they do drink. Wechsler and colleagues (2002) find that among college students an increase in abstinence, combined with an increase in frequent excess (binge) drinking, is in line with this dichotomy.

What Should Young People Learn About Alcohol?

Given that alcohol is ubiquitous in Western societies, it seems important (as well as accurate) to note its benefits along with its dangers. That is, moderate drinking increases longevity and can be psychologically beneficial for most drinkers. Learning these things implies the need to educate people in how to regulate their drinking. Indeed, even for high-school students in the United States, which alone among Western nations restricts legal drinking to those aged 21 years and older, there is ample opportunity to drink. Finally, given its likely presence throughout one's lifecycle, it seems worthwhile to inform the young that alcohol may be made an enjoyable part of life.

In addition to these points about personal pleasure, there are equivalent considerations concerning the social obligation for individuals to regulate their drinking. Even for those who drink excessively as youths, the goal should be to learn to drink moderately (Marlatt, 1999, refers to this as "secondary prevention"). The concept of moderate drinking is both possible and beneficial; it is beneficial for the individual and for those around the individual as well as for society at large. In other words, people should learn as an ethical tenet that excessive drinking and antisocial behavior while drinking are wrong.

Who Should Teach Positive Drinking Practices?

None of the primary institutions that present models for alcohol consumption has a special interest in conveying the benefits of moderate drinking and individual responsibility. Public health advocates, for their part, emphasize the dangers of drinking, including its ability to produce dependence and cause people to lose personal control. School-based education programs frequently rely on recovering alcoholics to present antidrinking messages. Like latter-day temperance lecturers, they teach children to associate drinking with excess, drunkenness, and loss of control. This may partially explain why young people in the United States increasingly display such loss of control and other dependence symptoms. Alcohol producers and advertisers speak about drinking responsibly. But alcohol advertising traditionally associates consumption with prestige purchases, social and sexual success and excess (particularly for young males), and other images of personal power and assertiveness. These images do not encourage moderate drinking, but rather the opposite.

How Are We Doing in Teaching the Young to Drink?

The data indicate that the young are not being taught how to regulate their drinking or how to drink moderately. Rather, they continue to practice relatively risky drinking. According to Plant (2001), such risk-taking may be a part of youthful development, one that can never be eliminated. Nonetheless, some basis should be laid for encouraging the emergence of regulated, pleasurable, and sensible drinking. As well as accelerating the development of sensible drinking, such knowledge should increase adults' skills in drinking responsibly, increasing the proportion of consumers who behave constructively and drink healthily.

Education in sensible drinking is not being conducted. The Monitoring the Future survey measures students' attitudes toward drinking, as well as their actual drinking. In 2001, although 69% of high school seniors disapproved of taking one or two drinks nearly every day, fewer (63%) disapproved of taking five or six drinks once or twice each weekend. That is, they disapproved as much or more of the kind of drinking likely to prolong life and encourage emotional well-being as they did of the weekend binge drinking so prevalent among the young (Johnston et al., 2002).

CONCLUSION: THE JOY OF DRINKING

This chapter has looked at how warnings about the dangers of alcohol and exploiting negative models of drinking have a limited impact on encouraging successful drinking patterns. In place of more elaborate and intensive communication of such negative models, we may gain more by presenting a positive model of drinking. Attributes of alcohol consumption can be identified in such a positive model, such as that it:

- brings pleasure, in both the short and the long run;
- facilitates social interaction, including both intimacy and friendship;

- is associated with physical well-being and health;
- contributes to positive thinking and intellectual pleasure;
- supports, rather than interferes with, other primary pleasures in life.

The year 2002 marked the anniversary—and the release of an updated version—of *The Joy of Sex*, a 1970s' manual on sexual pleasure designed for ordinary people, produced by an English physician, Alex Comfort (Comfort, 2002). The work was revised and reissued by the author's son, Nicholas Comfort, for the 30th anniversary of the original edition. Perhaps the time has arrived where we can try to overcome the aversion to acknowledging the pleasure in drinking, even in intoxication, just as we have become better at accepting sexual pleasure. In the service of this goal, we can rely on the mature examples provided by the Mass-Observation respondents quoted above, who so brilliantly describe the association of drinking with conviviality, relaxation, relationships, concentration, exercise, activity, physical contentment, and health.

REFERENCES

American Medical Association. (2002). *Partner or foe: The alcohol industry, youth alcohol policies, and alcohol policy strategies*. Policy Briefing Paper. Chicago: Author.

Brundtland, G. H. (2001, February 19). Address to the WHO European Ministerial Conference on Young People and Alcohol, Stockholm, Sweden. Retrieved June 17, 2004, from http://www.who.int/director-general/speeches/2001/english/20010219_youngpeoplealcohol.en.html.

Comfort, A. (2002). *The joy of sex: Fully revised and completely updated for the 21st century*. New York: Crown.

Chick, J. (1999). Can light or moderate drinking benefit mental health? *European Addiction Research, 5*(2), 74–81.

Hall, W. (1995). Changes in the public perceptions of the health benefits of alcohol use, 1989 to 1994. *Australian-New Zealand Journal of Public Health, 20*(1), 93–95.

Hall, W., Flaherty, B., & Homel, P. (1992). Public perception of the risks and benefits of alcohol consumption. *Australian Journal of Public Health, 16*(1), 38–42.

Hanson, D. J. (2001). Formal education. In E. Houghton & A. M. Roche (Eds.), *Learning about drinking* (pp. 193–208). Philadelphia: Brunner-Routledge.

Heath, D. B. (2000). *Drinking occasions: Comparative perspectives on alcohol and culture*. Philadelphia: Brunner/Mazel.

Johnston, L. D., O'Malley, P. M., & Bachman, J. G. (2002). *Monitoring the Future national results on adolescent drug use: Overview of key findings, 2001*. NIH Publication No. 02-5105. Bethesda, MD: National Institute on Drug Abuse.

Klatsky, A. L. (1999). Is drinking healthy? In S. Peele & M. Grant (Eds.), *Alcohol and pleasure: A health perspective* (pp. 141–156). Philadelphia: Brunner/Mazel.

Leigh, B. C., & Stacy, A. W. (1994). Self-generated alcohol expectancies in four samples of drinkers. *Addiction Research, 1*(4), 335–348.

Lender, M. E., & Martin, J. K. (1982). *Drinking in America: A history.* New York: Free Press.

Lowe, G. (1994). Pleasures of social relaxants and stimulants: The ordinary person's attitudes and involvement. In D. M. Warburton (Ed.), *Pleasure: The politics and the reality* (pp. 95–108). Chichester, United Kingdom: Wiley.

Lowe, G. (1999). Drinking behavior and pleasure across the life span. In S. Peele & M. Grant (Eds.), *Alcohol and pleasure: A health perspective* (pp. 249–263). Philadelphia: Brunner/Mazel.

Mäkelä, K., & Mustonen, H. (1988). Positive and negative consequences related to drinking as a function of annual alcohol intake. *British Journal of Addiction, 83*(4), 403–408.

Mäkelä, K., & Simpura, J. (1985). Experiences related to drinking as a function of annual alcohol intake and by sex and age. *Drug and Alcohol Dependence, 15*(4), 389–404.

Marlatt, G. A. (1999). Alcohol, the magic elixir? In S. Peele & M. Grant (Eds.), *Alcohol and pleasure: A health perspective* (pp. 233–248). Philadelphia: Brunner/Mazel.

Midanik, L. T., & Greenfield, T. K. (1997, November). *Trends in social consequences and dependence symptoms in the United States: 1984–1995.* Paper presented at the 125th annual Meeting of the American Public Health Association, Indianapolis, IN.

Midanik, L. T. & Greenfield, T. K. (2000). Trends in social consequences and dependence symptoms in the United States: 1984–1995. *American Journal of Public Health, 90*(1), 53–56.

Milgram, G. G. (2001). Alcohol influences: Role of family and peers. In E. Houghton & A. M. Roche (Eds.), *Learning about drinking* (pp. 85–108). Philadelphia: Brunner-Routledge.

National Center on Addiction and Substance Abuse (CASA) at Columbia University. (2002a). *Teen tipplers: America's underage drinking epidemic.* New York: Author.

National Center on Addiction and Substance Abuse (CASA) at Columbia University. (2002b). *CASA Report on Underage Drinking.* New York: Author. Retrieved December 16, 2004, from http://www.casacolumbia.org/absolutenm/templates/PressReleases.asp?articleid=271&zoneid=47.

Newman, I. (2001). Multiple influences on adolescents. In E. Houghton & A. M. Roche (Eds.), *Learning about drinking* (pp. 167–191). Philadelphia: Brunner-Routledge.

Nyström, M. (1992). Positive and negative consequences of alcohol drinking among young university students in Finland. *British Journal of Addiction, 87*(5), 715–722.

Peele, S., & Brodsky, A. (2000). Exploring psychological benefits associated with moderate alcohol use: A necessary corrective to assessments of drinking outcomes? *Drug and Alcohol Dependence, 60*(3), 221–247.

Pernanen, K. (1991). *Alcohol in human violence.* New York: Guilford.

Plant, M. (2001). Learning by experiment. In E. Houghton & A. M. Roche (Eds.), *Learning about drinking* (pp. 129–146). Philadelphia: Brunner-Routledge.

Room, R. (1989). Cultural changes in drinking and trends in alcohol problem indicators: Recent U.S. experience. *Alcologia, 1,* 83–89.

Sanchez-Sosa, J. J., & Poldrugo, F. (2001). Family and cultural influences on alcohol and young people. In E. Houghton & A. M. Roche (Eds.), *Learning about drinking* (pp. 57–83). Philadelphia: Brunner-Routledge.

Single, E., Robson, L., Xie, X., & Rehm, J. (1998). The economic costs of alcohol, tobacco and illicit drugs in Canada, 1992. *Addiction, 93*(7), 991–1006.

Stockdale, J. S. (2001). The role of the media. In E. Houghton & A. M. Roche (Eds.), *Learning about drinking* (pp. 209–242). Philadelphia: Brunner-Routledge.

Wechsler, H., Lee, J. E., Kuo, M., Seibring, M., Nelson, T. F., & Lee, H. (2002). Trends in college binge drinking during a period of increased prevention efforts. Findings from 4 Harvard School of Public Health College Alcohol Study Surveys: 1993–2001. *Journal of American College Health, 50*(5), 203–217.

Weiss, S. (2001). Religious influences on drinking: Illustrations from select groups. In E. Houghton & A. M. Roche (Eds.), *Learning about drinking* (pp. 109–128). Philadelphia: Brunner-Routledge.

Chapter 7

Drinking It In: Findings of the Valencia Meeting on Marketing and Promotion of Alcohol to Young People

Leanne Riley

The World Health Organization (WHO), as the leading international public health agency, is increasing its attention to the preventable risk factors associated with global morbidity and mortality. The *World Health Report* for 2002 (World Health Organization, 2002) focused on some of the key risks that predict the future course of death and disease for most of the world's population. These risks include tobacco, alcohol use, poor diet, and lack of physical activity. Alcohol consumption among young people is a significant cofactor in the leading causes of death among young people, including motor vehicle crashes, suicides, homicides, and drownings. Data from across the world suggest that a culture of sporadic heavy or binge drinking among young people is growing in developing countries as it has in developed countries.

In addressing the preventable risks to health, WHO and, indeed, the broader public health community are paying increasing attention to the impact of marketing to young people, both in promoting healthy behavior and in undermining health. Across the globe, children and young people are vulnerable targets for the new technologies of persuasion and marketing messages. Their direct buying power is increasing worldwide, and they exert considerable influence over household spending. Companies are keen to establish all-important brand loyalty to their products as early as possible, in the hope of maintaining it over the course of the young people's lives. It is in this context that concern has developed over the role that alcohol marketing plays in contributing to alcohol-related problems. This is not to suggest that marketing and promotion of alcoholic beverages are the most important cause or contributors to alcohol problems in young people. There are many interrelated factors, but these two elements play a significant and highly visible role and need attention, along with the attention paid to other factors and strategies.

In recent years, there has been a growing trend for alcohol marketing strategies to broaden their scope, complementing traditional forms of direct advertising in the print and broadcast media with other marketing activities, such as music, sports, or cultural sponsorship, Internet-based promotions and websites, product placements, youth-oriented new product development, and on-premise and special event promotions. Many of these new media are extremely attractive to young people, but are currently the subject of minimal regulation. The Internet is an interesting example: young people are the biggest users of the Internet and of advanced mobile phone technology. Industries, including the alcohol industry, have been quick to grasp the resulting marketing opportunity.

Beverage companies all over the world have created sophisticated websites for their most popular brands. They use the latest technology to produce interactive arenas with impressive graphics and eye-catching animation. The sophistication of these sites suggests that a great deal of money has been spent on their development. More important, their content is designed to tap into key aspects of youth culture, so that computer games, competitions, e-cards, and profiles of forthcoming sponsored events (e.g., parties, fashion shows, and sporting contest) are all common features.

Another piece of this marketing mix is the development of new products. Since the introduction of the first of the alcopops in 1995, the beverage industry has come up with a wide variety of alcoholic drinks that are likely to be attractive to children and young people. Alcopops, with their sweet taste and appeal to younger, inexperienced drinkers' palates, help to accustom this segment of the population to the taste of alcohol and propel them into the alcohol market. In fact, the sweet taste and the use of cartoon images, bright colors, psychedelic lettering, and glow-in-the-dark labels, together with rebellious, antiestablishment names, can only appeal to young people. Through the use of words such as "lemonade" and "cola," children can be easily misled by the packaging and may mistake these alcoholic beverages for soft drinks.

The increasingly widespread marketing of products leads to concern about its effects on the behavior of young people and on their attitudes toward alcohol. Although econometric studies may show only weak or little impact, survey data present evidence suggesting that young people do respond to this marketing on an emotional level, changing their beliefs and expectations about drinking. Marketing clearly influences a young person's decision to drink. Exposure to and enjoyment of alcohol advertising predicts heavier and more frequent drinking among young people. Marketing also contributes to young people overestimating the prevalence of heavy and frequent drinking among their peers and creates a climate for further increases in alcohol consumption by young people.

Equally important is the misleading picture of alcohol that marketing encourages. By presenting a very one-sided view of alcohol, linking it to fun, enjoyment, sexual and social success, marketing masks its contribution to morbidity, mortality, and social harm. Marketing's pervasiveness also serves to create the impression that drinking alcohol is the norm in all societies. It presents alcohol as a normal and integral part of young people's lives and cultures. In fact, more than half of the world's population aged 15 years and over are abstainers, and, of those who do drink, many are only very light or infrequent drinkers. This one-sided impression of the role of alcohol in society, fostered by marketing, contributes to an environment hostile to public health measures and messages.

Although global marketing and sales are increasing, it is clear that global and national regulation and education efforts are lagging or inadequate to address this issue, particularly in developing and transitional countries. Governments have traditionally employed a range of protective measures, including voluntary or self-regulatory codes of good advertising behavior, warnings in advertising, partial or complete restrictions on advertising and marketing in one or more media or venues, and counteradvertising. However, these current responses have done little to control the marketing of alcohol products, especially since many of them focus on advertising in the traditional media and miss many of the other marketing strategies already mentioned. In addition, technological innovations have increased the speed and intensity with which people receive information. Satellite television has made it possible to broadcast simultaneously in many different countries.

This globalization of the media has radically changed the face of advertising. As a result, a television commercial for an alcohol product can be received in a country where alcohol advertising is prohibited or restricted. For example, an alcohol commercial produced and transmitted from England could be picked up in Denmark, where alcohol commercials are actually forbidden. The use of a complete marketing mix of product pricing, easy availability, and promotion therefore requires a more comprehensive response, which can address all these marketing variables. The very global nature of marketing demands a response at international, national, and local levels.

In May 2002, in Valencia, Spain, WHO convened a meeting of public health experts and young people to review this area and make recommendations for further action and consideration. Over 50 representatives from 22 countries attended. The views of the alcohol industry were also presented through a paper prepared by International Center for Alcohol Policies (ICAP) on this issue. The participants at this meeting made the following four recommendations to WHO:

Noting the dangers inherent in the exposure of young people to alcohol marketing, that young people should not be exposed to promotional messages about alcohol in any medium and the general failure of industry self-regulation to limit the marketing of alcohol to young people,

• We recommend that the WHO assist countries in taking all legislative or regulatory steps necessary to ensure that young people are not exposed to promotional messages about alcohol.

Noting that the alcohol industry has achieved a high level of sophistication in its use of media to attract and encourage young people to drinking,

• We recommend that the WHO assist countries in raising awareness of these techniques, and developing best practices in media advocacy and counter-advertising programs, and that such practices be undertaken independently of commercial interests, and with participation of and leadership from young people themselves.

Noting the importance of young people's perspectives on this problem, and the creativity and unique knowledge of the situation that they possess,

• We recommend that young people play a central role in the work to free their generation from the illusions created by marketing and associated promotions of alcohol.

Noting the threats posed by trade agreements, negotiations and disputes to the ability of communities' jurisdictions to protect the public health through the regulation of the marketing of beverage alcohol, and that there is a particular potential threat from the current negotiations on the General Agreement on Trade in Services,

• We recommend that the WHO formulate a strategy to ensure that current negotiations on the services agreement does not undermine the rights and capacity of communities' jurisdictions to set appropriate and public health-oriented alcohol policies. (Global Alcohol Policy Alliance, 2002)

A response is clearly being demanded by the public health community and, indeed, by the affected and aware sections of civil society. So where does the alcohol industry figure in all this? Advice and leadership from WHO is being sought by a number of its member states that are concerned with this issue and want to review and develop more appropriate control measures. In formulating its own advice, WHO is committed to hearing the views of all key stakeholders, and this of course includes the alcohol industry. In February 2003, WHO invited a number of alcohol companies to a meeting at its headquarters in Geneva in order to provide the companies with a forum in which they could share their views on these issues and offer suggestions as to how they might contribute to a more appropriate response. It is clear that similar opportunities exist in specific countries where task forces or committees are being established to review existing situations and industry inputs, and perspectives are being invited as part of this process.

In the context of examining the roles and responsibilities of various stakeholders concerned with beverage alcohol, the industry is being presented with a choice and an opportunity: to be part of the problem or to be part of the solution. Those working at WHO sincerely hope that the beverage alcohol companies—either individually or collectively—will decide to be part of the solution. Enhanced global interaction and dialogue involving all key stakeholders will hopefully bring all the parties closer to an understanding of how to deal effectively with an increasing global public health threat. Strong, visible action now on this issue will lead to healthier, happier, and more productive communities.

REFERENCES

Global Alcohol Policy Alliance (GAPA). (2002). Declaration of the technical consultation to the WHO on the marketing and promotion of alcohol to young people [online version]. *The Globe: Drinking it in. WHO targets alcohol marketing.* Retrieved June 21, 2004, http://www.ias.org.uk/publications/theglobe/02issue2/globe0202_p5.html.
World Health Organization (WHO). (2002). *The World Health Report 2002: Reducing risks, promoting healthy life.* Geneva: Author.

Chapter 8

Government Regulation, Corporate Responsibility, and Personal Pleasure: A Public Health Perspective From New Zealand

Mike MacAvoy and Meg Mackenzie

This chapter approaches the topic of corporate social responsibility from a public health perspective. It assumes that alcohol use and misuse are so well entrenched in our culture that it does not contemplate anything other than a continuing presence. The issue then is how to live harmoniously with alcohol and not how to battle with it. From the perspective of those who have worked in the field of substance abuse for many years, and despite a huge and ever-expanding literature on the topic, it is astonishing how little is understood of the extraordinarily complex interactions between alcohol, the consumer, and the environment.

The negative impact of alcohol on individuals, societies, and, indeed, countries can be immense and is often unmeasured. Further, with changing global trade, marketing, and communication strategies, alcohol use has spread to wider sections of the population, in terms of both age and gender, and also to countries where alcohol was previously used minimally. It is, therefore, not surprising that the beverage alcohol industry should have come under increasing and often intense scrutiny for its alleged contribution to the negative aspects of alcohol use. Yet, the most striking feature in the whole debate around alcohol is the inability to form a balanced view of what an ideal society in which alcohol is present might look like. This failure has led to the polarization of views between the public health sector, other interest groups, and the alcohol industry. One of the few attempts to breach this divide resulted in the European Charter on Alcohol (World Health Organization Regional Office for Europe, 1995). In an effort to further the European Alcohol Action Plan, the charter calls on "Member States to draw up comprehensive alcohol policies and implement programmes that give expression, as appropriate in their differing cultures and social, legal and economic environments," to certain rights in relation to alcohol consumption, which it is the responsibility of the state to uphold. The European Charter sets out these rights as:

1. All people have the right to a family, community and working life protected from accidents, violence and other negative consequences of alcohol consumption.
2. All people have the right to valid impartial information and education, starting early in life, on the consequences of alcohol consumption on health, the family and society.
3. All children and adolescents have the right to grow up in an environment protected from the negative consequences of alcohol consumption and, to the extent possible, from the promotion of alcoholic beverages.
4. All people with hazardous or harmful alcohol consumption and members of their families have the right to accessible treatment and care.
5. All people who do not wish to consume alcohol, or who cannot do so for health or other reasons, have the right to be safeguarded from pressures to drink and be supported in their non-drinking behaviour. (World Health Organization Regional Office for Europe, 1995)

These rights adopt a population focus that lacks a holistic perspective of the society the charter intends to create, or of the responsibilities of the individuals who live within that society and choose to drink. If to the right to the minimization of alcohol-related harm (already within the charter) one adds the proviso that the potential social and health benefits of alcohol are also recognized, a vision emerges whereby alcohol can play an integral part in people's lives but in a manner that sustains society. If it is possible to define a society in which alcohol is used both safely and enjoyably and in which its use sustains and nurtures the culture of that society in a positive manner, who should be involved in determining that vision? How does one define what is acceptable drinking behavior and what is a tolerable level of harm arising from excessive use of alcohol?

For most governments, the sale of alcohol creates a major source of revenue through taxation. Few governments impose excise on alcohol products for the sole purpose of controlling consumption and consequently minimizing harm. This dependence on the product's potential for creating revenue has affected the ability of governments to assess objectively the impact of alcohol on their populations. Neither governments nor the alcohol industry can be seen as objective purveyors of an ideal society, but are those from the health sector any better equipped? Certainly, the health sector has contributed greatly, albeit reluctantly, to the identification of the risks generated through excessive alcohol use and the potential health benefits of moderate alcohol use. Much of the advice emerging from the public health sector is seen as negative, emphasizing attitudes and behaviors unwanted by the drinking public or the alcohol industry, or setting safe limits of consumption that appear to be well below those of the "normal" drinking experience.

No drinker sets out to damage his or her liver or become dependent on alcohol. Drinkers do set out to reduce anxiety, relieve emotional pain, or facilitate social intercourse and a host of other pleasurable effects through the use of alcohol. Relatively little attention has been paid to these social aspects of alcohol use in the literature (with the exception of Peele and Grant [1999]). The reality is that, apart from the interest in the product for itself (i.e., for the taste, smell, texture, and so forth), most people drink for the changes it induces in their emotional state or to engage more freely in certain behaviors, which are perceived as pleasurable. The alcohol industry wants to promote the beneficial effects of its products in the life of an individual. Governments want to control consumption of alcohol among certain groups, especially young people and people with diagnosed alcohol dependence or abuse disorders, and to avoid the costs of excessive consumption—both financial and social—while maintaining an effective revenue stream. Finally, the public health sector wants to alert the public to the risks of excessive consumption for the individual and society as a whole. On the receiving end of this bombardment of messages, it is little wonder that the average consumer remains largely unaffected by the proclamations from any of these groups and takes out of these proclamations only what he or she wants to hear. There is little in the way of a common partnership between these powerful groups, because most governments, representatives of the alcohol industry, and the public health sector cannot agree on a common vision. Any attempt by one or more of these groups to promote a collaborative vision is viewed with suspicion and cynicism by the others (Babor, 2000; David, 1999). In identifying a way forward, three important aspects emerge, based on the roles of individuals, governments, and the industry. These are:

- the rights and responsibilities of the individual;
- the role of governments in regulating those rights and responsibilities, while preserving the freedom of the individual as far as possible;

- the responsibility of the alcohol industry to ensure that communities, at the very least, are not harmed by alcohol in the drive for market share and shareholder satisfaction.

THE RIGHTS AND RESPONSIBILITIES OF INDIVIDUALS

A Right to Individual Pleasure

Many individuals consume alcohol to alleviate undesirable feelings and thoughts or to permit certain social behaviors to occur. These people may describe the resulting experiences as pleasurable, but it is not possible to derive a universally acceptable definition of pleasure, nor can we extrapolate from samples of individuals to the general population. Pleasure is not the same for all and, indeed, some "pleasures" may be positive experiences for some, yet negative experiences for others. The search for pleasurable feelings or experiences to alleviate emotional or physical pain is a natural phenomenon. The use of chemicals to achieve such a transition may become more common or socially tolerable as the levels of uncertainty, stress, and negative experiences in people's lives increase.

Since the terrorist attacks of September 11, 2001, for example, U.S. commentators and experts report that there has been a significant rise in "junk food consumption, pub crawling, late-night clubbing, casual sex," an increase in the sales of spirits by 25% compared to November 2000, and an increase in "determined drunkenness" (O'Neill, 2001). One commentator considered this to mean that "everyday Americans are coping with calamity through hedonism" to erase the painful concept that at any time, anyone could fall victim to an unpredictable and catastrophic event (Bockhorn, 2001). The fact that fear is driving this new hedonism throughout the world, not just in the United States, was confirmed by the attitudes of English and U.S. bar patrons interviewed by the *New York Times* after September 11 who commented that, "If we learn anything from what happened, it should be that you must live for the moment because tomorrow you could be toast" (O'Neill, 2001).

People in the United States who are using drugs and alcohol to cope or have relapsed from society after the national tragedy are the forgotten victims of September 11 (O'Neill, 2001). The hedonists, however, would not agree that they are simply using alcohol to "cope." They see the use and excessive use of alcohol as a valid pursuit that gives pleasure in itself, and they dislike the implication that they are drinking because they have "problems." Instant gratification has become part of a more general "psychoactive culture" among contemporary youth. Alcohol is the dominant psychoactive drug for people aged 18 to 30 years and is becoming more and more popular among young people of school age as well.

Libertarianism

The U.S. Libertarian Party's *Statement of Principles* holds that "all individuals have the right to exercise sole dominion over their own lives, and have the right to live in whatever manner they choose, so long as they do not forcibly interfere with the equal right of others to live in whatever manner they choose" (Libertarian Party, 2002). This core principle is translated into sovereignty over all aspects of one's life, including alcohol use and misuse. Thus, the "informed libertarian" reads or hears the public health warnings about the effects of excessive alcohol use on his or her health and considers the costs, risks, and benefits before making a choice about drinking. As for the short-term ill effects, these are just part of the price you pay, and different people will come to different conclusions about whether the price is worth paying.

In order to justify this viewpoint, libertarians tend to view promoters of public health messages as "puritans" who exaggerate research findings on the health effects of frowned-upon but so-called "pleasurable" pursuits, such as drinking alcohol or drinking to excess (Frederick, 1993). Indeed, they find these puritans making inroads into areas formerly known as "good clean fun," such as sport and recreation. Therefore, the libertarians view public health messages with suspicion, as antifun rather than antiharm, and the intention behind the messages is ignored. One author justifies his periods of excessive drunkenness in the face of public health messages by stating, "I'm here to enjoy life, not just to avoid dying" (Frederick, 1993, p. 5).

A Responsibility to Oneself and One's Society

Although many governments do not favor total abstinence from alcohol, scientific recognition of the harms caused by alcohol misuse or immoderate alcohol use has moved the promotion of self-regulation of alcohol use away from the individual and into the realms of public health systems and public policy. Nongovernmental organizations and public health agencies promote safe or responsible drinking guidelines, and public health researchers publish findings on the short- and long-term harms from immoderate alcohol use. An incessant clamor over disproportionate levels of harm linked to alcohol drowns out most of the research news about the social and health benefits of alcohol use. In an age when instant gratification is the norm, when the introduction of drugs of many different types has given rise to street-smart, savvy, educated, cynical, and hedonistic young people seeking "out of the norm" but presumably pleasurable experiences, there is, however, a lack of understanding as to what drives humans to seek pleasure and to seek out alcohol to achieve it. When confronted by lifestyle choices, and particularly when pleasure is involved, seemingly remote negative consequences may have little relevance (Brain, 2000).

Nevertheless, even libertarians agree that individuals give up certain rights and assume certain responsibilities as a condition of living in an organized society. In recent years, however, the rise of public health as a science has brought a whole new perspective to understanding the rights of individuals and the expectations that societies may have of those who reside in them. Luik (1999) concludes that much disease is caused by unhealthy lifestyle choices about pleasure and risk. Hence, adopting "appropriate" lifestyle choices can prevent much disease. Further, individuals have a moral obligation to live their lives in accordance with society's accepted norm of healthy behavior and should thus avoid inappropriate pleasures.

In an increasingly demanding society, it is generally accepted that services must be rationed and the needs of individuals prioritized. Individuals must accept that the right to live in a modern society brings with it a greater personal responsibility for their own health than ever before and that "a compromise must be reached between unbridled individual pursuits and social obligations" (Plange, 1999, p. 56). From this perspective, it is not unreasonable for the "accepted norms" of behavior to be encouraged or even imposed where the cost of "unacceptable" behaviors (such as risk-taking) to a society begins to challenge the ability of governments to provide basic resources to all. Examples of regulatory measures established to reduce the social cost of behaviors range from the compulsory wearing of seat belts in cars to attempts to eradicate smoking. In each case, these are lifestyle choices that, if left unregulated, have the capacity to impose considerable, yet avoidable, costs on society. It is abundantly clear that the imposition of a significant cost to society has been demonstrated in the case of alcohol.

Thus, the basic tenets of libertarian philosophy can be used to justify the regulation of alcohol in a society. According to libertarian thought, "the only purpose for which power can be rightfully exercised over any member of a civilized community, against his will, is to prevent harm to others" (Mill, 1859/2003, p. 94).

THE ROLE OF GOVERNMENT

Protecting the weak and vulnerable members of the community is a fundamental social responsibility. The role of the state is to impose its expectations of "acceptable behavior" on the individuals living within a society while preserving personal freedoms as far as possible (Gostin, 2000a, 2000b). In societies where the use of alcohol is under voluntary control, the frequency and quantity of consumption are the lifestyle choices of individuals. Therefore, these are matters in which the community and state can expect individuals to make "safe" and "healthy" choices reflective of their own interests and the interests of the community in which they live. The challenge is to balance the right of individuals to pursue their own nirvana while protecting the individuals and the wider society from unacceptable risks and cost. This challenge is predicated on the assumption that humans are rational and will act in their own self-interest and in the interest of the community in which they live. For most of the population alcohol is consumed safely and enjoyably. However, the reality is that the effect of alcohol on a person's judgment impairs his or her ability to analyze risk, making the individual more likely to make choices that are neither in his or her own self-interest, nor in the interest of his or her community. For the most part, people carry on having fun, even when they know the risks they are taking or the damage they are incurring (Frederick, 1993).

Harm Minimization

Throughout the world, governments are struggling with the concept of harm minimization in relation to legal drugs such as alcohol and tobacco. Although many governments state a commitment to harm minimization, it is the government's economic relationship with the alcohol industry that challenges this commitment. This is not a new challenge. The two principles of harm minimization in which governments can play a key role are supply control and demand reduction. Supply control strategies aim to reduce alcohol-related harm by restricting the availability of alcohol. One of the most effective ways in which governments can control the availability of alcohol is by passing and enforcing legislation that controls the production, sale, and supply of alcohol beverages. The demand reduction approach involves strategies that encourage reduced and responsible use of alcohol. The obvious example from a government's point of view is to ensure that there exists credible information to assist individuals in making healthy choices about their drinking and to discourage excessive consumption.

Demand reduction strategies also include encouraging effective self-regulation by the alcohol and hospitality industries in the areas of the promotion of alcohol, marketing of new beverages and product ranges, and host responsibility. However, it may also include the use of taxation to vary or maintain the price of alcohol in order to contain or decrease levels of alcohol consumption and related harms (Alcohol Advisory Council of New Zealand and Ministry of Health, 2001).

Information and Education

Consumers have the right to know the risks and benefits of any substance they ingest. Knowledge of the effects that a substance will have on health or behavior helps to inform an individual's decision as to whether or not to partake of that substance. Whether consumers choose to use the information is a matter of individual choice. Where the state considers that the risks of using a substance may impose costs to the individual or others, it may define certain conditions for the use of that substance. Educating the general drinker, however, is a relatively unsuccessful way of altering the drinker's attitudes and behavior. The complexity of the interaction between alcohol, the individual, and the situation in which alcohol is consumed makes it impossible to provide anything other than generalized advice. Most alcohol education is focused on the negative consequences of excessive consumption, and little information is provided to drinkers about patterns of acceptable use or levels of responsible consumption (Snel, 1999).

Likewise, evidence suggests that warning labels on alcohol products identifying the harms related to alcohol do much else but raise awareness (MacAvoy, 2002). "Labels that utilize a 'bumper sticker' approach, which are nebulous, inaccurate, or which tell people not to do something they may enjoy, do not assist individuals in making informed choices" (Alcohol Advisory Council of New Zealand, 1996, p. 33). The response of governments has been to counteract these simplistic messages with long-winded and complex truths but, when faced with overwhelming publicity from sectors of the alcohol industry and a public that wants to believe in good news stories, these have had little impact.

Regulating Advertising

The role of advertising in creating a certain mystique around the consequences of being seen with or consuming alcohol products has been a highly effective promotional strategy in capturing brand preference. The main function of alcohol advertising is to keep the market for alcohol products stable and saturated, and in ensuring an ongoing supply of new customers. Despite this, the evidence for the effectiveness of a ban on advertising as a harm minimization tool is equivocal. For many, proposals to ban advertising are viewed as protection where it is not needed, a solution looking for a problem, and an insult to the public's intelligence. The issue confronting makers of public policy is whether advertising encourages excessive consumption, creates an environment where alcohol use is normalized, or simply captures market share (Fisher & Cook, 1995; Nelson, 1990, 1997; Nelson & Moran, 1995; Saffer, 1991, 1995, 1997; Smart & Cutler, 1976; Wyllie, Zhang, & Casswell, 1994). Although the issue may appear simplistic, matters such as price, disposable income, and social factors may influence consumption decisions more directly than advertising.

Some countries ban advertising, while others, including New Zealand, have established codes to prevent the excesses in advertising (i.e., where it promotes fantasies or associates alcohol consumption with highly desirable outcomes or with behavior that society concludes is harmful) (Advertising Standards

Authority and Advertising Standards Complaints Board, 2002). Prohibition of alcohol advertising carries with it an assumption that the government can control all images of alcohol products and associations with the proposed drinker. This is simply not realistic. Increasing and uninhibited access to new technologies, such as the global Internet, text messaging, and viral marketing techniques, means that a total ban of advertising is not possible. With increased globalization, the use of an advertising ban to place alcohol imagery out of sight and, therefore, out of mind is a fantasy in itself.

Regulating Marketing

The alcohol industry attracts considerable criticism because some of its marketing strategies appeal to and recruit young drinkers. The appearance on the market of alcopops in the 1990s antagonized many governments of the day as much as it did parts of the beverage alcohol industry itself, although for different reasons. The production of highly flavored and colored drinks along with containers resembling, for example, syringes, sticks of gelignite, and hand grenades, often with high alcohol content, has been seen as a cynical exercise in recruitment. Moreover, novelty products such as alcoholic milk shakes and alcoholic jellies were clearly designed to create a fashion among the less sophisticated.

From the design and naming of a whole new set of alcohol products, most notably represented by alcopops, it has become clear that the alcohol industry has embraced youth drug culture. As Brain (2000) noted, "Early products in the alcopops range bore names such as 'Raver,' 'Blastaway,' 'DNA' (a play on the initials MDMA which denote the drug ecstasy)" (p. 5). These products and their marketing complete the move from alcoholic drinks simply mimicking the names and argot of the illicit drug culture to directly selling alcohol products as drugs. To the credit of the British alcohol industry, the creation of a code of practice by the Portman Group has done much to remove some of the more offensive products from the United Kingdom market. New Zealand has modeled its own self-regulatory guidelines on the Portman Group Code of Practice on the Naming, Packaging and Promotion of Alcoholic Drinks (Alcohol Advisory Council of New Zealand, 2000). However, the New Zealand experience has demonstrated that a voluntary code may prove effective in gaining the cooperation of its signatories but will do little to curb the behavior of others in the alcohol industry.

THE ALCOHOL INDUSTRY

The alcohol industry has succeeded, through its marketing and advertising strategies, in creating visions to attract consumers and maintain consumer loyalty to its products. This is evident in the growth and continuous introduction of new ranges of alcohol beverages. In part, it is the recognition of this success that drives the public health sector to block or obstruct these strategies.

Unlike many other aspects of alcohol-related harm, drink driving can have immediate negative consequences that are easy to demonstrate to the public. Unlike alcohol-related harms such as falls or self-harm, governments have built a strong statutory framework around drink driving, providing for associated punitive measures in legislation. The relative success of government and public health sector attempts to change drink driving behavior may also be due in part to the fact that the alcohol industry has supported or at least not undermined strategies to reduce drink driving in communities. If the industry were to support strategies to increase the age at which young people begin regular social drinking or to change the "binge" mentality of young people, for example, there could be an impact on the industry's profits.

The alcohol industry has been committing money to research into education about responsible drinking. The argument would "appear to turn not so much on whether education has contributed to convincing the majority to drink sensibly, clearly it has, but rather whether education is likely to effect changes in the minority who regularly drink excessively" (Hawks, 1993b, p. 131). If the aim of such education is as public health community and governments understand it (that is, to convince excessive drinkers to moderate their drinking to recommended upper limits), such an outcome would have a significant effect on the profits of the alcohol industry (Hawks, 1993b). After all, the 10% of drinkers who drink to excess consume between 50% and 70% of all alcohol beverages (Jacobson, Hacker, & Atkins, 1983). Unless the alcohol industry can convince the same number (or more) of lighter drinkers to drink up to those recommended upper limits, per capita consumption will decline significantly and the profit margin will plummet with it (Hawks, 1993b).

Consumer Seduction

The abstainer or nondrinker is an important potential consumer for the alcohol market. Thus, women and young people, who have made up a significant part of this population in the past, have become key targets for advertising and marketing strategies, with a range of new products being developed to cater to their tastes. The alcohol industry creates excellent conditions for consumer hedonism to flourish by supplying the market with a diverse range of high-strength psychoactive beverages. Understandably, the alcohol industry has seen the potential for market share and has attempted to use its products to meet this potential.

Does the alcohol industry have an ethical responsibility? The answer is most surely a resounding "yes." This includes not evading its responsibilities to its consumers and the wider community. The free enterprise system that drives most of the production and sale of alcohol products, like all such systems, is based on a foundation of ethics and expectations:

> There can be no ethics without taking responsibility. One of the older misunderstandings about responsibility is the idea that responsibility is a *burden* and that responsibility in business is largely a matter of liability for punishment. ... Responsibility is having a place ... in a community as a full-fledged participant. ... There is nothing negative about responsibility—except when it is a responsibility unfulfilled or neglected. (Solomon, 1994, pp. 71–72)

It is an accepted fact in the world of business that the primary obligation of large profit-driven companies is to their shareholders. Those companies also have obligations to their customers, suppliers, employees, and the community: "Loyalty is half of business ethics, but social responsibility is the other half" (Solomon, 1994, p. 71).

Hawks asks, "What would a friendly alcohol industry look like, since, unless we are to evidence irredeemable cynicism, a responsible industry must be conceivable" (Hawks, 1993a, p. 22). He concludes that an ethical, socially responsible, and "friendly" alcohol industry would be one that:

- advertises and promotes products in a truthful manner;
- does not make false associations;
- does not encourage overconsumption;
- does not target vulnerable populations;
- ensures to the best of its abilities that its products are sold and served responsibly;
- does not deliberately cultivate the culture of intoxication;
- agrees to a pricing policy that minimizes alcohol-related costs to society;
- does not resist or subvert public education messages or public health policies intended to ensure safer alcohol use;
- accepts that alcohol is a potentially dangerous product and, therefore, should not be regarded as a commodity to be sold cheaply and without restraint; and
- accepts that, to protect society, its products may attract further regulation resulting in a declining profit margin and a more modest return on investment. (Hawks, 1993a)

CONCLUSION

Peele (1999) explores

alternative models of drinking ... which emphasize healthy versus unhealthy consumption patterns as well as the individual's responsibility to manage his or her drinking. The ultimate goal is for people to see alcohol as an accompaniment to an overall healthy and pleasurable lifestyle, an image they enact as moderate, sensible drinking patterns. (Peele, p. 375)

This goal should be fundamental to any community in which alcohol is present. However, nurturing and maintaining a healthy community in which alcohol is present *can only* occur when the government, the individual, and the alcohol industry sacrifice certain self-interests for the common good. These sacrifices must be made by all three players for this ideal society to be created and maintained. How can these three elements of self-sacrifice be undertaken in balance so as to create and maintain the ideal society in which alcohol is present?

Ideal Government Behaviors

Public regulation of the alcohol industry is necessary for the promotion of a model of sustainable consumption (Brain, 2000). Economists and other policymakers have long argued that governments have an ethical responsibility to intervene when there is market failure, and this has been extrapolated to intervention in the case of other social failures. However, as democratic governments are voted into office in order to serve and protect a population and the rights of that population, it can be argued that governments also have an ethical responsibility to act to *prevent* market or social failure, while still preserving and protecting the rights of the individual as far as possible. This is surely the case where alcohol-related harms threaten to damage or impose huge costs upon a society: "The production, marketing and consumption of alcohol are therefore quite properly and, indeed, unavoidably matters of public policy" (Eurocare, 1995, p. 9).

Ideal Industry Behaviors

"The 'freedom' in free enterprise presumably includes the liberty to pursue goals other than profits" (Solomon, 1994, p. 216). This means that it is perfectly valid for the alcohol industry to pursue the goals of caring for its consumers and being socially responsible. Therefore, in addition to complying with government regulation, the alcohol industry can choose to self-regulate and can limit its own seduction of the consumer, thus preventing or limiting the repression of the consumer by the state and at the same time reducing the likelihood that the state will move to regulate the market.

Ideal Individual Behaviors

The individual can choose not to be seduced by the market, thus reducing the likelihood that he or she will be repressed by the state. But to make such a choice, communities and their individual citizens must be fully informed of the options available to them and must understand the reasons why choosing not to be seduced by the market is the best option for them. This must be an acceptable choice for societies and their individual members if it is to be a sustainable one, and individuals will need to realize that "responsibility does not restrict one's freedom; it *defines* it" (Solomon, 1994, p. 72). In order to choose this path, individuals must be offered an incentive. For some, the incentive of acting in the public interest will be enough. However, for many, this will not be an adequate reason to change attitudes and behaviors. In the past, public health messages have not been presented in an accessible way that offers interesting or pleasurable alternatives for the hedonist or the libertarian. Many individuals will need to be offered something of equal or greater value than the pleasure they receive from excessive alcohol consumption before they will consider making a positive change. It may be up to both the government and the industry to negotiate this replacement with communities and their members.

Collaboration and Acceptance Between Governments, Individuals, and the Industry

Clearly, the behaviors discussed above require each player to act in the interests of the public good and to exercise social responsibility. In most developed nations, the government is the body that has ultimate control over ethics and behaviors of both individuals and industry because it has the power to define, regulate, and enforce ethical or "appropriate" behaviors. Real reductions in levels of alcohol-related harm cannot occur until the government sacrifices self-interest by setting aside its attachment to revenue gained from the taxation of alcohol. Only after it puts this self-interest aside and considers the good of its constituents can the government make effective decisions that will result in significant reductions in alcohol-related harm.

Similarly, real changes with respect to excessive drinking cannot occur until the individual sees merit in adopting attitudes and behavior for the greater good rather than for self-interest. This means that individuals will need to accept that the government has a right to intervene where alcohol use causes harm to its consumers and can result in costs to others or the state. The alcohol industry must accept that it has a social responsibility over and above that of meeting shareholders' needs. At its most basic level, industry's social responsibility stems from the simple fact that, if the alcohol industry is seen to be behaving in a harmful manner, the consequent public, media, and public health backlash will damage its market share. Therefore, the alcohol industry is obliged to self-regulate in order to maintain market share and consumer goodwill. Moreover, if the alcohol industry regulates itself, it will have more control than if governments force regulation upon it (Hawks, 1993a; Jacobson et al., 1983). As Hawks puts it, until the industry demonstrates that it can regulate itself effectively, "the public have a right to demand that governments exercise more control of the industry" (Hawks, 1993b, p. 132).

REFERENCES

Advertising Standards Authority (ASA) and Advertising Standards Complaints Board. (2002). *Advertising codes of practice.* Wellington, New Zealand: Authors.

Alcohol Advisory Council of New Zealand (ALAC). (1996). *Submission to the review of the Sale of Liquor Act (1989).* Wellington, New Zealand: Author.

Alcohol Advisory Council of New Zealand (ALAC). (2000). *National guidelines on the naming, packaging and merchandising of alcoholic beverages.* Wellington, New Zealand: Author.

Alcohol Advisory Council of New Zealand (ALAC) and Ministry of Health (2001). *National alcohol strategy 2000–2003.* Wellington, New Zealand: Authors.

Babor, T. F. (2000). Partnerships, profit and public health. *Addiction, 95*(2), 193–195.

Bockhorn, L. (2001, December 10). The meaning of mashed potatoes [online version]. *The Weekly Standard.* Retrieved June 29, 2004, from http://www.weeklystandard.com/Content/Public/Articles/000/000/000/671tbsdw.asp.

Brain, K. J. (2000, January). *Youth, alcohol, and the emergence of the post-modern alcohol order.* Occasional Paper No. 1, New Series. London: Institute of Alcohol Studies.

David, J. P. (1999). Promoting pleasure and public health: An innovative initiative. In S. Peele & M. Grant (Eds.), *Alcohol and pleasure: A health perspective* (pp. 131–136). Philadelphia: Brunner/Mazel.

Eurocare. (1995). *Counterbalancing the drinks industry. A Eurocare report to the European Union on alcohol policy.* St. Ives, United Kingdom: Author.

Fisher, J. C., & Cook, P. A. (1995). *Advertising, alcohol consumption, and mortality: An empirical investigation.* Westport, CT: Greenwood.

Frederick, D. (1993). *The fun of alcohol: A rational defence of boozing against the anti-alcohol killjoys.* Political Notes No. 80. London: Libertarian Alliance.

Gostin, L. O. (2000a). Public health law in a new century: Part II: Public health powers and limits. *Journal of the American Medical Association, 283*(22), 2979–2984.

Gostin, L. O. (2000b). Public health law in a new century: Part III: Public health regulation: A systematic review. *Journal of the American Medical Association, 283*(23), 3119–3122.

Hawks, D. (1993a). What would a friendly alcohol industry look like? *Addiction, 88*(1), 22–23.

Hawks, D. (1993b). Taking the alcohol industry seriously. *Drug and Alcohol Review, 12*(2), 131–132.

Jacobson, M., Hacker, G., & Atkins, R. (1983). *Booze merchants: The inebriating of America.* Washington, DC: Center for Science in the Public Interest.

Libertarian Party. (2002). *Statement of principles: National platform of the Libertarian Party.* Indianapolis, IN: Author.

Luik, J. (1999). Wardens, abbots, and modern hedonists: The problem of permission for pleasure in a democratic society. In S. Peele & M. Grant (Eds.), *Alcohol and pleasure: A health perspective* (pp. 25–35). Philadelphia: Brunner/Mazel.

MacAvoy, M. G. (2002). *Report for the administrative appeals tribunal hearing on application A359 to the Australia and New Zealand Food Authority to include warning statements on alcohol beverage labels sold in Australia and New Zealand.* Wellington, New Zealand: Alcohol Advisory Council of New Zealand.

Mill, J. S. (2003). On liberty. In Warnock, M (Ed.), *Utilitarianism & On Liberty: Including Mill's "Essay on Bethan" & selections from the writings of Jeremy Bethan & John Austin.* 2nd ed. Malden, MA: Blackwell Publishing Limited. (Original work published 1859)

Nelson, J. P. (1990). State monopolies and alcoholic beverage consumption. *Journal of Regulatory Economics, 2*(1), 83–98.

Nelson, J. P. (1997, May). *Broadcast advertising and U.S. demand for alcoholic beverages: Systemwide estimates with quarterly data.* Washington, DC: U.S. Federal Trade Commission.

Nelson, J. P., & Moran, J. R. (1995). Advertising and U.S. alcoholic beverage demand: System-wide estimates. *Applied Economics, 27*(12), 1225–1236.

O'Neill, B. (2001, December 28). New hedonism: Flipside to fear [online version]. *Spiked.* Retrieved October 20, 2003, from http://www.spiked-online.com/Articles/00000002D381.htm.

Peele, S. (1999). Promoting positive drinking: Alcohol, necessary evil or positive good? In S. Peele & M. Grant (Eds.), *Alcohol and pleasure: A health perspective* (pp. 375–389). Philadelphia: Brunner/Mazel.

Peele, S., & Grant, M. (Eds.) (1999). *Alcohol and pleasure: A health perspective.* Philadelphia: Brunner/Mazel.

Plange, N. K. (1999). Pleasure and health. In S. Peele & M. Grant (Eds.), *Alcohol and pleasure: A health perspective* (pp. 55–57). Philadelphia: Brunner/Mazel.

Saffer, H. (1991). Alcohol advertising bans and alcohol abuse: An international perspective. *Journal of Health Economics, 10*(1), 65–79.

Saffer, H. (1995). Alcohol advertising and alcohol consumption: Econometric studies. In S. E. Martin & P. Mail (Eds.), *The effects of the mass media on the use and abuse of alcohol: Research monograph 28* (pp. 83–99). Bethesda, MD: National Institutes of Health, National Institute on Alcohol Abuse and Alcoholism.

Saffer, H. (1997, August). Alcohol advertising and motor vehicle fatalities. *Review of Economics and Statistics, 79*(3), 431–442.

Smart, R. G., & Cutler, R. E. (1976). Alcohol advertising ban in British Columbia: Problems and effects on beverage consumption. *British Journal of Addiction to Alcohol and Other Drugs, 71*(1), 13–21.

Snel, J. (1999). State-dependent lifestyles and the pleasure of alcohol. In S. Peele & M. Grant (Eds.), *Alcohol and pleasure: A health perspective* (pp. 277–289). Philadelphia: Brunner/Mazel.

Solomon, R. C. (1994). *The new world of business: Ethics and free enterprise in the global 1990's.* Lanham, MD: Rowman & Littlefield.

World Health Organization Regional Office for Europe. (1995). *European charter on alcohol.* Copenhagen, Denmark: Author. Retrieved December 13, 2004, from, http://www.euro.who.int/AboutWHO/Policy/20010927_7.

Wyllie, A., Zhang, J. F., & Casswell, S. (1994). *Response of 18- to 29-year-olds to alcohol and host responsibility advertising on television: Survey data.* Unpublished research report, University of Auckland Alcohol and Public Health Research Unit, New Zealand.

Chapter 9

Corporate Social Responsibility: A Context for Alcohol Policy

Peter H. Coors

Today, more than ever, many corporations are looking at their social obligations and examining what their ethical role should be in society. In this they are not alone, since governments, nongovernmental organizations, educators, special interest groups, and individuals are doing the same. The focus of their efforts is diverse, including economics, corporate governance, the environment, education, labor policies, health care, and nutrition. For those in the beverage alcohol industry, the role of alcohol in society has to be considered in the context of these broader issues.

PARTNERSHIPS IN ALCOHOL POLICY DEVELOPMENT

The global partnerships in alcohol policy development have a somewhat short but very productive history. The creation of the International Center for Alcohol Policies (ICAP) in February 1995 was a significant milestone in this history. This was followed in May 1997 by the development of what are now known as the Dublin Principles (International Center for Alcohol Policies and National College of Ireland, 1997); and then in May 2000 by the *Geneva Partnership on Alcohol: Towards a Global Charter* (International Center for Alcohol Policies, 2000), which set forth an ambitious agenda for partnerships, built on the Dublin Principles. ICAP then resolved to move forward by developing the themes of its first 5 years into the following activities:

- helping to develop alcohol policies that promote beneficial patterns of drinking and discourage unhealthy and risky patterns;
- establishing partnerships of diverse parties that, by working together, can reduce alcohol abuse;
- promoting self-regulation, which, in the appropriate context of governmental oversight, can be made more effective.

CORPORATE SOCIAL RESPONSIBILITY: THE ETHICAL ROLE OF CORPORATIONS

Many businesses have become more broadly involved in national or international coalitions that exchange best practices in corporate citizenship. ICAP represents one such grouping, dealing with corporate social responsibility related to alcohol. The need for collaboration in this field was illustrated in a Business for Social Responsibility poll of U.S. consumers, which found that:

- 90% of the respondents wanted companies to focus on more than profitability;
- 49% said that they form an impression of a company based on social responsibility;
- 39% said that they respond negatively to companies that are perceived to not be socially responsible;
- 20% said that they have avoided or have spoken out about products of companies that are perceived to be weak in the area of social responsibility. (Business for Social Responsibility website: www.bsr.org)

More and more companies are regarding corporate social responsibility an essential part of their business mission, strategy, and operations.

THE COORS BREWING COMPANY COMMITMENT

In addition to collective action, there is also a role for individual company action. Coors Brewing Company is an example of how an individual company can contribute to social responsibility. Those at Coors believe that it is their job to promote healthy lifestyles not only in the headquarters' state of Colorado, but also across the globe in all the places where it does business. This commitment is demonstrated in every aspect of its work:

- in advertising and marketing, promoting only responsible adult consumption of its products;
- in Coors' work with distributors and retailers, where it identifies appropriate ways to sell its beer;
- in its community initiatives, where Coors supports prevention, education, and intervention programs;
- in its support of legislation, where Coors backs measures to help get new drivers off to a good start and keep drunk drivers off the road.

It would be hypocritical to present this as totally altruistic. Being a good corporate citizen and having a positive corporate image actually promote product sales. Supporting sound alcohol policies is the right thing to do, with emphasis being placed on community involvement. There is no question that healthy, safe communities are better places to live and better places for business.

In some cases of abuse, a typically responsible person may make a rare mistake: an atypical lapse in good judgment about consuming alcohol. In other cases, the problem may be chronic. In any case, the result can be tragic and, therefore, absolutely unacceptable. That is why Coors is committed to doing whatever it can to make it universally understood that the consequences to the individual abuser can be swift and severe. Not only does Coors have the good name of its company to protect, but it also has a commitment to tackle abuse of its products in order to make sure that its business contributes to the health and happiness of the wider community, including colleagues, family, friends, and neighbors. Across the globe, ICAP sponsors are united in recognizing the need to fight all forms of alcohol abuse. So, in a very important sense, the commitment at Coors is both individual and collective, even if the industry does not agree on all the specific approaches to solving the problems. Significant progress has been made in many areas to promote positive and responsible behaviors in the selling, serving, and consuming of beverage alcohol and, perhaps most important, it is recognized that still more progress can be made.

PERSONAL ACCOUNTABILITY: THE "IT'S NOT MY FAULT" MENTALITY

As good corporate citizens, many companies do what they can to promote responsibility, but individuals have an important role to play as well. The litigious nature of the consumer products environment in the United States is familiar to most people. Unfortunately, the "It's not my fault" attitude—at least in U.S. society—has resulted in some quite bizarre lawsuits, demonstrating how reluctant some people are to assume responsibility for their own choices.

For example, an adult citizen recently filed a lawsuit in the U.S. courts claiming his many years of voluntarily dining in some of the country's popular fast-food restaurants had contributed to his profound obesity, diabetes, and heart disease, among other health problems. What is troubling about such examples is the suggestion that consumers, even those society would consider to be educated and well informed, are incapable of making responsible choices on their own about what they consume and in what measure.

Given people's creativity when it comes to dodging personal accountability, it is hard to imagine how this kind of silliness can be avoided completely. One way of contributing to healthy communities is to create an environment in which the acceptance of personal accountability is an integral part of the culture, although not forgetting that the industry, as good corporate citizens, should market its products responsibly and promote healthy, productive lifestyles. There are, however, many individuals and organizations that are very skeptical of the industry's efforts. Such skepticism can be destructive and unhelpful, but it can be useful if it encourages the industry to relentlessly reexamine its efforts to improve society. A willingness to accept and respect any and all constructive points of view may help, not only in making further progress, but also in the enlistment of future partners who can join in making the world a safer, healthier, and more productive place. These partnerships should be pursued, welcomed, and nurtured.

THE WAY FORWARD

From the formulation of the Dublin Principles to the Geneva Partnership, it is becoming increasingly clear that it is necessary to acknowledge and respect different points of view. The sponsors of ICAP, together with many other industry leaders, share a common purpose: promoting an understanding of the role of alcohol in society and reducing the abuse of alcohol worldwide. It may not be possible to reach a consensus on all the issues involved, but it is possible to learn from each other, reduce unproductive choices, and contribute to healthy communities. There are then major challenges: one is for the different parties, even when seemingly opposed, to respect each other's perspectives and then to look for common ground and work for some agreement on how to move forward. Progress should not be impaired or distracted by debate about *who* is right, but rather fueled by discussions about *what* is right.

NOTE

This chapter contains remarks made by Peter H. Coors, Chairman of Coors Brewing
   Company, to the "Alcohol, Ethics and Society" conference held in Dublin, Ireland in

October 2002. After the merger of Coors and Molson in 2005, Mr. Coors has served as Vice Chairman of Molson Coors Brewing Company.

REFERENCES

International Center for Alcohol Policies (ICAP). (2000). *The Geneva partnership on alcohol: Towards a global charter.* Washington, DC: Author.

International Center for Alcohol Policies (ICAP) and National College of Ireland. (1997). *The Dublin Principles of cooperation among the beverage alcohol industry, governments, scientific researchers, and the public health community.* Washington, DC: Authors.

Chapter 10

Corporate Social Responsibility in Practice Within the Beverage Alcohol Industry

John Orley

Although the central interest of the beverage alcohol industry (as with any business enterprise) lies in making a profit, many of the companies—as earlier chapters have made clear—recognize their obligation to be good corporate citizens. Industry members acknowledge that, although their products can offer considerable personal pleasure and social benefit, they can also cause serious personal and social harm if consumed irresponsibly. They also acknowledge that preventing misuse of their products is in their long-term strategic interest and is therefore consistent with their economic objectives, while turning a blind eye on misuse is ultimately bad for business. They are prepared, like many other businesses, to forgo short-term gains for more strategic long-term growth, recognizing that such growth is best built on an ethical and responsible foundation. Their social concern is also founded on the realization that reckless drinking, irresponsible advertising, or inappropriate promotional activities can lead to more restrictive government regulation, which can affect their business adversely. Similarly, the responsible service of alcohol to consumers is vital for the health of businesses that retail alcohol beverages. Therefore, it is appropriate to ask what the beverage alcohol industry has done to minimize the risks associated with its products. This chapter looks at industrywide interventions aimed at reducing the misuse of alcohol. Many of the interventions used to encourage or prescribe more moderate consumption patterns have been initiated by governments, but not exclusively so, and many have been developed by the industry in partnership with others. These interventions can be broadly divided into four categories:

1. *Controls over supply.* This includes, for example, legislation governing hours for selling, sale of licenses, price manipulation, and, in the extreme, product bans.
2. *Legislative controls over unacceptable alcohol-related behavior.* This incorporates penalties for drinking and driving, drunk and disorderly behavior, and so forth.
3. *The regulation of advertising and promotion.* It would be likely that the way in which a product is presented to consumers may affect the way it is consumed. For instance, some kinds of promotions can encourage people to drink excessively over a short time.
4. *Education to encourage more responsible use of alcohol.* The beverage alcohol industry has become a significant contributor to educational programs. This has been made possible because educational programs now rarely reflect a temperance view, but rather accept a harm minimization approach instead of attempting to prevent all consumption.

DEVELOPMENT OF SOCIAL ASPECTS ORGANIZATIONS

A number of companies have over the years made efforts to promote responsible drinking. The aim was to find a way that would not penalize the vast majority of drinkers who drink responsibly, but would nevertheless reduce alcohol misuse. By the late 1980s, this led to the creation of industry groups, which represented an approach by the beverage alcohol industry to promote responsible drinking. These groups came to be called social aspects organizations (SAOs) and they reflect the industry's wish to play a more proactive role in the area of alcohol-related social policy.

In 1989, there were just four SAOs: one in the Netherlands (founded in 1959), another in South Africa (founded in 1986), and the other two in the United Kingdom and in Canada (both founded in 1989). Today, over 30 SAOs exist, based mainly in Europe and North America, but also in Australasia and Africa.

Generally speaking, the activities of SAOs address four main topics:

- delivering better education to young people and promoting greater understanding of alcohol and sensible drinking;
- discouraging drinking and driving;

- disseminating the idea of sensible drinking for those who choose to drink;
- developing and enhancing mechanisms for self-regulation of industry marketing practices.

An important component of SAOs' activities lies in the establishment of partnerships. Those that have developed over the years are a testament to how seriously these organizations and, indeed, the beverage alcohol industry more generally have been taken. Partnerships include those with the Swedish government, the Ministry of Public Health in Thailand, the University of Melbourne in Australia, Canada's College of Family Physicians, the University of Illinois in the United States, the German and British Departments of Transport, the Ford Motor Company in Germany, the Spanish Association of Public Affairs, and the Institute of Traffic Safety in the Netherlands, to name but a few (Max & Willersdorf, 2001). The activities of SAOs have developed considerably over the past decade, but individual companies and trade associations have also been active partners in preventing alcohol abuse during this time.

Young People

As would be expected from industry-supported groups, social aspects organizations and trade associations that sponsor alcohol education programs try to convey positive messages about drinking to young people, while warning about risks. Rather than presenting a negative approach to alcohol, many of the current programs that the SAOs sponsor stress a message of moderation but also of individual and wider responsibility. As Peele points out in chapter 6, to stress total abstinence conveys a message that the choice has to be either not to drink at all or to abuse alcohol. The logical conclusion to be drawn from this message for anyone who chooses to drink is that their drinking must be "irresponsible," since the message of total abstention is that there is no such thing as moderate responsible consumption.

If, therefore, we want to encourage those who choose to drink to do so moderately, then educational programs, including programs for children, should convey the message that it is indeed possible to drink moderately. The programs should also provide children with the skills to hold to this once they are old enough for it to be an issue. In some countries, children are introduced relatively early to controlled moderate drinking with meals in the home with their parents. This can be likened to graduated driver licensing (GDL) in the United States, already referred to in chapter 3, where young drivers are gradually introduced to the responsibility of driving, allowing them to gain experience under low-risk conditions. When it comes to providing education in schools, the beverage alcohol industry has to work as a partner with the education system, or at least with individual schools, to implement programs.

Life skills education is an example of a positive approach, and one that is used in a variety of countries by nonindustry-funded groups as well. Its purpose is to equip young people with the kinds of skills they need to make responsible decisions about their lifestyles. For older children, a discussion of alcohol can be highlighted, but for younger ones at the start of primary school this is unlikely to be an issue yet.

Thus, the Industry Association for Responsible Alcohol Use (ARA) in South Africa sponsored a life skills program for primary school children that was not specifically about alcohol, but used several issues to help children to learn to make the kinds of decisions related to their current age. It is hoped that this will prepare them for making responsible decisions about drinking when they get older. The Stichting Verantwoord Alcoholgebruik (STIVA) in the Netherlands also funds life skills education in schools. Gode Alkoholdninger (Denmark) has produced high-school educational materials on alcohol that have been used to educate pupils in the historical and cultural dimensions and the social and psychological aspects of alcohol. Other countries that have used similar approaches include France, Germany, Spain, and the United Kingdom. Coors, a brewer based in the United States, sponsors a program called An Apple a Day, which aims to build literacy and critical thinking skills in young people and parents in that country. An example of an alcohol education program delivered on college campuses in the United States and sponsored by the distilled spirits industry is described by Cressy and Gourovitch in chapter 14.

Drink Driving

Major interventions by governments to deal with drink driving have included the introduction of random breath testing with significant penalties for failing the test, the reduction of legal blood alcohol levels to almost zero for probationary licensed drivers, together with a high level of enforcement in many countries. A number of industry-sponsored programs are trying to find innovative ways to approach drink driving issues. The response has been a variety of strategies to appeal to their target audiences. In Germany, for example, a disproportionate number of young drivers aged 18 to 25 years were involved in car accidents after leaving discotheques. A German SAO (DIFA FORUM) teamed up with the Ford Motor Company, the Department of Police, and other businesses to develop a program to address this problem, leading to a 10% reduction in alcohol-related accidents during the period of the program. Another approach—making the learning process as interactive and realistic as possible—was initiated by DIFA FORUM and replicated by a number of industry-sponsored groups in Austria, Belgium, Denmark, France, Ireland, and

Spain. These programs were funded in part by the Amsterdam Group, a pan-European SAO, and the European Road Safety Federation (Max & Willersdorf, 2001).

A number of SAOs in different countries sponsor taxi-cab services from bars and restaurants, as well as designated driver programs in which one of a party of drinkers takes responsibility for driving the others home and does not drink on that evening. In the United Kingdom, a SAO, together with the Ministry of Transport, sponsored a campaign called "If You Drink, Let Others Drive" (Portman Group, 1999). A similar program, funded by industry-sponsored organizations, called "Home Safely" was promoted in Australia. It involved a "Contract for Life" that set ground rules for getting home safely and encouraged parents/adults to provide a suitable role model for young people (Max & Willersdorf, 2001).

Server Training

Server training involves promoting the training of hospitality staff in bars and restaurants to deal with possible underage customers and to handle patrons who are drunk or behaving badly. In the United States, Anheuser-Busch, Coors Brewing Company, UDV North America, and Miller Brewing Company sponsor the Training for Intervention Procedures (TIPs) program. It is the most widely recognized alcohol server training program in the United States, with the aim of educating and training all facets of society in the responsible sale and consumption of alcohol. According to the program literature, there are over 500,000 TIPs-certified servers and 18,000 trainers in the United States. Servers trained in TIPs are also active in 22 other countries including Canada, Japan, the Netherlands, and the United Kingdom.

In Australia, a voluntary industry licensing scheme has been introduced in the state of Victoria by the Australian Hotels and Hospitality Association and the Licensed Clubs Association of Victoria. This is a self-regulating code of conduct endorsed by the relevant minister and the government's formal liquor licensing authority. It aims to raise the awareness of venue management and staff of their responsibilities under public liability law and as service providers to customers, in order to reduce alcohol-related harm in the community. A major impetus to formalize such codes of conduct has been the threat of legal action arising from failures to exercise a proper duty of care, particularly under regulations pertaining to alcohol service to intoxicated people and to underage drinkers, together with the consequent skyrocketing of insurance costs.

In Ireland, host responsibility is advanced through the Responsible Serving of Alcohol (RSA) program. Developed jointly by the Irish Health Promotion Unit in the Department of Health and Children and by the Drinks Industry Group of Ireland, the RSA is conducted by CERT, the national agency in charge of training and development in the hospitality industry (Health Promotion Unit, Department of Health and Children, 2002). Established in support of the national alcohol policy, which aims to reduce alcohol-related problems through an emphasis on moderating consumption, RSA helps license holders to develop appropriate guidelines and procedures for alcohol serving. The program takes the form of interactive workshops that use "real situations" or case studies to reinforce skills necessary to minimize or even prevent such alcohol-related problems as underage drinking, drunkenness, and drink driving. The workshop participants learn facts about alcohol and its effect on the body, become familiarized with the laws on driving under influence, and learn ways to prevent customers from becoming intoxicated, so that they leave the program with skills necessary to handle the following situations:

- how to prevent alcohol sales to minors (in Ireland, those under 18);
- how to identify signs of increasing intoxication;
- how to refuse to serve alcohol to intoxicated customers;
- how to handle "difficult" clients;
- how to cooperate with the authorities. (Mature Enjoyment of Alcohol in Society, 2003)

Moreover, the program organizers are working on delivering the RSA to a wider audience by gradually incorporating its principles in professional bar training courses and college programs around the country (CERT, 2003).

BRAND MARKETING AND ADVERTISING

The aim of advertising their products, according to the beverage alcohol companies, is to promote brand loyalty and to get existing drinkers to switch to their brands. The industry claims that it does not give messages encouraging people to drink more overall, nor would it expect nondrinkers to start drinking after seeing the advertisements (although both of these objectives would be perfectly legitimate). Many in the public health field doubt that the effects are as limited as the advertisers intend, even if the motivations behind them are limited. Certainly, advertisements for beverage alcohol, apart from promoting brands, do convey the impression to the public that drinking is a normal, pleasurable activity. There is, however, considerable debate about the extent to which advertising affects drinking behavior other than promoting brands.

Public health advocates have called for strict regulation or elimination of alcohol advertising (Mosher, 1994), and particular attention has been drawn to how alcohol advertising might affect young people (Atkin, 1993). The argument that alcohol advertising is intended to create brand preference and does not increase the likelihood of abuse by showing irresponsible consumption rings hollow among these critics, some of whom believe that advertising increases alcohol abuse and that self-regulation does little to prevent this (Hill & Casswell, 2001). A considerable body of literature, however, shows no causal link between alcohol advertising and particular (unsafe) drinking patterns and resulting problems (Fisher & Cook, 1995; Young, 1993).

In June 2000, the U.S. Department of Health and Human Services reviewed the evidence on the effects of alcohol advertising on alcohol consumption, alcohol-related problems, and drinking-related beliefs and attitudes (U.S. National Institute on Alcohol Abuse and Alcoholism, 2000). Studies were drawn from seven diverse fields. The overall conclusion was that survey research on alcohol advertising and young people "consistently indicates small but significant connections between exposure to and awareness of alcohol advertising and drinking beliefs and behaviors." The report adds that, taken as a whole, the survey studies provide some evidence that alcohol advertising may influence drinking beliefs but that this evidence is far from conclusive. The report states that with few exceptions, recent econometric research provides "very little consistent evidence that alcohol advertising influences per capita alcohol consumption, sales or problems" (U.S. National Institute on Alcohol Abuse and Alcoholism, 2000, p. 422). Indeed, it has been said, with some justification, that banning alcohol advertising is an intervention looking for a problem. It is on the face of it a relatively simple measure and has a certain political appeal, so that the pressure to apply it as a response to alcohol abuse is considerable, despite there being virtually no evidence for its effectiveness. This matter is also discussed in chapters 11 and 14 of this volume.

In part, the industry would claim that the lack of harm from advertising has been due to the control the industry has exercised over the content and placement of its advertisements. The companies acknowledge that their freedom to advertise their brands has to be balanced by their undertaking to advertise in a responsible manner, and this is best ensured through a process of self-regulation. This is the process whereby industry actively participates in and is actively responsible for its own regulation. The industry also participates in the self-regulation of advertising as a way of curbing the push for external controls by those who think that advertising has marked adverse effects on consumption. The ways that advertisements for beverage alcohol can convey harmful messages are well documented by Roche in chapter 11. The industry is mindful of the balance that has to be kept between having content that is eye-catching, memorable, and fun on the one hand, but responsible and free from content that could appear to condone illegal or risky behavior on the other. The process of self-regulation is in place to ensure that the industry keeps to its codes, which define the limits. In chapter 12, Burkitt warns the industry that a failure to adhere to its own guidelines could encourage a total ban on advertising beverage alcohol throughout the European Union.

SELF-REGULATION BY THE INDUSTRY

Self-regulation is the mechanism preferred by the industry for the control of its advertising. This requires two elements:

- a code of practice or a set of guiding principles governing the content and placement of advertisements;
- a process for the establishment, review, and application of the code or principles.

Impartiality is seen to be indispensable to the effective implementation of a code and public trust in it.

This is not to say that there is no role for legislation to play in relation to advertising and other forms of commercial communication. Indeed, self-regulation often exists in tandem with a broad legal framework that can be helpful in defining the boundaries within which self-regulation has to operate. One of the main purposes of self-regulation is to avoid cumbersome bureaucratic processes. It is an expression of responsible marketing practices, but there will always be rogue companies that will push the limits or even go beyond them, so that regulation needs to be within a framework that allows control over these elements. Even within companies there will inevitably be tensions between innovative/creative marketing departments (which will push the limits as far as they can) and those who oversee responsibility issues. Companies also therefore need effective internal controls to rein back excessive marketing enthusiasm that might stray beyond the accepted standards. It has been argued by the European Advertising Standards Alliance that "properly designed and well administered self-regulatory systems provide a swift, flexible, inexpensive and effective means of enabling the responsible majority of the industry to restrain the irresponsible minority" (European Advertising Standards Alliance, 1997, p. 19). The Federal Trade Commission (1999) in the United States echoes this view.

National self-regulatory codes have been developed by various SAOs, trade associations, and individual companies. In the United Kingdom, the Portman Group has issued a *Code of Practice on the Naming, Packaging, and Merchandising of Alcoholic Drinks*. This code was launched in 1996, then strengthened in 1997 to include a new independent complaints panel; the latest edition—the third—came into force in March 2003 (Portman Group, 2002). STIVA in the Netherlands also has such a code, as does the ARA in South Africa as well as industry groups in a number of other countries. Trade associations such as the Beer Institute and the Distilled Spirits Council of the United States also have codes, as do many individual companies.

In general the codes deal with advertising, but can also deal with promotions and presentation. They cover such issues as:

- Not targeting (or appearing to target) minors and those below the legal age of purchase for alcohol beverages, including:
  - not using media directed at minors;
  - not sponsoring events directed at minors;
  - not including minors (or anyone appearing to be a minor) in advertisements and promotions.
- Only depicting moderate and responsible consumption and avoiding promotions that might encourage rapid or excessive consumption.
- Not portraying abstinence or moderation in a negative way.
- Not suggesting any association with violent, dangerous, or antisocial behavior.
- Avoiding making any association between drinking and driving or any other activity where drinking alcohol could be dangerous.
- Not creating an impression that drinking alcohol is a requirement for success.

Although codes dealing with advertising and other promotional activities are desirable, many countries have neither statutory legislation nor self-regulation on this topic. A survey carried out in 1996 and presented by ICAP in its report on self-regulation indicated that 23 out of the 119 countries included had no controls. These were mostly among the emerging markets and developing countries. In an effort to redress this gap, ICAP (2002) has produced a document titled *Self-Regulation and Alcohol: A Toolkit for Emerging Markets and the Developing World*. This describes the steps for setting up a self-regulatory system and provides a model code as an annex.

An area of concern that is raised in various parts of this volume concerns advertising placed on the Internet. Because such advertising crosses national boundaries and because it is very difficult to limit access for those under the minimum drinking age, it poses considerable problems with regard to regulation. This of course is not just a problem in relation to alcohol, for Internet users have free access to all manner of potentially inappropriate information. The major industry partners and the Internet service providers must be responsible for regulating themselves in these matters.

RESEARCH

The place of the Alcoholic Beverage Medical Research Foundation (ABMRF) in supporting research on the effects of drinking alcohol has been briefly mentioned in chapter 4 as an example of cooperation between academia and industry. The example illustrates how it is possible to maintain an "arm's length" relationship between grantees and contributors. Industry members, representing those who provide the funds, hold minority seats on the Board of Trustees and do not participate in the grant selection process in any way. Grantees are encouraged to publish the results of their investigations without prior review or approval by the foundation. Another example from the field of research, described in more detail in chapter 16 on the feedback from the Framework for Responsibility, is the support provided by the South African industry through its SAO (ARA) to the Foundation for Alcohol Related Research (FARR). This support is primarily to cover the Foundation's administrative costs, while money for projects (for instance its pioneering work on fetal alcohol syndrome) is obtained from other sources (e.g., NIAAA and the Centers for Disease Control and Prevention in the United States and the Department of Health in South Africa). This arrangement is intended to safeguard the integrity of the foundation's research agenda. Further details on FARR are provided in Case Study 1 in chapter 16.

There are, therefore, numerous potential and actual programs that help prevent harm from the consumption of alcohol in which industry members can participate as partners. Chapters 11, 12, and 13 deal with responses to potential harms that might derive from the advertising of alcohol and how these should be dealt with, while chapters 14 and 15 expand on what has been done in education. Chapter 16 reviews industry programs in emerging markets and developing countries.

REFERENCES

Atkin, C. K. (1993). Effects of media alcohol messages on adolescent audiences. *Adolescent Medicine, 4*(3), 527–542.

CERT (Fáilte Ireland). (2003, June 6). *Bar staff training vital for responsible drinking environment.* Press release. Retrieved June 21, 2004, from http://www.cert.ie/about_cert/Press_Releases100.html.

European Advertising Standards Alliance. (1997). *Advertising self-regulation in Europe* (2nd ed.). Brussels: Author.

Federal Trade Commission. (1999). *Self-regulation in the alcohol industry: A review of industry efforts to avoid promoting alcohol to underage consumers.* Washington, DC: Author.

Fisher, J. C., & Cook, P. A. (1995). *Advertising, alcohol consumption, and mortality: An empirical investigation.* Westport, CT: Greenwood.

Health Promotion Unit, Department of Health and Children. (2002). *Strategic task force on alcohol: Interim report.* Dublin: Author.

Hill, L., & Casswell, S. (2001). Alcohol advertising and sponsorship: Commercial freedom or control in the public interest? In N. Heather, T. J. Peters, & T. Stockwell (Eds.),

International handbook of alcohol dependence and related problems (pp. 823–846). Chichester, United Kingdom: John Wiley.

International Center for Alcohol Policies (ICAP). (2002). *Self-regulation and alcohol: A toolkit for emerging markets and the developing world.* Washington, DC: Author.

Mature Enjoyment of Alcohol in Society (MEAS). (2003). *MEAS initiatives: Responsible serving of alcohol programme.* Retrieved June 21, 2004, from http://www.meas.ie/.

Max, G., & Willersdorf, G. (2001). The beverage alcohol industry and learning about drinking. In E. Houghton & A. M. Roche (Eds.), *Learning about drinking* (pp. 267–281). Washington, DC: Brunner-Routledge.

Mosher, J. (1994). Alcohol advertising and public health: An urgent call for action. *American Journal of Public Health, 84*(2), 180–181.

Portman Group. (1999). *Ten years and counting: A review of progress towards sensible drinking.* London: Author.

Portman Group. (2002, September). *Code of practice on the naming, packaging, and merchandising of alcoholic drinks* (3rd ed.). London: Author.

U.S. National Institute on Alcohol Abuse and Alcoholism (NIAAA). (2000, June). Alcohol advertising: What are the effects? In *10th special report to the U.S. Congress on alcohol and health* (pp. 412–426). Bethesda, MD: Author.

Young, D. J. (1993). Alcohol advertising bans and alcohol abuse [Comment]. *Journal of Health Economics, 12*(2), 213–228.

Chapter 11

Establishing Good Practice in Responsible Drinks Promotion: Illustrations of Good and Bad Practice From a Public Health Perspective

Ann Roche

This chapter is presented in six sections dealing with the following topics:

- Background and contextual factors that have an impact on alcohol advertising and promotions.
- Product innovations in marketing and promotions.
- Internet sales, promotion, and distribution: staking a claim in cyberspace.
- Television, film, and music video advertisements and product placement.
- Print media advertisements.
- General principles of good alcohol advertising.

The third, fourth, and fifth sections offer descriptions of advertising or promotional activities in a specific medium and then highlight key areas of concern to the public health field, providing examples of good and bad practices. It has not always been possible to cite examples of good practice in each category and to that extent the chapter may appear to be negatively biased. The final section distills elements of good and bad practice and sets out some key principles that may be useful as a basis for further debate and discussion.

BACKGROUND AND CONTEXTUAL FACTORS

Advertising and promotion of alcohol is a vexatious issue and has been for many decades. Since the 1950s, there have been claims and counterclaims as to the effect, positive or negative, of advertising (Atkin, Hocking, & Block, 1984). Largely disparate and, at times, adversarial views are currently held by the beverage alcohol industry and the public health community. This chapter tries to move forward the dialogue around the issue of alcohol advertising and promotions, as well as to lay the groundwork by which to delineate what constitutes good, bad, or inappropriate advertising. It does this by focusing on what might be considered a broad and widely accepted view of responsible consumption.

Many of the issues raised decades ago in relation to alcohol advertising remain with us today, together with new and emerging areas of concern that reflect factors associated with technological development and globalization. This chapter explores some of these issues and articulates areas of concern from a public health perspective. Although the chapter is not an academic study in the traditional sense, it does attempt to map out some of the key issues that continue to confront the public health field and that, in turn, challenge the beverage alcohol industry. In this way, it is intended that a typology of good practice may be developed that can provide a practical framework for future activities in this area.

The chapter takes the view that the issues currently at stake are wider than those traditionally defined as "alcohol and advertising." It, therefore, also incorporates an examination of wider factors, such as the role and place of alcohol "promotions" in their broadest sense, and considers the newly emerging role of product placement, the Internet, and other electronic means of communication and commercialism.

Historical Approaches

For some time, and especially throughout the 1970s and 1980s, the debate around advertising tended to be predicated on the syllogism that *advertising increases alcohol consumption; increased consumption increases alcohol abuse.* There is a body of literature that has focused on establishing or, conversely, refuting whether alcohol advertising does indeed increase consumption (Atkin et al., 1984; Atkin, Neuendorf, & McDermott, 1983; Hastings, MacKintosh,

& Aitken, 1992; Lipsitz, Brake, Vincent, & Winters, 1993; Wyllie, Zhang, & Casswell, 1998). This approach, often based on econometric analyses, has led to much debate, friction, conflict, and unhelpful attempts to disparage opposing arguments, often generating more heat than light. Researchers have attempted to ask and answer global questions through surveys, econometric studies, and, occasionally, experimental designs. Research findings gathered to answer these broad questions have, not surprisingly, been equivocal and inconclusive. As suggested above, the approach was predicated on the notion that increased consumption invariably led to increased abuse of alcohol or higher levels of alcohol-related problems. Again, this is a complex and controversial area underpinned by a particular set of epidemiological principles that remain hotly debated (Roche, 1997). It appears unhelpful therefore to revisit these issues. Rather, a more pragmatic approach is required that can identify methods and principles for the creation of a new generation of responsible marketing strategies, established around a common set of ethical standards that accept and reflect public health interests and concerns.

From an Econometric to an Ethical Approach to Advertising

Advertising does work, and space will not be taken here to argue the issue or weigh the "evidence." What is meant by "it works" is that it not only promotes brand identification and preference, but that it also works in the way it is largely intended to work: that is, to make a company's alcohol beverages more appealing and more widely consumed. With this agreed on, it is possible to move to the more important question of what type of advertising communities should accept or reject on ethical grounds. This issue forms the core of this chapter, which is an attempt to articulate what constitutes good and bad advertising practices, albeit from a public health perspective. Admittedly, if it were from a marketing or commercial perspective, the task would be simpler and would comprise assessment against specific economic goals. Here the task is more complex, subtle, and inevitably subjective as it involves delineation of human and social values. Moreover, it involves a process of identifying what forms of advertising and promotion are considered acceptable or unacceptable from a "values" perspective.

Codes of Practice, Self-Regulation, and Legal Sanctions

Laws and voluntary codes of practice regulate alcohol advertising. Further details of codes of practice and related self-regulatory mechanisms have been addressed in an International Center for Alcohol Policies (2001) report. Hence, the central issues will not be reiterated here, but it is noted that there is considerable variability with regard to regulation and pressure in some parts of the world, such as within the European Union, to adopt more consistent approaches (Beccaria, 2001). Although a range of codes of practice and other self-regulatory mechanisms exist in various countries around the world, these codes are increasingly criticized for their tardiness and lack of effectiveness (Jones & Donovan, 2002), and they need to be critically assessed. In addition, the adequacy of the scope of self-regulatory mechanisms also requires urgent review, especially in light of the substantial changes experienced internationally in the past 3 to 5 years in relation to the Internet and other forms of mass communication. In Friedman's (2000) words, "there is no more First World, Second World or Third World. There is now just the Fast World."

Addressing Different Media Used in Advertising and Promotions

This chapter discusses examples of good and bad advertising practices from print-based and electronic media (such as the Internet). Comparatively less attention will be directed to audiovisual materials because of the limitations entailed in a printed publication. However, it is noted that the majority of alcohol advertising expenditures in, for instance, North America and Europe have been in the medium of television (Besen, 1997). Moreover, some would argue that there is a persuasive case to be made that this form of media is in fact the most effective (Saffer, 1997). There is a countercase to be made that in recent years other forms of media, especially the electronic media, may have superseded the potency of television. Hence, what is presented here should be seen as an initial examination, warranting further development and expansion to fully address issues that are specific to different types of media, including television and film advertising.

PRODUCT INNOVATIONS IN MARKETING AND PROMOTIONS

From time to time, new alcohol products are marketed that raise serious concerns in terms of responsible serving and consuming behaviors. Most of these products involve a new, innovative form of packaging or delivery, which is the manner in which the alcohol product is designed to be ingested. Many such products raise concerns from a public health perspective. Some examples are outlined below, together with the reasons why they give rise to such concerns.

Zulu 42

A recent example of an innovative product is a spray can version of vodka called Zulu 42. This product, produced in Germany, is a 50-ml aerosol can designed to be sprayed directly into the mouth. It has a very high alcohol content of up to 26% and comes in gimmicky packaging with obvious appeal to young people. There are clear health and safety concerns about such a product. Apart from the high alcohol content, the unusual and novel delivery system is of concern because of its apparent appeal for young people, and particularly young people legally unable to purchase beverage alcohol. Young people are more likely to be attracted to Zulu 42, since it is difficult to envisage sophisticated over-30-year-olds using such a product. The similarity of Zulu 42 and its delivery mode to illicitly used psychoactive volatile substances (such as those contained in aerosol containers) is of particular concern to the public health community, as well as to the general public.

Volatile substance use is an especially dangerous recreational drug problem in both developed and developing communities, and one that is mostly associated with 10- to 14-year-olds. A deliberately designed beverage alcohol that can easily be associated with this form of drug use is a matter of considerable concern. This is particularly important given that the beverage alcohol industry is keen not to be associated with the use of illicit drugs. In addition, it is particularly worrisome that this manner of delivery of beverage alcohol removes any possibility of the drinkers being able to assess and monitor how much alcohol they have consumed. It is contrary to all international efforts to establish standard measures of consumption and to educate drinkers and servers about standard drinks.

In light of such concerns, Zulu 42 was the subject of a September 2000 Retailer Alert Bulletin issued by the Portman Group in the United Kingdom on account of its gimmicky packaging, which may encourage irresponsible consumption and appeal to the under 18s in breach of the Portman Group Code. However, the process of banning or restricting such products is time-consuming (often with a sufficient time lag to allow the product to reach vulnerable members of the public), expensive, and conveys especially negative and irresponsible images of the alcohol industry *as a whole*, regardless of which sectors of the industry may have been involved in the product's production. It is, therefore, in the best interests of the industry as a whole to take an active role in monitoring and regulating such products before they reach the marketplace.

Alcopops

In the late 1990s, strong concern was expressed in various quarters about a range of products collectively referred to as alcopops (McKeganey, Forsyth, Barnard, & Hay, 1996). Although it has been argued that these types of products were transient and a brief aberration, there is sufficient evidence that similar products are continuing to emerge and that ongoing monitoring and vigilance are required.

Recent examples cited by the Portman Group include products with brand names such as Delirium Tremens (a small bottle in the shape of a beer bottle, but brightly colored and containing a high level of alcohol by volume) and Jello Shot (a product in a small transparent plastic cup containing a bright red jelly-like substance with a 15% alcohol content). Both of these products had claims upheld against them by the Portman Group Independent Complaints Panel and were subsequently removed from the marketplace.

Complaints continue to be lodged against products with novel marketing features. A press release by the Portman Group in May 2002 identified complaints against a range of products (Portman Group, 2002). Claims that were upheld were those where miniature spirits bottles had been prepackaged with confectioneries and where alcohol beverages were being sold at the front of a supermarket at the cash register among the confectionery. The concern in both cases was the ease with which the products could appeal to and be accessed by children. The general principle of avoiding packaging, presenting, marketing, displaying, or selling alcohol products in a manner resembling a confectionery line is consistently highlighted. There is no reason to assume that these types of products will cease to emerge, even if not from industry leaders. In fact, there is good evidence to the contrary. Principles of good promotional and advertising practice must address the serious and valid concerns associated with any such products.

INTERNET SALES, PROMOTION, AND DISTRIBUTION: STAKING A CLAIM IN CYBERSPACE

The commercial potential of the Internet would not have been accurately predicted a decade ago. In the past 5 years, however, the world has witnessed an unprecedented level of growth in electronic media as a mechanism for commercial transactions. This is equally—if not more—true in commodity product areas such as the promotion, sale, and distribution of beverage alcohol. The rapid expansion of this medium has caught many off guard. Although it has become a significant vehicle for the promotion of alcohol, there are questions about the extent to which the Internet is covered by current self-regulatory codes and legal restrictions. For this reason, and also partly because of its novelty, less diligence has been applied to ensuring that appropriate standards are met in this medium.

Since the late 1990s, a number of studies have been undertaken to investigate the style of commercial advertisement and promotions found on the Internet (Center for Media Education, 1996, 1997, 1998). Again, studies from the Center for Media Education (1999) showed that virtually every major beverage alcohol company has staked its claim in cyberspace. Such studies have identified a range of new interactive advertising and marketing techniques developed specifically for the promotion of alcohol through this medium and reported that a number of practices would violate long-standing safeguards intended to protect young people and children (Carroll & Donovan, 2002). The Center for Media Education (1998) reported in one of its studies that the following range of techniques was used in alcohol advertisements that would appeal to young people: use of cartoons or motion video, branded sites, games or contests, youth-oriented language or slang, and use of downloadable sound.

Carroll and Donovan (2002) published an analysis of a selection of Internet sites established with the specific purpose of promoting the sale and distribution of particular alcohol beverages. They identified a range of deceptive forms of advertising and online infomercials and noted that a number of alcohol companies were using the Internet to advertise and promote their products through a variety of marketing techniques that take advantage of the Internet's strong and special attraction to young people. The authors examined six Internet sites. A brief summary is set out below, particularly noting the extent to which they would comply with codes of practice and the areas in which they raise public health concerns. Given the dynamic nature of the Internet, all the sites examined by the authors have changed since the original study. The sites examined were:

- www.carltoncold.com.au
- www.jimbeam.com
- www.strongbow.com.au
- www.wickedwines.com.au
- www.midori.com.au
- www.subzero.com.au

Carlton Cold

This is a beer site that had a strong focus on music and music concerts called "Cold Live at the Chapel." The only way tickets to these concerts could be obtained was through the site, which also invited the user to participate in competitions to win CDs. In addition, visitors could download screen savers and software to mix their own music, and attend an "awesome party" featuring "extreme sports exhibitions and hot local and international DJ's."

Jim Beam

This site had a strong extreme sports focus and includes skateboarding, motor cross, and bicycle motocross (BMX) racing—activities with clear and strong appeal to youth. The site featured a Jim Beam bar described as "a place where you can hang out with your friends and enjoy great music, classic games, and a casual atmosphere" and "sit back and relax with a refreshing drink or get a little crazy listening to electrifying sound clips from some great unsigned band" or "try your hand at the ever growing selection of classic arcade games." A section called "Get Local" referred to the Jim Beam Planet X Tour 2001–2002. Visitors were informed that Planet X (an extreme sports website—www. planetx.net.au) and Jim Beam "are stoked to bring you the Jim Beam Planet X Tour national party series," which will feature "freestyle sports demos—freestyle moto x, BMX, skate and breakers, live bands, top Aussie DJ's, big screen video walls, Planet X celebrity appearances and interactive competitions and give-aways." The site further noted that "some of the Jim Beam Planet X Tour Events will be 18 years and over ONLY." Visitors were informed that identification would need to be produced on entry.

In addition to the strong association with high-risk activities, it is noteworthy that the Planet X television program was screened at 12:30 on a Sunday afternoon. The associated Jim Beam bimonthly free magazine—now *Xpression Mag*—depicted a series of six photos with a bottle of Jim Beam riding on, and then falling off, a skateboard. There was also a promotion on the Jim Beam site where drinkers received a token to race their friends in a race-car simulator, thus raising concerns about the strong and inappropriate association with drink driving.

Strongbow Cider

This Australian site featured links to a 2002–2003 advertising campaign "Drink Fresh. Think Fresh." It included a spoof television commercial in which a mother finds her son's pornographic magazine collection. Another section contained a series of swimsuit models and the visitor was invited to "burst some swimsuit bubbles" in a downloadable game. There was also a gallery of swimsuit models with a screen saver. The site used an element of dare in its wording, "I am an adult. I can do what I want. If I want to stay up late, I can. I am also over the legal drinking age. ... I am over 18 years."[1]

Wicked Wines

Carroll and Donovan (2002) report that the trade press describes this "as set to arouse younger wine lovers." It consists of a range called Wicked Wines, which included "Flirt," "Lust," "Greed," and "Envy." The site stressed that you must be over 18 years old to click on enter and stated that, "This site contains

---

[1] It should be noted that this information was contained on a website for an Australian product; the legal age of purchase in Australia is 18 years.

wads of wickedness. If you're easily offended or not in the mood for some harmless fun, you'd better get out of here really quick." Brand names were described in colorful language and included words such as "desire," "impulse," and "passion." The "Lust" brand asserted:

> So what does drinking "Lust" say about you? Yellow or gold is a stimulant. It drives desire and not surprisingly, prompts quick action. The cool rose motif? Well, surely the rose is the most famous symbol of love and desire. After all, don't men the world over think giving a dozen red roses is foreplay? So what does the combination of "lustrous" gold and the romantic red rose say about you? Right here, right now. I'm ready and I'm tingling all over.

The wine company brand manager stated that, "We're aware that we are pushing things to the extreme here, but there is a strong and somewhat ignorant market for the younger generation. As they get older, their palates become more sophisticated. Until then, we are making a smooth, approachable wine for our target audience" (Schou-Clarke, 2001, p. 22). The approach taken with Wicked Wines was highly questionable, given the pervasive sexual innuendoes associated with its consumption. It was also inconsistent with most tenets of self-regulatory codes of practice.

Midori

The Midori website offered visitors the opportunity to sign up for the Club Midori, where as a member you would "be the first to know when the Midori Guys and Girls are in town. You'll gain access to the Club Midori Competitions where you can win loads of cool prizes. You can find out about the hottest night-spots and when Midori is on special in a liquor outlet near you."

Sub Zero

This product is an alcoholic soda. The website included an interactive game, Sub Space, to play with Sub Zero bottles as well as the latest advertising campaign for the flavors "remix," "pink grapefruit," and "lemon." There was a photo page featuring the Pink Police female promotional models.

Besides the above six websites, other examples included the use of existing video games and their websites as a venue for alcohol advertising and promotional activity. For instance, Jack Daniels had a 3-month product placement on www.shockwaves.com, a popular youth website, with a section called "real pool" video games. Miller Beer used video race-car driving on its website, again causing concern because of the appeal to youth and the direct association between drinking and driving.

At present, there appear to be no effective legal sanctions or self-regulatory controls over alcohol advertising and promotion via the Internet. The case illustrations above highlight the pressing need for an effective regulatory mechanism to be established. The Internet presents a set of special challenges in terms of monitoring its appropriate use, and it is increasingly the subject of international scrutiny. The limitations inherent within existing codes of practice for the print media and television become even more obvious when transposed to the context of the Internet. In the latter instance, the medium is often used interactively, making it potentially more powerful compared to the passive media of print and television. Clearly, particular attention needs to be directed to the issue of alcohol advertising and promotion via the Internet. This issue is all the more important because of the age profile of heavy Internet users, which is skewed toward the younger age groups. Young people's drinking patterns, as well as their access and initiation to drinking, have always been matters of concern, and this is more so today than ever before. Their unlimited and unsupervised exposure to beverage alcohol advertising on the Internet, unconstrained by any mechanism, is therefore a matter for public health concern.

TELEVISION, FILM, AND MUSIC VIDEO ADVERTISEMENTS AND PRODUCT PLACEMENT

As noted above, until recently, a very large proportion of alcohol advertisements were broadcast through the medium of television. For a number of reasons, it is possible that this level of exposure may change in the near future. For instance, increasing controls are being imposed on the extent and nature of television alcohol advertisements in many countries. Perhaps more significantly, the Internet may radically change the nature of mass communication. As pointed out in the previous section, beverage alcohol advertising and promotional activities have already made substantial inroads on the Internet. Nonetheless, an examination of television alcohol advertisements, as well as the broader question of the role and impact of product placement, is warranted.

Given the limitations of presenting any analysis of television advertisements in a printed volume such as this book, it is perhaps best just to describe particular examples and then highlight the public health concerns that might arise from them. In Table 11.1, the left-hand column summarizes the contents of a series of television alcohol advertisements used in a study by Parker (1998). The right-hand column indicates the public health concerns or responses associated with each of the advertisements. The advertisements referred to in the

TABLE 11.1. Advertisements and Related Public Health Concerns

Descriptions of Selected Advertisements	Public Health Concerns
Stairway, 30 seconds: a young woman follows beer can trail to a roof party where two young men are waiting.	Using alcohol as a lure is considered inappropriate. The fact that only three people form the party suggests a sexual rendezvous rather than a party. Finally, since the woman is outnumbered, the question of her personal safety arises.
Bar scene, 30 seconds: quick cuts of people at a bar, shots of beer bottles and empty mugs, shown to the song, "Come on let me show you where it's at."	Concerns relate to encouraging people to drink to excess.
Space creatures, 60 seconds: space creatures dance and drink beer to the song, "Come on let me show you where it's at." Announcer says, "Looks like there's intelligent life out there, after all."	Concerns relate to the portrayal of alcohol consumption as a requisite for intelligent or clever behavior.
Barrel, 30 seconds: snowy scenes with a barrel of beer, beer splashing into icy glasses. Announcer says, "Get out of the cold and into the cold."	In many countries with cold weather, there is a significant death rate from alcohol-related exposure. This has included children in some communities where intoxicated parents have locked them out of the house.
Cactus, 30 seconds: a young beer truck driver stops in the desert. Animated cactus removes six-pack of beer from the truck. Music is, "On the Road Again," by Canned Heat.	Any association with drink driving is of concern and to be avoided at all times—especially with young drivers, as depicted here. In this particular instance, the driver is on his own, so clearly there is no replacement driver. Breaking open a six-pack offers the opportunity to consume a large amount of alcohol.
Race car, 30 seconds: a racing car is speeding around an empty track when a woman appears in the stands. The car becomes a stealth fighter plane and wins the race. Announcer mentions Bobby Rahal, a former Indy car driver.	Any association with drinking and driving should be avoided. Where the type of driving involved is car racing, even greater concern is warranted. Associations between alcohol and driving, and especially car racing, are ill advised. Added to this already potential mix is the hint of sexual success. Again, these are elements to be avoided.
Gator, 30 seconds: young men rescue a woman trapped on a houseboat in a lagoon full of alligators, all to the song, "Mississippi Queen."	Apart from the stereotypical gender roles and the association of alcohol with male heroism, no obvious public health concerns.

table are relevant only in terms of the general principles they illustrate, since it is unlikely that they are still in use.

In terms of product placement, numerous issues arise, some of which have already been noted in the section above, where placement of products at the point of sale has come under criticism. Perhaps a subtler and, some would argue, more insidious form of product placement is that which occurs increasingly within the context of television programs and films. Even though the research undertaken in relation to alcohol advertising has become increasingly sophisticated and methodologically rigorous, relatively little of this work has focused on media and television portrayals of alcohol (Furnham, Ingle, Gunter, & McClelland, 1997). Most research undertaken has, until recently, focused on advertising and has paid little attention to general images of alcohol and drinking in the media. Again, this is an area that has changed sharply in the past few years. For instance, reports from Britain indicate that alcohol portrayal and drinking in television soap operas had increased in the 10 years up to 1997 (Furnham et al., 1997). The U.S. Federal Trade Commission reported in 1999 that eight of the largest alcohol companies had considered making product placements in PG and PG-13 movies[2] with youth-oriented themes and large youth audiences and on eight of the 15 television shows most popular with teenagers (U.S. Federal Trade Commission, 1999). Rock music videos have also been increasingly used as a vehicle for the promotion of alcohol. The entertainment industry at large has often been accused of promoting adolescent health risk and problem behaviors (Hansen & Hansen, 1990; DuRant et al., 1997).

Few laws or self-regulatory systems address product placement, although this is likely to change in the future as concerns mount over its excessive, inappropriate, and uncontrolled use. The scope for associating alcohol beverages with high-profile media figures and programs is self-evident, and there is growing concern over the subtle, and at times less than subtle, way it is done (Furnham et al., 1997; Wallack, Grube, Madden, & Breed, 1990; Yoast, Lamkin, & Sherman, 2001). There is a view that the general public is becoming increasingly media savvy and is less tolerant of being exploited or manipulated.

PRINT MEDIA ADVERTISEMENTS

The print media have attracted much attention with regard to alcohol advertisements. Described below are a series of print advertisements that highlight

---

[2] PG and PG-13 movies are those that advise parental guidance for children. Clearly, many children attend movies for which parental guidance is suggested.

various positive and negative aspects of alcohol advertising. The advertisements are grouped into those that:

- give cause for concern for the public health field, particularly around the themes of youth, sex, and women, or involve combinations of them;
- are considered neutral or benign from a public health perspective;
- illustrate positive associations, such as wine taken in conjunction with a meal.

Youth, Sex, and Women Themes Raising Public Health Concerns

Kirov Vodka

One Kirov Vodka ad depicts a colored photo of a young woman, evidently a teenager. She is wearing skimpy clothes comprising a bra top and a very short hipster kilt, typical of adolescent party gear. The pose is sexually provocative, as is the caption appearing above the photo, "No, I am not wearing any," which is an allusion to question, "Is anything worn under the kilt?" The sexual imagery also includes the strategic positioning of the letter "i" in the word "Kirov" between the young woman's thighs, creating a highly phallic image. On several counts, this advertisement represents several aspects of bad or unacceptable alcohol advertising, in that it depicts a very young person and it is heavy with sexual and seductive imagery on various levels.

James Boag's Premium Beer

An extensively used Boag's beer advertisement—with a caption, "Who is James Boag?"—shows the faceless back view of a woman from the waist down bent over a railing. She is dressed in a black dress that is split up to the top of her thigh, revealing a lace-topped stocking. This advertisement for a beer product is of particular concern. It captures many of the elements of sexist advertising, despite many attempts to eradicate them in the past few years (Woodruff, 1996). It contains no redeeming features; it is dehumanizing and is the type of advertisement shown to be associated with violence against women. Clearly, this type of advertisement cannot be said to be responsible, safe, and harm-reducing.

Tanqueray Gin

One Tanqueray Gin ad shows Hugh Hefner, dressed in a velvet smoking jacket, juxtaposed with young blonde twin women. The women are dressed in skimpy satin slips with their bodies pressed together; between their legs is positioned the bottle of gin. In small, almost illegible print in the lower left-hand corner is a message, with an apparently implied double message, which advises, "Sip responsibly." This advertisement has no redeeming features and is an excellent example of the type of advertising that is considered irresponsible and inappropriate on numerous counts.

Neutral Advertisements

When the diverse array of print-based alcohol advertisements was examined, many of the advertisements encountered were considered neutral and largely acceptable from a public health perspective. A range of different alcohol advertisements was found that depicted products in a visually attractive but inoffensive manner. Most of these display sophistication, with strong visual appeal, but they do not actively contravene advertising codes or raise public health concerns. However, there is scope for these advertisements to be improved by including more, or better, information about safe drinking, standard drinks information, and so on. There is clearly no sexual allusion, demeaning depiction of women, or involvement of, or appeal to, young people in any way at all.

Low-Risk and Contextual Images

Some advertisements depicted images reflecting low-risk drinking patterns, placing drinking in the context of eating food, or, more specifically, consuming good-quality food with good-quality alcohol. Some of these types of advertisements showed the production of alcohol beverages within an earthy context, and while they may be deliberately manipulative, they do not contain the type of highly problematic material outlined above. Advertising images that illustrate the consumption of a beverage within the context of a meal are particularly supported, as drinking during meals can obviate some of the potential hazards of alcohol. Drinking in the context of a meal also reflects positive social norms and desirable patterns of consumption. None of these imply drinking to excess or to the point of intoxication.

GENERAL PRINCIPLES OF GOOD ALCOHOL ADVERTISING

Outlined above are some of the key issues of concern from a public health perspective that arise in relation to alcohol advertising and promotions. An attempt has been made to delineate areas of concern associated with various forms of advertising and promotions. None of the content of these areas of concern is new. From a public health perspective, there has been a high level of consistency with regard to what is inappropriate advertising. This chapter is a further attempt to highlight, through the use of specific examples, the areas in which concern has been expressed and action is likely to be taken. In addition, the examples have also illustrated features of advertising that do not raise public health concerns. In this way, it is hoped that a clearer, more positive articulation of what is considered acceptable, appropriate, and ethically defensible might emerge. It is also hoped that this exercise may lead to a more proactive and prosocial response on the part of the alcohol industry overall to curb inappropriate activities of colleagues (the notion of "rogue players" holds little credibility for the general public). This section attempts to crystallize some of the key features of alcohol advertising and promotions and to capture the essence of safe and responsible advertising.

Tackling the Issue of Youth Head-On

One of the most important and sensitive groups in relation to alcohol and advertising is young people. It is this age group, as well as women, that forms the focus of most concern from the public health field. One viewpoint suggests that:

> drinking is a learned behavior. In many ways, it is much like learning to drive or ski. It entails instruction, modeling, and even some experimentation, as part of the process of learning how to undertake the activity efficiently and without problems. (Grant, 2001, p. xi)

It seems both helpful and consistent for the alcohol industry to ensure that alcohol advertising and promotions reflect that view. As drinking is a learned behavior, which entails the contributions of parents, family, school, and the broader community, there is clearly an important prosocial role to be played in relation to advertising and promotions. The most responsible position that could be adopted by the alcohol industry would be a "hands-off" stance in relation to youth, that is, a complete moratorium on *any* activities that address, involve, or target youth. To be fully self-initiating and truly self-regulatory in this regard would win great social acclaim. If young people are to learn safe, low-risk drinking behaviors, and if the industry position is to be that the family is the place where this should predominantly take place, then logically there is no scope for advertising and promotional activities that negate this view. The following represents an advertising and promotions checklist.

Things Not to Do

- Alcohol advertisements and promotions should not appeal to or involve children and young people.
- The use of child-friendly images such as cartoon characters, animals, and fast-paced animation should be avoided.

- The advertisement or promotional efforts should in no way suggest or imply the condoning of drinking to excess or drinking to the point of intoxication.
- Alcohol advertisements should not have an implicit or explicit association with illicit drugs.
- Any association with sexual success should be avoided.
- Demeaning depiction of women in relation to beverage alcohol should not occur.

Things to Do

- Ensure that the product is clearly and unambiguously indicated to be an alcohol beverage (for self-evident harm reduction reasons, but also to prevent inadvertent poisonings).
- Clearly and legibly display the alcohol concentration level of the beverage within any given container.
- Clearly indicate the number of standard drinks contained in a package of beverage alcohol.
- Provide prospective consumers with information and advice about potential negative effects of the product.
- Provide potential consumers with recommended strategies to avoid alcohol-related problems.
- Depict the consumption of alcohol in the social context considered desirable. From a public health perspective, this would be friendly social and especially family settings in physical environments not conducive to harm, injury, or threat to one's person.
- Emphasize ways to drink alcohol safely, including attention to transportation needs and avoiding the potential for injury.
- Use neutral imagery.

The not-to-do list above is of the type available in many places, especially those countries with self-regulatory systems in force (hence, there is little value in reproducing a full list here). Even though injunctions not to do this or that in relation to alcohol advertising have been extensively developed, the issue of compliance with—and, perhaps, comprehension of—these injunctions is the important point.

It is noted again, however, that the self-regulatory mechanisms in place in most countries do not adequately, if at all, address product placement issues, the use of the Internet and related electronic media for alcohol advertising and promotions, and a sufficiently wide range of social and ethical concerns. Hence, considerably more work is required in these areas, even in countries where substantial efforts may already have been directed to such questions.

In addition, the constantly changing nature of this field necessitates continual updates, reviews, and critiques.

At the Broader Level

There is great scope for the alcohol industry to create a positive public image, in contrast to its historically negative reputation in relation to alcohol advertising and promotion. An opportunity exists to reverse the commonly held view that the alcohol industry contributes to alcohol problems, not to their resolution. There is scope for this to be done in constructive and meaningful ways. The challenge is to reframe the industry's approaches so that it can work proactively to create an environment that supports healthy and safe drinking behavior.

REFERENCES

Atkin, C., Hocking, J., & Block, M. (1984). Teenage drinking: Does advertising make a difference? *Journal of Communication, 34*, 157–167.

Atkin, C., Neuendorf, K., & McDermott, S. (1983). The role of alcohol advertising in excessive and hazardous drinking. *Journal of Drug Education, 13*, 313–325.

Beccaria, F. (2001). The Italian debate on alcohol advertising regulation. *Contemporary Drug Problems, 28*, 719–737.

Besen, D. (1997). US alcohol beverage advertisers sharpen their focus on core brands. *Impact, 27*, 1–5.

Carroll, T. E., & Donovan, R. J. (2002). Alcohol marketing on the Internet: New challenges for harm reduction. *Drug and Alcohol Review, 21*, 83–91.

Center for Media Education. (1996). *Web of deception: Threats to children from online marketing*. Washington, DC: Center for Media Education.

Center for Media Education. (1997). *Alcohol and tobacco on the Web: New threats to youth*. Washington, DC: Author.

Center for Media Education. (1998). *Alcohol advertising targeted at youth on the Internet: An update*. Washington, DC: Author.

Center for Media Education. (1999). *Youth access to alcohol and tobacco Web marketing. The filtering and rating debate*. Washington, DC: Author.

DuRant, R. H., Rome, E., Rich, M., Allred, E., Emans, S. J., & Woods, E. R. (1997). Tobacco and alcohol use behaviors portrayed in music videos: A content analysis. *American Journal of Public Health, 87*, 1131–1135.

Friedman, T. L. (2000). *The Lexus and the olive tree: Understanding globalization.* New York: Anchor Books/Random House.

Furnham, A., Ingle, H., Gunter, B., & McClelland, A. (1997). A content analysis of alcohol portrayal and drinking in British television soap operas. *Health Education Research, 12*, 519–529.

Grant, M. (2001). Foreword. In E. Houghton & A. M. Roche (Eds.), *Learning about drinking* (pp. xi–xiii). Washington, DC: Brunner-Routledge.

Hansen, C. H., & Hansen, R. D. (1990). Rock music videos and antisocial behavior. *Basic Applied Social Psychology, 11*, 357–369.

Hastings, G. B., MacKintosh, A. M., & Aitken, P. P. (1992). Is alcohol advertising reaching the people it shouldn't reach? *Health Education Journal, 51*, 38–42.

International Center for Alcohol Policies (ICAP). (2001). *Self-regulation of beverage alcohol advertising*. ICAP Report No. 9. Washington, DC: Author.

Jones, S. C., & Donovan, R. (2002). Self-regulation of alcohol advertising: Is it working for Australia? *Journal of Public Affairs, 2*(3), 153–165.

Lipsitz, A., Brake, G., Vincent, E. J., & Winters, M. (1993). Another round for the brewers: Television ads and children's alcohol expectancies. *Journal of Applied Social Psychology, 23*, 439–450.

McKeganey, N., Forsyth, A., Barnard, M., & Hay, G. (1996). Designer drinks and drunkenness amongst a sample of Scottish schoolchildren. *British Medical Journal, 313*, 401.

Parker, B. (1998). Exploring life themes and myths in alcohol advertisements through a meaning-based model of advertising experiences. *Journal of Advertising, 27*, 97–112.

Portman Group. (2002, May 20). *Top retailers rapped by drinks industry code of practice*. Press release. Retrieved June 28, 2004, from http://www.portman-group.org.uk/newsdesk/66.asp?coid=144&recordcount=4.

Roche, A. M. (1997). The shifting sands of alcohol prevention: Rethinking population control approaches. *Australian and New Zealand Journal of Public Health, 21*, 621–625.

Saffer, H. (1997). Alcohol advertising and motor vehicle fatalities. *Review of Economics and Statistics, 79*, 431–442.

Schou-Clarke, J. (2001, September 20). Wicked goes wild. *AdNews*, 22.

U.S. Federal Trade Commission. (1999, September). *Self-regulation in the alcohol industry: A review of industry efforts to avoid promoting alcohol to underage consumers*. Washington, DC: Author.

Wallack, L., Grube, J. W., Madden, P., & Breed, W. (1990). Portrayals of alcohol on prime-time television. *Journal of Studies on Alcohol, 51*, 428–437.

Woodruff, K. (1996). Alcohol advertising and violence against women: A media advocacy case study. *Health Education Quarterly, 23*, 330–345.

Wyllie, A., Zhang, J. F., & Casswell, S. (1998). Responses to televised alcohol advertisements associated with drinking behaviour of 10–17 year olds. *Addiction, 93*, 361–371.

Yoast, R. A., Lamkin, L., & Sherman, J. (2001). *Alcohol issues: Partner or foe? The alcohol industry, youth alcohol problems, and alcohol policy strategies*. Policy Briefing Paper. Chicago: American Medical Association.

Chapter 12

Are Alcohol Advertisers Drinking in the Last Chance Saloon?

Hugh Burkitt

This chapter is written from the perspective of someone who has spent 30 years in advertising (during the past 20, working on alcohol brands), from the perspective of a regulator who served 6 years on the Council of the Advertising Standards Authority (ASA) and is currently serving on the Independent Complaints Panel of the Portman Group, and from the perspective of a father of a 15-year-old boy who is learning how to drink alcohol.

Alcohol brings great pleasure to an enormous number of people, but it is also dangerous. Young people in particular need to learn how to drink it sensibly. The "advertiser" in me recognizes that the specific rules on alcohol advertising are generally being followed, although the "regulator" fears that the *spirit* of these rules is being widely ignored, especially on television, which is the most powerful advertising medium. Seen within a European context, British drink advertisers may be behaving unwisely. This makes a ban or serious restriction on television advertising for alcoholic drinks a real possibility. A ban already exists in many European countries, and it would be easy for those opposed to alcohol advertising to argue that the United Kingdom should be "harmonized" with these markets.

From an advertiser's perspective, this would be a pity because, in principle, there should be commercial freedom to advertise products that are legally sold. It would also be true to say that television viewers would miss drink advertisements because they are funny. Drink advertisers, unlike many other marketers, are actually trying to *entertain* their target audience as part of the advertising process, because they want consumers to identify with their ads and to feel comfortable drinking their brand. One has to ask the question, however, "Are alcohol advertisers drinking in the last chance saloon?"

There are three main interrelated issues to consider: targeting young drinkers, binge drinking, and sexual success. Fifty years ago, young men were usually initiated into drinking through beer. It seemed bitter, metallic, and disgusting at first, but one learned to drink it—slowly and with difficulty—because it was a necessary requirement of growing up and becoming a man. Youths of today have a large choice of fruit-flavored drinks, which have no unpleasant taste, contain 5% alcohol, and are increasingly acceptable as "proper" drinks for young men. Two famous spirit brands have come to dominate this premium packaged spirits market in recent years: Bacardi and Smirnoff. Although neither would dream of intentionally targeting drinkers under 18, it is very difficult to exclude under-18-year-olds from a television media schedule and from access to the product itself. The commercial logic of targeting 18- to 24-year-old drinkers is irrefutable, and an examination of a television commercial for Bacardi Breezer, "The Daughter-in-Law," shows that it does a very good job of suggesting that it is the young who know how to enjoy themselves. In the commercial, scenes of a woman's meeting with her prim mother-in-law are constantly set against images of wild fun that the young woman and her friends have in their "real life"—with the help of Bacardi Breezer, of course.

From an advertiser's perspective this commercial is funny and right on brief. A regulator, however, might feel a twinge of concern that there may be a suggestion of, on occasion, drinking to excess. The advertising for Bacardi Breezer has evolved skillfully over the years with the use of a cat called Tom who has become a metaphor for youthful (especially male) misbehavior. Tom has been seen in a number of commercials out "on the tiles" and in one ("Tom—the Morning After") he faces the consequences on the morning after a night of dancing, drinking, and socializing. Although one can only admire the lateral creativity of the cat, the "regulator" in me finds himself wondering whether it is right to make a joke out of feeling terrible on the morning after partying with Bacardi Breezer. Would Tom have felt like this if the amount he had drunk were sensible?

When it comes to targeting youth, the rules have always been clear that characters that appeal especially to people aged under 18 years should not be used in commercials, and the United Kingdom's rules also state that people shown drinking should not be, nor should they look, under 25. This seems odd because the heroes of the young are, surely, likely to be a bit older than they themselves are, in order to be aspirational. Indeed, one of the dangers that premium packaged spirits brands face is that they will become too obviously popular with very young drinkers and therefore lose their alcohol brand credibility.

One commercial for the parent brand Bacardi uses as its central character someone who has definite "street cred" with young males: the footballer-turned-actor Vinnie Jones. Vinnie Jones is a man who had a particularly violent reputation as a professional soccer player, and who was brilliantly, and unexpectedly, cast as one of the villains in the cult movie *Lock, Stock and Two Smoking Barrels*. The "advertiser" in me can only admire the casting of Vinnie in this commercial. He represents masculinity, toughness, and aggression in spades. He would not necessarily appeal *more* to under-18-year-olds than to young legal-age drinkers; he is well into his 30s and he is no longer an active sporting hero, but he will definitely be machismo personified to the majority of young men aged 18 to 24. The letter of the code may not have been breached, but Vinnie does not sit comfortably within the code's spirit.

Bacardi and Bacardi Breezer are not alone in suggesting that their brands are good ones with which to "party." In Scotland, Tennants has been suggesting to drinkers that they "Murder a few tonight," and Coors Light has built a whole campaign around the idea of drinking late into the night. Both of these are perfectly logical campaigns from a brand owner standpoint, and neither shows excessive consumption taking place. Yet, from a regulator's point of view, the wording in the first commercial and the action in the second could suggest unwise drinking.

Turning to the notion of sexual success, it is perhaps worth noting the guidelines put forth by the Broadcast Advertising Clearance Centre (BACC) in the United Kingdom:

> "Sexual success" goes beyond the basic idea of alcohol as an aid to seduction. It also includes any suggestion of enhanced sexual attractiveness through the consumption of a particular drink and of drink as an accessory to sexual relationships. Sexual innuendo should be handled with extreme care as it will more often than not be deemed to contravene this rule. (Broadcast Advertising Clearance Centre, 1994/August 1999)

Another commercial is worth examining with this thought in mind: Smirnoff Ice's "Faked Pregnancy," which shows a couple disturbing a stage performance by suggestive moans from their theater box. When the ushers interfere, the woman appears to be having a baby. Once the couple is escorted safely into a cab, it becomes clear that it was all a joke, as the woman pulls the man's jacket out from under her shirt. The commercial is funny, and it studiously avoids showing the actual consumption of the product anywhere in the plot so that it in turn avoids the direct accusation of "sexual success." Yet, it certainly does not avoid innuendo. In fact, innuendo is unendingly "in your face" throughout the current alcohol advertising scene in the United Kingdom. This is hardly surprising. Indeed, one of the many reasons why relatively old regulators disapprove of the behavior of the 18- to 24-year age group is that they not only spend a lot of time getting drunk, they also spend a lot of time (the regulators nostalgically imagine) pairing up and having sex.

Another commercial, this time for Gordon's gin, shows a young couple playing chess in a house made out of ice ("Ice Chess"). Sensual interaction between the two players does not convey the impression that they are having a deep and meaningful discussion about winning match strategies. It is certainly quite clear what they are likely to do once the game is over. The attraction here seems suitably modern and mutual. It would not of course be acceptable if the man were in any way taking advantage of the woman.

It is, however, the consumer who needs to be listened to, whether as drinker, parent, or voter, and, in the United Kingdom, the Independent Television Commission (ITC) and the Advertising Standards Authority (ASA) act as the consumers' watchdogs. There do not seem to be any great signs of unrest in the country's society at large about the effect of advertising on drinking behavior. The level of complaints about alcohol brands to either of these two consumer watchdogs is generally very low. Out of more than 12,000 complaints received by the ASA in 2002, only 179 were about alcoholic drinks.

Until recently, the situation was similar with television. Total consumer complaints were low, and in 5 years only one commercial has had a complaint upheld. That was until a commercial for Carling lager titled "Frustrating" began to be screened. In it, a woman is furious at her boyfriend, who has not cleaned the apartment. She then goes around the rooms spilling his favorite Carling lager, while the man follows her licking everything that the beer touches. Once the house is sparkling clean, the woman is prepared to pour the remaining lager on herself—but, to the couple's distress, there is no lager left. This commercial received a large number of complaints from the public, who were concerned with the obvious reference to oral sex and the fact that it was shown throughout the football World Cup, when a lot of children were watching. The ITC upheld the complaint, but imposed only the mild sanction of requiring the commercial to be shown exclusively after 9 P.M. Still, the ITC has signaled informally to the advertising business that it is unhappy with a number of current drink advertisements and will be looking much more closely at this sector.

The ASA has upheld more complaints than the ITC in the past few years, but it tends to be more concerned about general issues of taste and decency than about the specific rules concerning alcohol. Recently, the ASA Council has upheld several complaints against alcohol advertisements on the grounds of implied sexual success, sexual innuendo, encouraging drunken behavior, and suggesting an association with drugs.

There is certainly a need for watchdogs to be vigilant because all agencies and brand marketers will strive as hard as they can to gain the maximum competitive advantage for their own beverage brand. The financial rewards of success in this market can be substantial indeed. It would be good to see the BACC (which clears commercials for British television) take a tougher line. The ASA could also look more closely at the specific rules on alcohol when considering complaints about print advertisements. More important, however, the major United Kingdom drinks advertisers need to take stock at the moment. In particular, they should review their collective output on television and carefully consider this output against public concern, particularly in the context of the European political scene, with a view to moderating their behavior.

At present, the advertisers of a lot of drinks brands are talking very effectively to the young audience, which they have researched very thoroughly and understand very well. These advertisers have a great responsibility to encourage their consumers to drink wisely, and it is not clear that they are doing this. More alcohol advertisers need to understand that they *are* drinking in the last chance saloon.

NOTE

Since this presentation was delivered much has changed in the marketing of alcoholic drinks in the UK, and from a regulator's perspective much has improved. Two of the companies whose advertising is strongly criticized in the presentation—Diageo and Bacardi—have issued new social responsibility guidelines to all their staff and have followed up these with training programs and advertising approval systems to try to ensure that inappropriate advertising and promotions are no longer produced.

Meanwhile the whole advertising regulatory system has changed. A new regulatory authority, Ofcom, has issued new rules and guidelines on alcohol advertising which came into force in January 2005. These specifically emphasize the need for the rules to be observed in the spirit as well as the letter ("whether or not the product is shown") and also require that there be no link between alcohol and sexual activity.

Responsibility for enforcing the Ofcom rules in the UK is now the responsibility of an enlarged Advertising Standards Authority, which acts as the regulator for both television and print advertising. This should remove some of the anomalies that have occurred in the past when different authorities have sometimes take different view of the same campaign.

Around the time of my presentation in October 2002, a number of brand marketers and regulators realized that advertising controls had become too lax in the UK, and both sides have worked hard since to improve the situation. Currently, alcohol brand marketers still have the freedom to use all adult advertising media in the UK. I believe that all the major alcohol brand owners realize that this freedom needs to be collectively guarded by a responsible approach to advertising.

REFERENCE

Broadcast Advertising Clearance Centre (BACC). (1994/August 1999). *Notes of guidance*. Section 4.9.2 (g). Retrieved June 16, 2004, from www.bacc.org.uk.

Chapter 13

Setting the Standards for Responsible Consumer Marketing in Beverage Alcohol

Chris Britton

Paul Walsh, Diageo's[1] chief executive officer, has said, "We're proud of our brands. We want Diageo's marketing and promotional activities to be recognized as the best in the world. That means demanding great results for our brands." He has, however, added, "but doing so in a way which sets the industry standards for responsible marketing." This last part is becoming a mantra in Diageo, which believes that responsible marketing is good business practice. Marketing is an understanding of what motivates a person to consume and buy, and of when that person consumes and buys. Consumer insight is the deep understanding of the values, attitudes, and preferences that motivate the current and future behavior of a brand's key target group. Marketing is about trying to generate a consumer insight and then leveraging it. It is about finding out what the trend is and then understanding how it can be utilized. Marketing never creates trends. The consumer insights are researched to see how they play out in different markets to assess the value that each one can create. At the heart of it all is consumer insight, and great marketing is based on con-

---

[1] Diageo plc, a sponsor of ICAP, is an international beverage alcohol company headquartered in the United Kingdom.

sumer insight brand-building programs. Behind a piece of advertising, behind a piece of public relations (PR), behind a piece of sponsorship, there is a consumer insight.

The role of the consumer is paramount in a consumer-oriented company. Marketing organizations have to be passionate about their consumers, who are put at the heart of everything that is done. After all, without consumers there is no business at all. An increasing consumer orientation has become very evident in recent years: it is the consumers who are now driving marketing initiatives and business strategies. Consumers were often the preserve of marketing, but now they drive the whole business. As far as marketing is concerned, though, the optimum goal is brand loyalty, and this applies equally to marketing soap powder, marketing a sports team, or marketing beverage alcohol. Every brand has to be produced and marketed to the highest standards of social acceptability and responsibility. That is a critical consumer insight that creates real value for the business. Without it, it is very difficult to win brand loyalty.

As far as alcohol beverages are concerned, there must be sensitivity to marketing only to adult consumers of legal purchase age, and efforts should be made to avoid marketing to nondrinkers. Drinks marketers need to achieve even higher standards of integrity and social responsibility. Alcohol marketing and advertising are about encouraging drinkers to develop, change, or maintain brand preferences. They are about brand switching, about things that go on in a category, and about the creation of loyalty. There is no conclusive evidence to prove that marketing and advertising encourage nondrinkers to drink, nor do they encourage drinkers to increase consumption or discourage drinkers from cutting consumption. Marketing is all about brand competition and that is why marketers are entirely focused on the "market share."

The decision to drink or not to drink is an individual's choice, and that choice must be respected. Consumers know that drinking responsibly can provide enjoyment, and they should be empowered to learn to drink well, maximizing enjoyment and avoiding misuse. Marketing in the beverage alcohol industry can have a role in the process of encouraging consumers to drink well through communicating positive brand and product attributes. This concept of responsible marketing dictates promotion of positive drinking patterns and responsible drinking occasions as part of a balanced, healthy lifestyle. It is about understanding responsible drinks marketing and then positioning brands within it through their marketing.

Responsible marketing must be in compliance with existing regulations, whether statutory or voluntary. This compliance can be ensured through self-regulation, but self-regulation works only when it is backed by a broad legal framework. All parties must agree and adhere to the standards, and there must be a proper process to channel complaints and execute removal of offending marketing and/or penalties for behavior that violates the agreed standards. There must also be regular audits by external independent bodies.

The process of self-regulation can vary, reflecting market cultural traditions and legal frameworks, but there are some general principles that apply globally. Self-regulation, however, must always evolve and be strengthened, especially outside Europe and the United States, where there is a need to introduce or update some of these systems. Responsible consumer marketing companies need to observe the spirit as well as the letter of the code. Marketing is a creative process within which one is always trying to set the boundaries. There is a tension between working within the boundaries and circumventing them, but it is not acceptable to circumvent.

Baileys Irish Cream, for instance, is a sensuous product. It is the only spirit brand in which consumers will dip their fingers. They will not normally do that with a scotch or vodka. Those who market Bailey's are trying to convey sensuousness. Baileys is not about sex, nor about sexual success. It is about sensuousness, about friends, about warmth, and about sociability. A lot of effort is now going into making both the marketers and the advertising agency really understand the difference and getting the spirit and the letter of responsible marketing absolutely in line.

Consumers also want to be well informed. They need basic information in terms of beverage strength and serving size that enables them to be responsible about their drinking behavior. Drinks marketers have a role to play in informing the consumers about responsible drinking patterns. But consumers can also be more involved in the discussions on responsibility. Better consumer communication in this area will enable them to influence future marketing practices. At the moment, that is not happening regularly.

Moreover, responsible drinks marketing needs to move from being an issue or a constraint for a company to being recognized as an effective, proven practice. Responsible drinks marketing needs to be explicitly linked to a company's performance, giving the industry the incentive to pursue it. The industry needs to train its employees in responsible drinks marketing, and that effort needs to be highly visible and supported widely, so that the industry uses its considerable marketing skills to promote responsible drinking.

Diageo is trying to do this. Its employees have a part to play in managing the company's corporate reputation and creating value in the external environment. A company's actions as a corporate citizen can differentiate it from its competitors in the minds of its stakeholders. Diageo has had a code of marketing practice since it was first established in 1997. It has now appointed an independent auditor to report on its compliance to the code. Twenty-seven brands in 47 countries outside the United States have been reviewed, while inside that country the auditor has reviewed 600 advertisements for 36 brands. The code is published on the company's corporate website (Diageo plc, 2003).

Diageo is involved in many social aspects organizations—about 20 around the world—such as the Portman Group in the United Kingdom and the Century Council in the United States. The company itself is supporting alcohol education initiatives, drink-driving initiatives, and responsible server programs. It is also looking at how pure marketing initiatives can help, using direct social responsibility advertising. In the United States now, the goal is that one in five of Diageo's broadcast advertisements should be centered on social responsibility. As for marketing to those under the legal purchase age, the company is absolutely attuned not to do it. Diageo does not commission research into underage drinkers, nor does it glamorize excessive drinking, make drunkenness attractive, or encourage reckless behaviors. Nevertheless, the company needs to set and improve standards all the time. Responsible marketing will be central to the way that Diageo does its business. That is part of the company's wider commitment to leadership in corporate social responsibility. As part of this stance, Diageo is a signatory to the United Nations Global Compact on Corporate Social Responsibility, which covers issues such as human rights, labor, and the environment. It was the first drinks company to sign the Global Compact—a major step forward in showing its commitment to this area.

In conclusion, alcohol beverages bring pleasure to millions of adults every day all over the world, and they have done so for thousands of years. The industry is proud of the unique part that alcohol plays in the social lives and celebrations of many cultures, but it also recognizes that alcohol beverages may be consumed irresponsibly and create problems for the individual and society as a whole. The industry, therefore, has a responsibility to ensure that all its brands are advertised and marketed responsibly. This is something to be taken very seriously. Brand advertising that depicts responsible drinking as a relaxed, sociable, and enjoyable part of the human experience is not only an appropriate means of marketing, but can also help promote a responsible approach to alcohol consumption. Responsible marketing of alcohol beverages should encourage responsible drinking, but this is a shared responsibility, applying not only to brand owners, but also to the consumers.

REFERENCE

Diageo plc. (2003). *The Diageo code of marketing practice for alcohol beverages: "Diageo Marketing Code."* London: Author.

Chapter 14

Developing Solutions for Abusive Drinking on Campus: A Campus-Community-Industry Collaborative Model

Peter Cressy and Monica Gourovitch

There is widespread agreement that underage and abusive drinking on U.S. college campuses is a serious social problem. In order to make an impact, all constituencies that are involved—including the campus, the broader community, and the beverage alcohol industry—must make a long-term commitment to work together and implement science-based solutions. In this chapter, we briefly discuss the scope of underage drinking and abuse, the state of research on contributing factors, and the ongoing efforts and best practices. Finally, we will describe a successful ongoing model program by the distilled spirits industry that illustrates the effectiveness and impact of collaboration and implementation of science-based programs.

In the United States, there are several university and federal agencies that compile data through surveys on college drinking and consequences.[1] Some relevant statistics are:

---

[1] Since the drinking age in the United States is 21 years, most college students are legally underage.

- 67% of college students reported drinking in the past month (Johnston, O'Malley, & Bachman, 2002).
- In 2001, 44% of college students had consumed five drinks in a row at least once in the past 2 weeks. However, the percentage of college students who abstain is increasing (Wechsler et al., 2002).
- 24% of crash fatalities involving a 16- to 20-year-old driver are alcohol related (National Highway Traffic Safety Administration, 2004).

Although these numbers indicate that underage and abusive drinking remain high, there are statistics that clearly show that progress has been made. According to the 2001 Monitoring the Future survey (Johnston et al., 2002), the percentage of college students who reported drinking in the past month had declined 15% since 1980 (the year in which the survey began collecting data on college students). According to the data from the National Highway Traffic Safety Administration (2004), the number of fatalities in teen drink-driving crashes had declined 2% since 2000 and 60% since 1982, going from 4,214 fatalities in 1982 to 1,681 fatalities in 2003 (see Figure 14.1).

In the United States, there has been a great deal of recent publicity centered on the view that the beverage alcohol industry is targeting youth and may be encouraging them to drink. The beverage alcohol industry does not target youth in its marketing. Moreover, it is working hard to strengthen its already effective advertising codes to ensure that all advertising is responsible. Furthermore, as pointed out in other chapters in this volume, the scientific studies are clear in the finding that advertising has no causal impact on a youth's decision to consume or abuse, but is an effective method for influencing decisions on type and brand of alcohol products consumed. Despite the limitations of any individual study, the overall conclusion drawn from current econometric research is that alcohol advertising has little, if any, effect on total levels of alcohol consumption and related problems (Grube, 2000).

The evidence also indicates that a complete ban on broadcast advertising of all alcohol beverages has no effect on consumption in comparison with countries that do not ban broadcast advertising. Equally important for alcohol policy, the results fail to provide evidence that advertising bans have significant negative effects on alcohol abuse outcomes, including cirrhosis, mortality, and road fatalities. This finding suggests that advertising bans do not have a large impact on drinking patterns, although bans may affect brand and beverage choices (Nelson & Young, 2001).

A definitive review of research from around the world found that advertising has virtually no influence on consumption and no impact on either experimentation or abuse; this conclusion is consistent with other reviews of the research (Fisher, 1993, pp. 150–151).

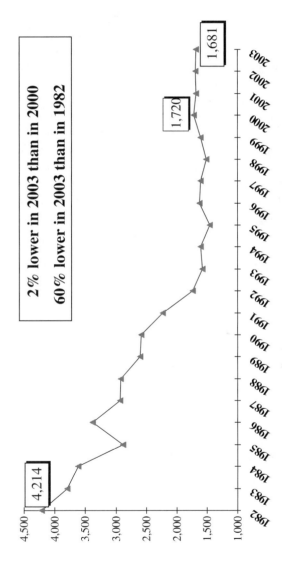

FIGURE 14.1. Total Fatalities in Teen Drink-Driving Crashes. Teen drink-driving crashes represent the total number of people (occupants and nonoccupants) killed in motor vehicle traffic crashes in which at least one teenage (16–20) driver had a BAC of .08 or higher.

Source: Alcoholstats.com. Data from the National Highway Traffic Safety Administration (2004).

The notion that advertising influences consumption is further contradicted by the information presented in Figure 14.2. As the graph clearly shows, while advertising expenditures have dramatically risen since 1992, overall consumption in the United States has remained flat.

The National Center on Addiction and Substance Abuse (CASA) at Columbia University, New York, carried out a survey of adults in 2002 to ascertain their beliefs about who has primary responsibility for underage drinking and what the main influences are on this behavior. The research results set out in Table 14.1 indicate that most of the people surveyed believed that the main responsibilities for and influences on a youth's decision to drink are in fact parents and peers (National Center on Addiction and Substance Abuse, 2003).

In 2002, the U.S. National Institute on Alcohol Abuse and Alcoholism (NIAAA) released its task force's report *A Call to Action: Changing the Culture of Drinking at U.S. Colleges* (National Institute on Alcohol Abuse and Alcoholism, 2002). The objective of the report was to offer recommendations on the potential effectiveness of current strategies and guidance for future research. It clearly states that success depends on comprehensive programs that address all constituencies, including individuals, the student population as a whole, the college, and the surrounding community. Included in the surrounding community is the beverage alcohol industry. According to the NIAAA report, the evidence supporting various substance abuse prevention

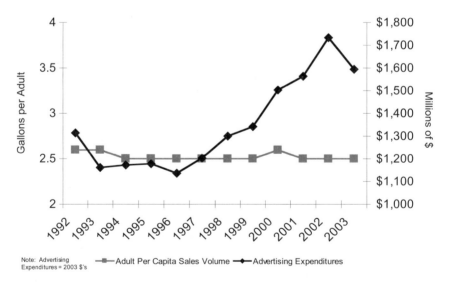

FIGURE 14.2. Per Capita Sales Volume Versus Advertising Expenditures
Source: Adams Beverage Handbook (2004).

TABLE 14.1. Responsibility and Influence on Young People's Decision to Drink

Responsibility (%)		Influence (%)	
Parents	50.4	Peer group	69.3
Peer culture	29.1	Parental influence	10.8
Establishments that sell alcohol	6.8	Depression or emotional problems	5.5
Inadequate law enforcement	2.9	Restlessness	5.4
Media	2.5	Wish to relax or be less inhibited	3.0
Alcohol industry	2.2	Media/entertainment industry	2.2
Political leaders	1.0	Alcohol use by adults	0.9
		Alcohol advertising	0.9

Source: National Center on Addiction and Substance Abuse, 2003.

strategies in the literature varies widely. These differences do not always mean that one strategy is intrinsically better than another. They may reflect the fact that some strategies have not been as thoroughly studied as others or have not been evaluated for application to college drinkers. To provide a useful list that accounts for the lack of research as well as negative findings, task force members placed prevention strategies in descending tiers on the basis of the evidence available to support or refute them. Below is a summary of their research-based strategies.

TIER 1. EVIDENCE OF EFFECTIVENESS AMONG COLLEGE STUDENTS

- Combining cognitive-behavioral skills with norms clarification and motivational enhancement interventions.
- Offering brief motivational enhancement interventions.
- Challenging alcohol expectancies.

TIER 2. EVIDENCE OF SUCCESS WITH GENERAL POPULATIONS THAT COULD BE APPLIED TO COLLEGE ENVIRONMENTS

- Increased enforcement of minimum drinking age laws.
- Implementation, increased publicity, and enforcement of other laws to reduce alcohol-impaired driving.
- Restrictions on alcohol retail outlet density.

TIER 3. EVIDENCE OF LOGICAL AND THEORETICAL PROMISE, BUT REQUIRE MORE COMPREHENSIVE EVALUATION (THESE WERE CAMPUS-BASED POLICIES)

- Adopting campus-based policies and practices that appear to be capable of reducing high-risk alcohol use (i.e., reinstating Friday classes and exams; scheduling Saturday morning classes; implementing alcohol-free, expanded late-night student activities; eliminating keg parties on campus; establishing alcohol-free dormitories; employing older, salaried resident assistants or hiring adults to fulfill that role; further controlling or eliminating alcohol at sports events and prohibiting tailgating parties that model heavy alcohol use; refusing sponsorship gifts from the alcohol industry; banning alcohol on campus, including alcohol at faculty and alumni events).
- Increasing enforcement at campus-based events that promote excessive drinking.
- Increasing publicity about and enforcement of underage drinking laws on campus and eliminating "mixed messages."
- Consistently enforcing disciplinary actions associated with [drinking age] policy violations.
- Provision of "safe rides" programs.
- Regulation of happy hours and sales.
- Informing new students and their parents about alcohol policies and penalties before arrival and during orientation periods.

TIER 4. EVIDENCE OF INEFFECTIVENESS

- Conducting informational, knowledge-based, or values clarification interventions about alcohol and the problems related to its excessive use, when used alone.
- Providing feedback to students on blood alcohol content.

The Distilled Spirits Council of the United States (DISCUS) has agreed that a combined, committed effort of all constituencies is needed to make an impact on abusive college drinking. In 2000, the council began a program that attempted to maximize collaboration, assist universities in gaining knowledge on how to apply the best practices illustrated by NIAAA, and help universities to develop effective and sustainable plans for their campus and surrounding community.

DISCUS, working with George Washington University, in Washington, DC, the University of Massachusetts Dartmouth, the University of Massachusetts

Amherst, Eastern Connecticut State University, and the University of Louisville, Kentucky, convened a 3-day conference on The American Campus and Alcohol in October 2000. Thirty-four universities attended with their campus/community teams.

Each team came to the conference having already identified a specific alcohol abuse problem on its campus that it wanted to address. At the conference, nationally recognized speakers from universities, the government, and alcohol-related organizations presented information on a range of programs and best practices being used successfully on campuses to reduce alcohol abuse among college students. The conference also included team planning sessions in which the teams worked independently to develop specific, action-oriented plans to take back and implement in their communities. On the last day of the conference, several teams presented the plans they had devised for their own community. These included:

- setting up integrated campus/community teams;
- integrating vertically: from college president to student;
- integrating horizontally: from responsible retailer to student to parent to law enforcement;
- developing sustainable team-based plans at a working conference coached by experts;
- providing resources for implementation, such as matching grants;
- following up through regional conferences.

At the end of the conference, teams were encouraged to apply for a matching grant from the beverage alcohol industry in an amount of up to US$20,000. Seventeen universities applied and were awarded grants. Part of each grant came from DISCUS and part came from a local retailer or wholesaler in each university's community. A total of US$300,000 was awarded as grants.

Some of the best-practice programs implemented with matching grants included an alcohol screening and brief intervention, a variety of regional interventions, interventions in middle and high schools, designated driver programs, fraternity and sorority online alcohol education, and a comprehensive freshman year experience effort. Several universities decided to use grants to replicate the national conference in their immediate region, and the results of both the national and regional conferences have been very encouraging. Important lessons have been learned during this continuing process.

Underage and abusive drinking on college campuses in the United States remains a serious problem, but progress has been made to counter it. Continued progress necessitates collaboration among all interested constituencies, including the beverage alcohol industry, and requires the implementation of science-based programs. The American Campus and Alcohol program is one example, which provides a framework for developing sustainable, science-based plans through collaboration with the campus, community, and beverage alcohol industry to make an impact on college alcohol abuse.

REFERENCES

Adams Beverage Group, (2004). *Adams Beverage Handbook*. Palm Springs, CA: Author.

Fisher, J. C. (1993). *Advertising, alcohol consumption, and abuse: A worldwide survey*. Westport, CT: Greenwood.

Grube, J. W. (2000, June). Alcohol advertising: What are the effects? In *10th special report to the U.S. Congress on alcohol and health: Highlights from current research* (pp. 412–426). Bethesda, MD: National Institute on Alcohol Abuse and Alcoholism.

Johnston, L. D., O'Malley, P. M., & Bachman, J. G. (2002). *Monitoring the future: National survey results on drug use, 1975–2001. Volume II: College students and adults ages 19–40*. NIH Publication No. 02-5107. Bethesda, MD: National Institute on Drug Abuse.

National Center on Addiction and Substance Abuse (CASA) at Columbia University. (2003, February). Appendix B: CASA National Underage Drinking Survey. In *Teen tipplers: America's underage drinking epidemic* (revised ed., pp. 69–103). New York: Author.

National Highway Traffic Safety Administration (NHTSA). (2004). *Persons killed in motor vehicle traffic crashes involving a 16–20 year old driver by state and the highest 16–20 year old driver BAC in the crash. 1982–2003 Fatality Analysis Reporting System (FARS)*. Retrieved December 22, 2004, from: http://www.alcoholstats.com/documentsVirtual/teendrunkdrivingchartupdated9-10-2004.pdf

National Institute on Alcohol Abuse and Alcoholism (NIAAA). (2002, April). *A call to action: Changing the culture of drinking at U.S. colleges*. NIH Publication No. 02-5010. Bethesda, MD: Author.

Nelson, J. P., & Young, D. J. (2001). Do advertising bans work? An international comparison. *International Journal of Advertising, 20*(3), 273–296.

Wechsler, H., Lee, J. E., Kuo, M., Seibring, M., Nelson, T. F., & Lee, H. (2002). Trends in college binge drinking during a period of increased prevention efforts. Findings from 4 Harvard School of Public Health College Alcohol Study surveys: 1993–2001. *Journal of American College Health, 50*(5), 203–217.

Chapter 15

Alcohol Education

**Marjana Martinic, Daniya Tamendarova,
and Eleni Houghton**

Education is a much-used tool in the prevention of alcohol problems. It exists
in a variety of forms and contexts, and is aimed at a broad range of target
audiences. While there are many formal applications of alcohol education,
much of it is informal. "It could be argued that an individual's alcohol education encompasses all of the alcohol-related experiences of a lifetime" (Plant &
Plant, 1997, p. 195). However, there is considerable debate over whether alcohol education is an effective approach to preventing problems that may arise
from certain drinking patterns and whether it can be viewed in isolation from
other policy and prevention measures.

Much work has been done in this area over the years. A comprehensive
analysis of methodology and evaluation is beyond the scope of this chapter.
What is offered, instead, is a broad overview of the concept of alcohol education and efforts that have been implemented around the world. Drawing upon
available evidence, the discussion focuses on general approaches to different
aspects of alcohol education and the specifics of selected efforts.[1]

---

[1] The text of this chapter was first published as Issue 16 of the *ICAP Reports* series. Its
publication and review process raised a number of issues that are the topics of a debate
published in the journal *Addiction* (2005, forthcoming).

EDUCATION, AWARENESS, AND BEHAVIOR CHANGE

In its broadest role, alcohol education seeks to raise awareness around issues relating to alcohol consumption. These include the social and health effects of alcohol and awareness about recommendations regarding potential risks and benefits for particular groups of individuals (International Center for Alcohol Policies [ICAP], 2003b). A second and more specific role of alcohol education is to change particular drinking patterns and behaviors, especially where these carry potential risk for harm. The end goal of such efforts is to encourage responsible and positive choices and to discourage irresponsible and negative ones. Ultimately, alcohol education should equip individuals with the skills needed to make informed decisions around whether or not to drink and provide information about the drinking patterns most likely to keep them out of harm's way.

In addition to general efforts, alcohol education can be delivered in a targeted fashion. Various approaches have been developed to reach population groups in need of particular advice and guidance. These groups include individuals who may be at increased risk and whose drinking patterns make them particularly susceptible to harm, such as young people, pregnant women, indigenous populations, individuals with alcohol problems, and others (Perkins, 2003; Alcohol Concern, 2002; Hankin, 2002; ICAP, 2001; Copans, MacNamee, Burkle, & Goodstein, 2000). Targeted approaches are also aimed at particular drinking patterns or behaviors that accompany alcohol consumption and that should be discouraged. For example, specific efforts are aimed at reducing binge drinking, intoxication, or drinking and driving.

One of the central questions in alcohol education is who should provide it. Governments and quasi-governmental organizations are major sources of education and information (ICAP, 2003b). Others include health workers and medical practitioners, the media, educators, non-governmental and civil society organizations, and advocacy groups. Many alcohol education efforts have also been developed and implemented by the private sector, notably the beverage alcohol industry and its related organizations and bodies. Yet much of what can be considered alcohol education is imparted through informal channels. In particular, family and peers play a key role in the development of attitudes, awareness, and behaviors around drinking (Houghton & Roche, 2001). There is evidence that socialization and trial by error play a powerful role in educating young people in particular about various risk-taking behaviors, including drinking (Hellandsjo Bu, Watten, Foxcroft, Ingebrigtsen, & Relling, 2002; Plant, 2001).

APPROACHES TO ALCOHOL EDUCATION

Promising approaches to alcohol education exist. It is important to bear in mind, however, that evaluating them is often a difficult proposition (Holmila,

2003; Carmona, Stewart, Gottfredson, & Gottfredson, 1998). Many efforts—formal and, in particular, informal ones involving family, peers, religion, and general socialization—have not been fully assessed or may rely on qualitative indicators. Among those initiatives that have been evaluated, a number suffer from methodological problems that confound results about their effectiveness (Foxcroft, Ireland, Lister-Sharp, Lowe, & Breen, 2003; Gorman, 2003, 2002, 1996; Midford & McBride, 2001; White & Pitts, 1998; Foxcroft, Lister-Sharp, & Lowe, 1997; Hansen, 1993; Schaps, DiBartolo, & Moskowitz, 1981).

It should also be noted that not all alcohol education has the same end goal. Informing the public, building awareness through reminders, and changing behavior are three quite different goals, and a different yardstick is needed for each. It is important not to view individual measures in isolation, but rather within the context of other efforts, broader trends, and cultural influences.

Generally speaking, approaches to alcohol education can be divided into two broad categories, each defined by its desired end goal. The objective of the first position is abstinence, designed to eliminate the demand for alcohol altogether. The second approach views abstinence as an unrealistic goal and relies on minimizing the potential for harm by encouraging responsible and low-risk drinking patterns.

Another essential difference among education approaches is how information about alcohol and drinking is imparted. Many measures can be described as "top-down." They are generally authoritative and didactic in nature, relying on experts to share information, and may involve political intervention or legislation to achieve desired outcomes. Such measures can be regarded as non-specific in that they target the population as a whole. Others are more aptly described as "bottom-up," relying on the active participation of those they are trying to reach and with an emphasis on choice, awareness of consequences, and the assumption of responsibility (Centre for Addiction and Mental Health, 1999; Marlatt, 1998). These approaches target the individual and are aimed at raising awareness and changing specific behaviors.

Alcohol Education for the General Public

Information about alcohol is often delivered through guidelines and recommendations regarding alcohol consumption levels and drinking patterns. For example, governments and quasi-governmental organizations in countries around the world issue formal guidelines intended to provide the public with balanced and scientifically based information about alcohol (ICAP, 2003b; Stockwell, 2001). These guidelines advise about the levels of drinking considered to be "safe" or "low-risk" and those at which risk increases. Other information might include the differential effects of alcohol on men and women, caveats for particular populations, or potential risks associated with certain situations, such as driving, drinking in the workplace, or operating heavy machinery (ICAP, 2003a). Alcohol education seeks to remind and raise awareness of benefits and harms among those who receive it.

The effectiveness of drinking guidelines in changing behavior and preventing harm has been questioned (Babor, Caetano, Caswell, Edwards, Giesbrecht, Graham et al., 2003). At the same time, there are those who argue a moral imperative to produce such recommendations so that citizens can be better informed about decisions governing their own drinking (Plant & Plant, 1997).

Alcohol education is often conveyed through general public service announcements (PSAs) or responsibility messages. PSAs are offered by health agencies, government bodies, non-governmental organizations, and others and generally include information about drinking or particular patterns. A variation of this approach is the counter-advertisement that focuses on the harm that can be caused by the misuse of a particular product. Responsibility messages are often also included on advertising for beverage alcohol. These messages encourage consumers to drink in moderation or to behave responsibly when drinking.

The evidence on the effectiveness of such messages is mixed. It has been argued that they are not effective in changing behavior (Wechsler, Nelson, Lee, Seibring, Lewis, & Keeling, 2003; Austin, Pinkleton, & Fujioka, 1999; Slater, 1999), although they can be useful in increasing awareness and understanding of the issues (Clapp, Lange, Russell, Shillington, & Voas, 2003; Pinkleton, Austin, & Fujioka, 2001; Gotthofer, 2000). Other studies make a case that such measures can be successful and should be used more widely (Babor, Caetano, Caswell, Edwards, Giesbrecht, Graham et al., 2003; Perkins, 2003; Bauerle, 2002; Saffer, 2002). The impact of PSAs and responsibility messages also appears to differ among target groups: for example, while they may not be as useful for young people, there is evidence that they may be helpful in educating parents (Honik, Maklan, Cadell, Prado, Barmada, Jacobsohn et al., 2002).

Labels that include information and health warnings are another public information tool and are mandated by a number of governments around the world (ICAP, 1997). The labels may be placed on beverage alcohol packaging as well as on advertisements. Information on these labels may include the alcohol content of a beverage or how many standard drinks/units a given container holds (Stockwell & Single, 1997; Cutler & Thomas, 1994; Stockwell & Lemmens, 1994). The size of a drink or unit has been defined in a number of countries, although these definitions cover a broad range (ICAP, 1998).

Other labels alert consumers to potential adverse effects of alcohol consumption on health, or in regard to drinking and driving or drinking during pregnancy. Evidence from several countries suggests that the effectiveness of health warning labels is modest. While labels do seem to have some impact on increasing awareness (Agostinelli & Grube, 2002; Greenfield, Graves, & Kaskutas, 1999; Greenfield & Kaskutas, 1998; Kaskutas & Greenfield, 1997; Hankin, Sloan, Firestone, Ager, Sokol, & Martier, 1996), this has generally not translated well into changing behavior (MacKinnon, Nohre, Cheong, Stacy, & Pentz, 2001; Stockley, 2001; Hankin, Firestone, Sloan, Ager, Goodman, Sokol, & Martier, 1993).

Alcohol Education for "At-Risk" Populations

Alcohol policy measures often include provisions about how to address so-called "at-risk" populations. These include groups of individuals who are deemed to be at particular risk for harm from alcohol consumption: young people, those with health issues that may make them vulnerable to the effects of alcohol, indigenous and other socially marginalized populations, the elderly, individuals with a predisposition to dependence, or pregnant women whose drinking may put their unborn children at risk for harm (ICAP, 2004, 2001; Daugherty, James, Love, & Miller, 2002; Copans, MacNamee, Burkle, & Goodstein, 2000). Special education measures have been implemented to help raise the awareness among these groups about alcohol consumption and to help them modify harmful drinking patterns.

Young People

Raising awareness among young people about alcohol issues and encouraging responsible and low-risk choices is one of the main focus areas of alcohol education. These efforts can be divided into two major categories: (1) formal alcohol education through schools and other channels and (2) informal approaches that are imparted through the socialization process by family, peers, and others who are or might be influential in the development of young people. Some new approaches fall in between the two categories. For example, Internet- or computer-based approaches can combine the formal and informal aspects of alcohol education and may resonate well with young people (Reis & Riley, 2002).

Curriculum-based programs are among the most popular and most studied forms of alcohol education at the primary and secondary school level. In many countries, some young people begin drinking around the ages of 13 or 14 and at times earlier (Hibell, Andersson, Bjarnason, Ahlström, Balakireva, Kokkevi et al., 2004; Smart & Ogborne, 2000). As a result, efforts are made to integrate programs that can address alcohol issues into school curricula. Depending on the country, the approach used is usually either one that recommends abstinence until the legal drinking age has been reached or one that accepts that some underage drinking will occur but attempts to minimize any potential for harm.

School-based programs have been widely criticized as ineffective, in particular, those approaches that advocate abstinence. The argument brought is that the goal of abstinence is not an achievable one and is unrealistic given the actual behavior of young people and the reality that alcohol is often introduced to them within the home by parents for cultural and/or religious reasons (Milgram, 2001; Centre for Addiction and Mental Health, 1999; Paglia & Room 1999; Hanson, 1996). Similarly, delaying the initiation of drinking until the legally mandated drinking age may be unrealistic in some instances, given the disparate drinking ages that exist around the world as a reflection of prevailing drinking cultures (ICAP, 2002). In particular, where the drinking age is high (for example, age 21 in the United States), delaying all drinking for all young people has not been realistically achievable. Other shortcomings of school-based programs include inadequate training of teachers to implement them, insufficient time allocated to them within the curriculum, and the absence of reasonable and measurable goals. Many curriculum-based programs have also been criticized for being "top-down," relying on messages that do not resonate well with young people and not allowing much direct involvement by students (Centre for Addiction and Mental Health, 1999; Marlatt, 1998; Somers, 1996).

However, there is evidence that some school-based measures *can* be effective. They appear able to raise awareness and even change behavior, at least in the short term (Kanof, 2003). Preliminary evidence suggests that some education approaches to addressing substance abuse may be cost-effective, due to their ability to avert future social cost (Caulkins, Liccardo Pacula, Paddock, & Chiesa, 2004; Flisher, Brown, & Mukoma, 2002).

On the whole, education that relies on reducing the potential for harm may be useful for increasing awareness and changing the behavior of young people. Here, the emphasis is on encouraging responsible drinking behavior and avoiding risk. One such example is Rethinking Drinking: You're in Control, an Australian joint initiative of industry, public health, and educators. The program is aimed at older students and involves parents as well as teachers in activities like role-playing, lesson plans and interactive teaching, and computer materials and has been applied among both indigenous and non-indigenous populations (*c.f.*: http://www.dest.gov.au/schools/drugeducation/rethinkingdrinking.htm). The program has been approved by state education authorities and taken up by over two thirds of secondary schools in Australia. The Rethinking Drinking program has also been adapted for use elsewhere in the world. In Costa Rica, virtually all public secondary schools run a program called "If it has alcohol, it's not for me," based on the Australian example (Worldwide Brewing Alliance, 2003).

Also in Australia, the School Health and Alcohol Harm Reduction Project (SHAHRP) is a direct result of the Rethinking Drinking program, but is aimed at younger students and involves a broader range of audiences and participants

(McBride, Farringdon, Midford, Meuleners, & Phillips, 2004, 2003; McBride, Farrington, & Midford, 2000). The focus of SHAHRP is to enhance students' ability to identify and deal with risky drinking situations, thereby reducing possible harm. Measures include supervised drinking with a parent or other adult present, reducing the number of drinks consumed per occasion, being able to identify standard drinks for different types of alcohol beverages accurately, and learning the skills that reduce the impact of harm once it has occurred (for example, first aid and communication techniques). The approach has shown promise in influencing drinking behavior among young people (McBride, Farringdon, Midford, Meuleners, & Phillips, 2004, 2003), yet some criticism has been raised regarding SHAHRP's evaluation and the interpretation of its results.

Another framework for education is the life skills approach (Botvin, Griffin, Paul, & Macaulay, 2003; ICAP, 2000; Botvin, Baker, Dusenbury, Botvin, & Diaz, 1995), which aims to provide a context for promoting healthy lifestyles in children—and often adults (Wald, Flaherty, & Pringle, 1999)—and has been applied across cultures. It focuses on teaching a range of skills that address decision-making, communication, and handling emotions. Life skills curricula can address general lifestyle issues or focus specifically on drinking. These programs have been widely implemented in a number of public health areas, notably sexual behavior and HIV/AIDS. A similar approach has been applied to alcohol in a number of developing and industrialized countries.

Several life skills programs implemented in a school setting have been formally evaluated. Results regarding their effectiveness are mixed (Foxcroft, Ireland, Lister-Sharp, Lowe, & Breen, 2003; Gorman, 2002; Plant & Plant, 1999). In the United States, for example, where much of the existing evaluation of alcohol education has been conducted, some life skills programs received a poor assessment (Kanof, 2003; Burke, 2002; Brown, 2001), largely for their lack of rigorous evaluation and methodological shortcomings (Gorman, 2003, 2002). Other programs, such as the Student Training through Urban Strategies Program (STATUS) or the Alcohol Skills Training Program (ASTP), have been positively reviewed (Burke, 2002; Miller, Kilmer, Kim, Weingardt, & Marlatt, 2001; Fromme, Marlatt, Baer, & Kivlahan, 1994). There is evidence from other countries, including Australia, Belgium, and the United Kingdom, that similar approaches also work there (Godfrey, Toumbourou, Rowland, Hemphill, & Munro, 2002; Lloyd, Joyce, Hurry, & Ashton, 2000; Bils, 1999). Life skills education has the potential to be an effective tool in addressing various high-risk behaviors and situations, including the incidence of binge drinking (Eisen, Zellman, & Murray, 2003). Such results may be attributable to improved coping and refusal skills or to changes in perceptions of harm and peer norms.

Educational approaches that rely on life skills may be especially promising in developing countries and countries in transition and in contexts where various social factors, such as poverty, social exclusion, or fragile family structure, are prevalent. Early education that integrates alcohol with other health and social issues, as well as an approach that involves parents and peers and is community-based, seems especially worth pursuing (Marlatt, Larimer, Mail, Hawkins, Cummins, Blume et al., 2003; Godfrey, Toumbourou, Rowland, Hemphill, & Munro, 2002; Spoth, Guyll, & Day, 2002; ICAP, 2000).

Alcohol education extends well beyond school or other "formal" settings. An individual's everyday encounters and experiences with alcohol within a particular culture also constitute "alcohol education." It is impossible to ignore these influences when trying to assess the effectiveness of particular approaches. They shape beliefs around alcohol, the social framework around acceptable drinking behavior, and impart a value system that will ultimately persist through adulthood.

Families are the single most influential factor in a young person's decision whether or not to drink (Allen, 2003; Bjarnason, Andersson, Choquet, Elekes, Morgan, & Rapinett, 2003; Duncan, Duncan, & Strycker, 2003; Miller & Plant, 2003; Sanchez-Sosa & Poldrugo, 2001; Akers, 1985), followed by the influence of peers and friends (Andrews, Tildesley, Hops, & Lu, 2002; Barnow, Schuckit, Lucht, John, & Freyberger, 2002; Geckova & Van Dijk, 2001; Houghton & Roche, 2001). This appears to hold true across different cultures (Hellandsjo Bu, Watten, Foxcroft, Ingebrigtsen, & Relling, 2002; Halmi & Golik-Gruber, 2002). Socialization is an important part of alcohol education in which rules, values, and attitudes are passed from parents to their children, who then internalize them, integrating them into their own behavior (Sanchez-Sosa & Poldrugo, 2001; Sroufe, Cooper, & DeHart, 1996). This transfer occurs informally but values and attitude learned can be strong protective factors through adolescence into adulthood and may help reduce the potential for harm. Strong relationships between parents and children, family discipline structure, communication, monitoring, and supervision, and parental involvement can positively influence alcohol consumption choices by young people (Brower & Carey, 2003; Bry, Catalano, Kumpfer, Lochman, & Szapocznik, 1998; Etz, Robertson, & Ashery, 1998; Costa, Jessor, & Turbin, 1999; Jessor, 1998). Where the family structure is missing and there is weak support through other influences, negative drinking patterns and related problems are more likely to surface (Foxcroft & Lowe, 1997).

Building on the informal involvement of parents in their children's skill development, more formal approaches may be used to help strengthen the role of the family. Various programs exist that help encourage the family's role in influencing behaviors around drinking. Some of these, like the Strengthening Families Program: For Parents and Youth 10–14 (SFP 10–14), have shown considerable promise (Foxcroft, Ireland, Lister-Sharp, Lowe, & Breen, 2003; Kumpfer, Alvarado, & Whiteside, 2003; Spoth, Redmond, & Lepper, 1999;

Ashery, Robertson, & Kumpfer, 1998). The programs, which include behavioral training for parents, family skills training, education, support, and brief therapy, appear to be helpful even when applied across different cultures. It has been shown that the impact of such programs is enhanced when they are combined with those that focus on young people themselves (Kumpfer, Alvarado, & Whiteside, 2003; Kumpfer, Alvarado, Tait, & Turner, 2002).

There is evidence that family-based education approaches may be cost-effective, and may help to avoid significant future social and economic costs (Spoth, Guyll, & Day, 2002). Yet, despite promising evidence, the influence of family is often neglected in research and in recommendations around alcohol education and prevention.

Peers are second only to families as a major influence on the drinking behavior of young people (Beccaria, Amici, Bonello, Maggiorotti, & Tomaciello, 2003). The need to conform to what is acceptable to their peers drives much of young people's behavior, both positive and negative. This concept has been used in developing an approach to alcohol education based on what is known as the Social Norming Theory. Initially developed in the United States, the approach relies on changing the attitudes and norms that exist around drinking behaviors, particularly on university campuses. The underlying premise is that drinking among young people is influenced by their perceptions of how their peers drink. Studies show that students tend to have an exaggerated view of the quantities of alcohol being consumed by their peers. Making students aware of this misperception can help change behavior and reduce drinking (Mattern & Neighbors, 2004; Lilja, Larsson, Wilhelmsen, & Hamilton, 2003; Perkins, 2003; Perkins & Craig, 2002).

The social norms approach relies largely on intensive publicity campaigns on university campuses to educate students about how much their peers actually drink (and do not drink) and to correct existing misperceptions. Information about how much alcohol students actually consume, how many of them suffer negative outcomes, and basic information relating to drinking are part of the approach. Information is disseminated through ads in school newspapers, on billboards and posters in student halls, through presentations, and by other students. Results at Northern Illinois University and the University of Arizona in the United States, where the approach has been used extensively, have been encouraging (Johannessen & Glider, 2003) and positive results have also been seen elsewhere (Perkins, 2003; Bauerle, 2002).

As is the case with any educational measure, the social norms approach has its critics who may not agree with the messages it delivers or its basic premise or are not convinced by the results of its application (Clapp, Lange, Russell, Shillington, & Voas, 2003; Wechsler, Nelson, Lee, Seibring, Lewis, & Keeling, 2003; Granfield, 2002). Currently, some 20% of universities in the United States incorporate some aspects of social norms in their prevention efforts, and the approach has also been used in the United Kingdom in somewhat different settings (Hancock, Higson, Ryan, Smith, & Smith, 1999).

It is important not to overlook another critical element in how young people learn to drink and how they learn to seek or avoid risk. Like most other behaviors, learning about drinking involves experimentation and trial and error (ICAP, 2004; Plant, 2001; Lindberg, Boggess, Porter, & Williams, 2000; Finken, 1997; Fossey, Loretto, & Plant, 1996). Risk-taking is an integral component of growing up and helps us learn what to seek out and what to avoid. Understanding that young people are likely to experiment with drinking and with many other behaviors could help in developing ways to educate them and make this transition process a safer one.

A final approach to educating young people about alcohol integrates schools, peers, parents, and the wider community, using a number of different strategies to raise awareness and change behavior. This approach relies on information campaigns, life skills education, parent training, and peer leadership. While such campaigns are complex, labor intensive, and expensive, evidence shows they can produce positive results on attitudes, knowledge, and behavior related to drinking, such as driving (Holder, Gruenewald, Ponicki, Treno, Grube, Saltz et al., 2000; Wagenaar, Murray, & Toomey, 2000; Williams & Perry, 1998).

An example of one such approach is Project Northland, implemented in several communities in the United States (Perry, Williams, Veblen-Mortenson, Toomey, Komro, Anstine, et al., 1996; Perry, Williams, Forster, Wolfson, Wagenaar, Finnegan et al., 1993). The goal of the approach is to prevent or delay drinking among students in a number of primary and secondary schools. Using education both at the individual level and within the community, the approach targets families, peer groups, teachers, business and community leaders, government, and mass media. While the scope of Project Northland is limited to a number of small rural communities, it does suggest that an integrative approach can have an impact. Knowledge about alcohol and the involvement of the family, in particular, were positively affected. Students were also less likely to drink and reported changes in attitudes and beliefs about alcohol (Williams, Perry, Farbakhsh, & Veblen-Mortenson, 1999). These effects of the Project Northland, however, may not be sustainable over the long term and may be weakened in the absence of continuous intervention throughout adolescence (Perry, Williams, Komro, Veblen-Mortenson, Stigler, Munson et al., 2002; Perry, Williams, Veblen-Mortenson, Toomey, Komro, Anstine, et al., 1996).

Other "At-Risk" Populations

While young people are the focus of a large proportion of alcohol education efforts aimed at so-called "at-risk" populations, there are also other groups for whom specialized and targeted interventions have been developed, largely because measures aimed at the general population may not be adequate to meet their needs.

One such group includes pregnant women. There is evidence that certain drinking patterns during pregnancy (for example, heavy chronic and binge drinking) may have adverse effects on the developing fetus. Special education measures have been developed for pregnant women in a precautionary effort to raise awareness and change potentially harmful behaviors. This includes providing information about alcohol and pregnancy through government-issued guidelines (ICAP, 2003b, 1999) and by medical and health personnel (Loop & Nettleman, 2002), mass media campaigns, and warning labels (Hankin, 2002). However, research has shown that raising general awareness does not seem to translate effectively into changing some pregnant women's own behaviors and attitudes towards drinking during pregnancy (Kesmodel & Kesmodel, 2002; Andersen, Olsen, & Gronbaek, 2001).

Targeted approaches appear to be more effective. Pregnant women who are deemed to be at high risk (for example, those who have previously abused alcohol or already have a child with alcohol-related effects) may be the focus of educational measures that involve counseling and information about health-related behaviors including drinking (Andrulis & Hopkins, 2001; Drinkard, Shatin, Luo, Heinen, Hawkins, & Harmon, 2001). Project CHOICES (Changing High-risk alcOhol use and Increasing Effectiveness Study), for example, is aimed at reducing the incidence of fetal alcohol syndrome (FAS) by increasing knowledge about alcohol and pregnancy (Floyd, Ebrahim, & Boyle, 1999). This approach appears to be particularly appropriate when individuals who are important in the mothers' lives are involved and can offer support (Abela, 2000; Allard-Hendren, 2000) and when education is provided in face-to-face sessions with counselors, and not in a "top-down" approach relying solely on written materials and messages (Calabro, Taylor, Kapadia, 1996).

Other groups within the "at-risk" category include indigenous populations and groups with a particularly high prevalence of alcohol problems. In the United States and Canada, education efforts have been developed to target Native communities. Educational efforts have been used effectively to reduce the incidence of FAS among these populations (Westphal, 2000; Williams & Gloster, 1999), and other approaches are aimed at education about drinking patterns and at drinking and driving. The impact of such initiatives seems to hinge upon whether or not they are culturally appropriate and whether they address issues relevant to a particular target community (Moran & Reaman, 2002; Okamoto, Hurdle, & Marsiglia, 2001; National Resource Center on Native American Aging, 2001). Similarly, Australia has used some promising educational measures for dealing with alcohol abuse among its aboriginal population and changing risky behaviors among adults and young people (Sheehan, Schonfeld, Hindson, & Ballard, 1995; Hazlehurst, 1986).

Targeting Behaviors

A final approach to alcohol education focuses on certain behaviors and attempts to make changes that can reduce risk for harm and encourage positive patterns of drinking. An important prerequisite for the success of this approach is the education of those who are in a position to provide information about drinking to particular audiences. They include health workers, medical practitioners, social workers, police, and others. The involvement of these professionals can effectively raise awareness and knowledge about alcohol and also influence behavioral change among those in their care (Weintraub, Saitz, & Samet, 2003; D'Onofrio, 2002; Giannetti, Sieppert, & Holosko, 2002; Kaner, Wutzke, Saunders, Powell, Morawski, & Bouix, 2001).

For example, knowledgeable health workers trained in providing counseling about drinking and in offering brief interventions to those whose drinking is problematic have shown potential across different cultures and "at-risk" populations (Beich, Thorsen, & Rollnick, 2003; Fleming, 2003; Patton & Touquet, 2003; Seppa, 2003; Chang, 2002). Even a short 20-minute session in which an individual is educated about his or her drinking can have dramatic effects on behavior. The approach has shown success with adults, as well as with young people (Kypri, McGee, Saunders, Langley, & Dean, 2002; Kypri, Langley, McGee, Saunders, & Williams, 2002; Murphy, Duchnick, Vuchinich, Davison, Karg, Olson et al., 2001; Dimeff, Baer, Kivlahan, & Marlatt, 1999). A detailed discussion of this topic lies beyond the scope of this chapter. However, it is important to bear in mind that in order to educate others about responsible drinking, those providing such assistance also need to be knowledgeable about alcohol issues.

Harmful drinking behaviors can be addressed through a number of venues and channels. Much alcohol education, for instance, is provided through the workplace. The focus of these measures is largely on alcohol abuse and harmful patterns that can affect work performance. It has been shown that informing individuals about drinking and providing them with appraisals of their own risk can positively influence their behavior and motivation to change (Lapham, Gregory, & McMillan, 2003; Hurtado, 2002).

Interventions in schools and universities, addressed earlier, have also been used to educate about specific drinking patterns in an attempt to change behavior and reduce the risk for harm. Binge drinking, for example, is one of the major topics addressed through educational approaches on campuses around the United States. While many of these initiatives have not been evaluated thoroughly and have been criticized for being inadequate (Glassman, 2002), there is evidence that educational measures can help reduce binge drinking among student populations (Donohue, Allen, Maurer, Ozols, & DeStefano, 2004; Eisen, Zellman, & Murray, 2003; Ziemelis, Bucknam, & Elfessi, 2002). Numerous targeted educational approaches to addressing drinking patterns and harm reduction have focused on drinking and driving and responsible hospitality. Both areas have yielded promising results and have provided common ground for involvement by many different sectors with an interest in reducing alcohol problems—governments at the local and national levels, non-governmental organizations, the media, health professionals, the beverage alcohol industry, alcohol industry-sponsored social aspects organizations (SAOs), law enforcement, and others.

Drinking and Driving

The problems and potential outcomes of drinking and driving are a popular focus for alcohol education in many countries, including the developing world. Few would disagree with the need to reduce injuries and deaths associated with drinking and driving and with the main message that these two activities are not compatible. This approach, therefore, enjoys much public support. Education around drinking and driving includes public information campaigns in the print and electronic media, the use of driving simulators to demonstrate first-hand the effects of alcohol consumption on driving, school-based programs, and testimonials by survivors of drunk driving crashes. Many campaigns rely on general messages that discourage alcohol-impaired driving. Others attempt to inform the public about legal blood alcohol content limits and legislation around drinking and driving that exist within a particular country or region.

Many campaigns against impaired driving have been implemented around the world. One example is "Euro-Bob," a designated driver program that involves a continuous awareness-raising campaign through the mass media, increased police controls around drinking and driving, and local initiatives in pubs and bars (Directorate-General for Energy and Transport, European Commission, 2002). Each week, the Bob bus, a van decorated in Bob colors and equipped with a driving simulator, supports local events. The campaign also provides informational materials and administers blood alcohol tests. Since its inception in Belgium in 1995, variations of the "Bob" program have been adopted in Denmark, France, Greece, the Netherlands, Portugal, and Spain, with similar programs started in other EU member states.

Partnerships have played a key role in the success of initiatives against drunk driving and include transport agencies, law enforcement, the alcohol beverage industry, civic organizations, and retail bodies. They operate in tandem with government regulations governing drinking age laws and blood alcohol limits that are in place in many countries. However, enforcement of existing laws, for example through random breath testing, is an essential adjunct to education and an important factor in reducing alcohol-related crashes (Baum, 1999).

Recent findings indicate that mass media campaigns can contribute to reducing alcohol-related crashes and the incidence of drunk driving (Elder, Shults, Sleet, Nichols, Thompson, & Rajab, 2004; Morrison, Petticrew, & Thomson, 2003; McCammon, 2001). The campaigns were found to reduce social costs related to injuries, lost productivity, pain and suffering, and property damage. It appears that campaigns can achieve positive results regardless of whether the focus is on legal consequences of drunk driving or on negative social and health aspects. However, all of the campaigns were implemented in conjunction with other prevention activities, which may have contributed to their success.

Responsible Hospitality

A second popular and effective approach that addresses behavior targets those who sell or serve beverage alcohol. The objective of this approach is to make the drinking environment safer. Responsible hospitality education has shown considerable promise in this regard. It attempts to educate wait staff, bartenders, and servers about potential risks, drinking patterns, and outcomes and teaches them skills necessary to deal with intoxicated patrons. The goal is to educate servers and bar staff about the legal and social responsibilities of serving alcohol and how to intervene effectively when problems occur. Responsible hospitality and server training are clearly areas in which the beverage alcohol industry has a role. In fact, most SAOs in existence around the world have implemented programs around this approach.

Specifics differ from one program to another. Some focus on educating servers about liability issues, while others emphasize the importance of server judgment in reducing harmful outcomes. Programs have been implemented in many countries, but not all have been evaluated. On the whole, however, server training has received a positive response, especially when combined with enforcement (Babor, Caetano, Caswell, Edwards, Giesbrecht, Graham et al., 2003; Stockwell, 1997). It can raise awareness, but also reduce heavy drinking, the numbers of intoxicated patrons, and occurrences of negative outcomes including drunk driving accidents (Babor, Caetano, Caswell, Edwards, Giesbrecht, Graham et al., 2003; Graham, 2000).

CONCLUSIONS: WHAT WORKS?

Alcohol education is a complex and challenging area. It involves formal measures, as well as informal influences, all of which help to shape attitudes towards drinking and risk, encourage certain drinking patterns, and discourage others. More importantly, alcohol education is an approach that, like other policy and prevention measures, cannot be viewed or implemented in isolation but depends on a comprehensive approach.

The central question with regard to alcohol education remains whether it works and is effective. As the debate around the issue clearly demonstrates, the answer is likely to be, "It depends." While some alcohol education measures have been found to have an effect on awareness and behavior, others are demonstrably less useful.

Yet research into the effectiveness of alcohol education suggests that there are several lessons to be learned. First and foremost, targeted interventions may be more likely to effect change than broad-based measures. It is important to clearly identify the target audience and match it with the appropriate approach. As with any alcohol policy or prevention measure, cultural considerations and the relevance of the approach need to be recognized. Second, the goal of a particular approach needs to be clearly defined so that its impact can be assessed. It may be unrealistic, for example, to expect a program that is designed to raise awareness to change behavior. Third, combined interventions have been shown to have greater impact than single approaches and benefit from the inclusion of multiple groups to ensure their success. Programs should be comprehensive in nature and be given time to become integrated into the system. Finally, alcohol education programs need realistic goals, corresponding to the needs of those whom they are intended to target, with measurable objectives and evaluation criteria built into the program design.

The evidence also shows that, like most other measures, alcohol education should not be viewed and evaluated in isolation. Outside influences, often not quantifiable, play an important role in whether an approach is effective. Other policies and prevention approaches applied around the implementation of an educational program will also have a strong impact on the outcome. Similarly, the prevailing political climate and trends around alcohol consumption are key determinants in whether certain approaches are necessary, adequate, or successful.

Alcohol policies are demonstrably more successful when they are targeted and when several targeted interventions can be successfully combined. No single measure on its own is able to change the face of problems or attitudes around alcohol. Alcohol education is no different in this regard. The effectiveness of alcohol policy hinges upon its ability to integrate many components and to be flexible and realistic. Alcohol education is but part of the larger picture along with legislation, enforcement, and other policy and prevention efforts.

REFERENCES

Abela, M.B. (2000). Factors associated with alcohol consumption: From a developmental perspective. *Dissertation Abstracts International, 61*(3), 1667B.

Agostinelli, G., & Grube, J.W. (2002). Alcohol counter-advertising and the media: A review of recent research. *Alcohol Research & Health, 26*(1), 15–21.

Akers, R.L. (1985). *Deviant behavior: A social learning approach.* Belmont, CA: Wadsworth.

Alcohol Concern (2002). *Alcohol and teenage pregnancy.* London: Author.

Allard-Hendren, R. (2000). Alcohol use and adolescent pregnancy. *MCN: The American Journal of Maternal Child Nursing, 25*(3), 159–162.

Allen, D. (2003). Treating the cause not the problem: Vulnerable young people and substance misuse. *Journal of Substance Use, 8*(1), 47–54.

Andersen, A.M., Olsen, J., & Gronbaek, M.N. (2001). Impact of changes in sensible drinking limits for pregnant women's alcohol intake. *Ugeskr Laeger, 163*(11), 1561–1565.

Andrews, J.A., Tildesley, E., Hops, H., & Lu, F. (2002). Influence of peers on young adult substance use. *Health Psychology, 21*(4), 349–357.

Andrulis, D., & Hopkins, S. (2001). Public hospitals and substance abuse services for pregnant women and mothers: Implications for managed-care programs and Medicaid. *Journal of Urban Health: Bulletin of the New York Academy of Medicine, 78*(1), 181–198.

Ashery, R.S., Robertson, E.B., & Kumpfer, K.L. (Eds.). (1998). *Drug abuse prevention through family interventions.* NIDA Research Monograph 177. Rockville, MD: National Institute on Drug Abuse.

Austin, E.W., Pinkleton, B., & Fujioka, Y. (1999). Assessing prosocial message effectiveness: Effects of message quality, production quality, and persuasiveness. *Journal of Health Communication, 4*(3), 195–210.

Babor, T., Caetano, R., Casswell, S., Edwards, G., Giesbrecht, N., Graham, K. *et al.* (2003). *Alcohol: No ordinary commodity.* Oxford: Oxford University Press.

Barnow, S., Schuckit, M.A., Lucht, M., John, U., & Freyberger, H.J. (2002). Importance of a positive family history of alcoholism, parental rejection and emotional warmth, behavioral problems and peer substance use for alcohol problems in teenagers: A path analysis. *Journal of Studies on Alcohol, 63*(3), 305–315.

Bauerle, J. (2002). Social norms marketing: Reducing high risk drinking among undergraduates. *American Journal of Health Promotion, 16*(6), 366.

Baum, S. (1999). Self-reported drink driving and deterrence. *Australian and New Zealand Journal of Criminology, 32*(3), 247–261.

Beccaria, F., Amici, S., Bonello, M., Maggiorotti, P., & Tomaciello, M.G. (2003). "Listen to me, I have something to tell you:" Young people, alcohol and drugs. Peer education. *Nordisk Alkohol- & Narkotikatidskrift (Nordic Studies on Alcohol and Drugs), 20* (English Suppl.), 110–115.

Beich, A., Thorsen, T., & Rollnick, S. (2003). Screening in brief intervention trials targeting excessive drinkers in general practice: Systematic review and meta-analysis. *BMJ: British Medical Journal, 327*(7414), 536–540.

Bils, L. (1999). Prevention primaire en Belgique francophone (Primary prevention in French-speaking Belgium). *Alcoologie, 21*(HS), 187–192.

Bjarnason, T., Andersson, B., Choquet, B., Elekes, Z., Morgan, Z., & Rapinett, G. (2003). Alcohol culture, family structure and adolescent alcohol use: Multilevel modeling of frequency of heavy drinking among 15–16 year old students in 11 European countries. *Journal of Studies on Alcohol, 64*(2), 200–208.

Botvin, G.J., Baker, E., Dusenbury, L., Botvin, E.M., & Diaz, T. (1995). Long-term follow-up results of a randomized drug abuse prevention trial in a white middle-class population. *JAMA: Journal of the American Medical Association, 273*(14), 1106–1112.

Botvin, G.J., Griffin, K.W., Paul, E., & Macaulay, A.P. (2003). Preventing tobacco and alcohol use among elementary school students through life skills training. *Journal of Child and Adolescent Substance Abuse, 12*(4), 1–1.

Brower, K.J., & Carey, T.L. (2003). Racially related health disparities and alcoholism treatment outcomes. *Alcoholism: Clinical and Experimental Research, 27*(8), 1365–1367.

Brown, J.H. (2001). Youth, drugs and resilience education. *Journal of Drug Education, 31*(1), 83–122.

Bry, B.H., Catalano, R.F., Kumpfer, K.L., Lochman, J.E., & Szapocznik, J. (1998). Scientific findings from family prevention intervention research. In R.S. Ashery, E.B. Robertson, & K.L. Kumpfer (Eds.), *Drug abuse prevention through family interventions* (pp. 103–129). NIDA Research Monograph No. 177. Rockville, MD: National Institute on Drug Abuse.

Burke, M.R. (2002). School-based substance abuse prevention: Political finger-pointing does not work. *Federal Probation, 66*(2), 66–71.

Calabro, K., Taylor, W.C., & Kapadia, A. (1996). Pregnancy, alcohol use and the effectiveness of written health education materials. *Patient Education and Counseling, 29*(3), 301–309.

Carmona, M.C., Stewart, K., Gottfredson, D.C., & Gottfredson, G.D. (1998). *CSAP Technical Report: Guide for evaluating prevention effectiveness.* Rockville, MD: Center for Substance Abuse Prevention.

Caulkins, J. P., Liccardo Pacula, R., Paddock, S., & Chiesa, J. (2004). What we can—and cannot—expect from school-based drug prevention. *Drug and Alcohol Review, 23*(1), 79–87.

Centre for Addiction and Mental Health (1999). *Alcohol and drug prevention programs for youth: What works?* Toronto: Author.

Chang, G. (2002). Brief interventions for problem drinking and women. *Journal of Substance Abuse Treatment, 23*(1), 1–7.

Clapp, J.D., Lange, J.E., Russell, C., Shillington, A., & Voas, R.B. (2003). Failed norms social marketing campaign. *Journal of Studies on Alcohol, 64*(3), 409–414.

Copans, S., MacNamee, H., Burkle, F., & Goodstein, R. (2000). Special populations. In J. Kinney (Ed.), *Loosening the grip: Handbook of alcohol information* (pp. 358–433). Boston: McGraw-Hill.

Costa, F.M., Jessor, R., & Turbin, M.S. (1999). Transition into adolescent problem drinking: The role of psychosocial risk and protective factors. *Journal of Studies on Alcohol, 60*(4), 480–490.

Cutler, B.D., & Thomas, E.G. (1994). "This is your brain on drugs:" A review of the marketing literature on alcohol/drug abuse. *Health Marketing Quarterly, 11*(3/4), 9–25.

Daugherty, M., James, W.H., Love, C.T., & Miller, W.R. (2002). Substance abuse among displaced and indigenous peoples. In W.R. Miller, & C.M. Weisner (Eds.), *Changing substance abuse through health and social systems* (pp. 225–239). New York: Kluwer Academic/Plenum Publishers.

Dimeff, L.A., Baer, J.S., Kivlahan, D.R., & Marlatt, G.A. (1999). *Brief Alcohol Intervention and Screening for College Students (BASICS): A harm reduction approach.* New York: Guilford Press.

Directorate-General for Energy and Transport, European Commission (2002, December). *"Euro Bob" European designated driver campaign against drinking and driving, 2001–2002.* Final Report. Retrieved on December 3, 2004, from http://europa.eu.int/comm/transport/road/roadsafety/behaviour/campaigns/doc/eurobob_2001_2002.pdf

D'Onofrio, G. (2002). Improving emergency medicine residents' approach to patients with alcohol problems: A controlled educational trial. *Substance Abuse, 23*(2), 125.

Donohue, B., Allen, D.A., Maurer, A., Ozols, J., & DeStefano, G. (2004). A controlled evaluation of two prevention programs in reducing alcohol use among college students at low and high risk for alcohol related problems. *Journal of Alcohol and Drug Education, 48*(1), 13–33.

Drinkard, C.R., Shatin, D., Luo, D., Heinen, M.J., Hawkins, M.M., & Harmon, R.G. (2001). Healthy pregnancy program in a national managed care organization: Evaluation of satisfaction and health behavior outcomes. *American Journal of Managed Care, 7*(4), 377–386.

Duncan, S.C., Duncan, T.E., & Strycker, L.A. (2003). Family influences on youth alcohol use: A multiple-sample analysis by ethnicity and gender. *Journal of Ethnicity in Substance Abuse, 2*(2), 17–33.

Eisen, M., Zellman, G.L., Murray, D.M. (2003). Evaluating the Lions-Quest "Skills for Adolescence" drug education program: Second-year behavior outcomes. *Addictive Behaviors, 28*(5), 883–897.

Elder, R.W., Shults, R.A., Sleet, D.A., Nichols, J.L., Thompson R.S., & Rajab, W. (2004). Effectiveness of mass media campaigns for reducing drinking and driving and alcohol-involved crashes: a systematic review. *American Journal of Preventive Medicine, 27*(1), 57–65.

Etz, K.E., Robertson, E.B., & Ashery, R.S. (1998). Drug abuse prevention through family-based interventions: Future research. In R.S. Ashery, E.B. Robertson, & K.L. Kumpfer (Eds.), *Drug abuse prevention through family interventions* (pp. 1–11). NIDA Research Monograph No. 177. Rockville, MD: National Institute on Drug Abuse.

Finken, L.L. (1997). Developmental extension of the propensity-event theory to adolescents' reckless behavior. *Dissertation Abstracts International, 57*(8), 5358B–5359B.

Fleming, M.F. (2003). Brief interventions and the treatment of alcohol use disorders: Current evidence. In M. Galanter (Ed.), *Recent developments in alcoholism: Volume 16. Research on alcoholism treatment* (pp. 375–390). New York: Kluwer Academic/Plenum Publishers.

Flisher, A.J., Brown, A., & Mukoma, W. (2002). Intervening through the school system. In W.R. Miller & C.M. Weisner (Eds.), *Changing substance abuse through health and social systems* (pp. 171–182). New York: Kluwer Academic / Plenum Publishers.

Floyd, R.L., Ebrahim, S.H., & Boyle, C.A. (1999). Preventing alcohol-exposed pregnancies among women of childbearing age: Necessity of a preconceptional approach. *Journal of Women's Health and Gender-Based Medicine, 8*(6), 733–736.

Fossey, E., Loretto, W., & Plant, M. (1996). Alcohol and youth. In L. Harrison (Ed.), *Alcohol problems in the community* (pp. 52–75). London: Routledge.

Foxcroft, D.R., Ireland, D., Lister-Sharp, D.J., Lowe, G., & Breen, R. (2003). Longer-term primary prevention for alcohol misuse in young people: A systematic review. *Addiction*, *98*(4), 397–411.

Foxcroft, D.R, Lister-Sharp, D., & Lowe, G. (1997). Alcohol misuse prevention for young people: A systematic review reveals methodological concerns and lack of reliable evidence of effectiveness. *Addiction*, *92*(5), 531–537.

Foxcroft, D.R., & Lowe, G. (1997). Adolescents' alcohol use and misuse: The socializing influence of perceived family life. *Drugs: Education, Prevention and Policy*, *4*(3), 215–229.

Fromme, K., Marlatt, G.A., Baer, J.S., & Kivlahan, D.R. (1994). Alcohol Skills Training Program: A group intervention for young adult drinkers. *Journal of Substance Abuse Treatment*, *11*(2), 143–154.

Geckova, A., & Van Dijk, J.P. (2001). Peer impact on smoking alcohol consumption, drug use and sports activities in adolescents. *Studia Psychologica*, *43*(2), 113–123.

Giannetti, V.J., Sieppert, J.D., & Holosko, M.J. (2002). Attitudes and knowledge concerning alcohol abuse: Curriculum implications. *Journal of Health and Social Policy*, *15*(1), 45–58.

Glassman, T. (2002). Failure of higher education to reduce the binge drinking rate. *Journal of American College Health*, *51*(3), 143–144.

Godfrey, C., Toumbourou, J.W., Rowland, B., Hemphill, S., & Munro, G. (2002). *Drug education approaches in primary schools*. West Melbourne, Australia: Drug Info Clearinghouse.

Gorman, D.M. (1996). Do school-based social skills training programs prevent alcohol use among young people? *Addiction Research*, *4*(2), 191–210.

Gorman, D.M. (2002). "Science" of drug and alcohol prevention: The case of the randomized trial of the Life Skills Training program. *International Journal of Drug Policy*, *13*(1), 21–26.

Gorman, D.M. (2003). Alcohol and drug abuse: The best of practices, the worst of practices: The making of science-based primary prevention programs. *Psychiatric Services*, *54*(8), 1087–1089.

Gotthofer, A.R. (2000). Effects of fear, localization, and injury threat in public service advertisements (PSAs) on intention to drink and drive among college students. *Dissertation Abstracts International*, *60*(9), 3185A.

Graham, K. (2000). Preventive interventions for on-premise drinking: Promising but underresearched area of prevention. *Contemporary Drug Problems*, *27*(3), 593–668.

Granfield, R. (2002). Believe it or not: Examining to the emergence of new drinking norms in college. *Journal of Alcohol and Drug Education*, *47*(2), 18–31.

Greenfield, T.K., Graves, K.L., Kaskutas, L.A. (1999). Long-term effects of alcohol warning labels: Findings from a comparison of the United States and Ontario, Canada. *Psychology & Marketing*, *16*(3), 261–282.

Greenfield, T.K., & Kaskutas, L.A. (1998). Five years' exposure to alcohol warning label messages and their impacts: Evidence from diffusion analysis. *Applied Behavioral Science Review*, *6*(1), 39–68.

Halmi, A., & Golik-Gruber, V. (2002). Prevention and reduction of the consumption of alcohol and any other drugs among a high-risk group of youths through improving family resilience. *Alcoholism: Journal on Alcoholism and Related Addictions*, *38*(1–2), 41–55.

Hancock, J., Higson, C., Ryan, T., Smith, I., & Smith, M. (1999). Community Reinforcement Approach (CRA) as applied to alcohol and drug services in Trafford Manchester. *Alcohol and Alcoholism: International Journal of the Medical Council on Alcoholism, 34*(1), 101–102.

Hankin, J.R. (2002). Fetal alcohol syndrome prevention research. *Alcohol Research and Health, 26*(1), 58–65.

Hankin, J.R., Firestone, I.J., Sloan, J.J., Ager, J.W., Goodman, A.C., Sokol, R.J., & Martier, S.S. (1993). Impact of the warning label on drinking during pregnancy. *Journal of Public Policy and Marketing, 12*(1), 10–18.

Hankin, J.R., Sloan, J.J., Firestone, I.J., Ager, J.W., Sokol, R.J., & Martier, S.S. (1996). Has awareness of the alcohol warning label reached its upper limit? *Alcoholism: Clinical and Experimental Research, 20*(3), 440–444.

Hansen, W.B. (1993). School-based alcohol prevention programs. *Alcohol Health and Research World, 17*(1), 54–60.

Hanson, D. (1996). *Alcohol education: What we must do.* Westport, CT: Praeger.

Hazlehurst, K.-M. (1986). Alcohol, outstations and autonomy: An Australian Aboriginal perspective. *Journal of Drug Issues, 16*(2), 209–220.

Hellandsjo Bu, E.T., Watten, R.G., Foxcroft, D.R., Ingebrigtsen, J.E., & Relling, G. (2002). Teenage alcohol and intoxication debut: The impact of family socialization actors, living area and participation in organized sports. *Alcohol and Alcoholism, 37*(1), 74–80.

Hibell, B. Andersson, B., Bjarnason, T., Ahlström, S., Balakireva, O., Kokkevi, A., Morgan, M. (2004). *The ESPAD Report 2003: Alcohol and other drug use among students in 35 European countries.* Stockholm, Sweden: The Swedish Council for Information on Alcohol and Other Drugs (CAN).

Holder, H.D., Gruenewald, P.J., Ponicki, W.R., Treno, A.J., Grube, J.W., Saltz, R.F., *et al.* (2000). Effect of community-based interventions on high-risk drinking and alcohol-related injuries. *JAMA: Journal of American Medical Association, 284*(18), 2341–2347.

Holmila, M. (2003). Evaluation of the Metropolitan project; process and causality. *Nordisk Alkohol- & Narkotikatidskrift (Nordic Studies on Alcohol and Drugs), 20* (English suppl.), 81–90.

Honik, R., Maklan, D., Cadell, D., Prado, A., Barmada, C., Jacobsohn, L. *et al.* (2002). *Evaluation of the National Youth Anti-Drug Media Campaign: Fourth semi-annual report of findings.* Bethesda, MD: National Institute on Drug Abuse (NIDA).

Houghton, E., & Roche, A.M. (Eds.). (2001). *Learning about drinking.* Philadephia: Brunner-Routledge.

Hurtado, S.L. (2002). *Effectiveness of an alcohol abuse secondary prevention program among Marine Corps aviation personnel.* San Diego, CA: Naval Health Research Center.

International Center for Alcohol Policies (ICAP). (1997). *ICAP reports 3: Health warning labels.* Washington, DC: Author.

International Center for Alcohol Policies (ICAP). (1998). *ICAP reports 5: What is a "standard drink"?* Washington, DC: Author.

International Center for Alcohol Policies (ICAP). (1999). *ICAP reports 6: Government policies on alcohol and pregnancy.* Washington, DC: Author.

International Center for Alcohol Policies (ICAP). (2000). *Life Skills Education in South Africa and Botswana.* Washington, DC: Author.

International Center for Alcohol Policies (ICAP). (2001). *ICAP reports 10: Alcohol and "special populations." Biological vulnerability.* Washington, DC: Author.

International Center for Alcohol Policies (ICAP). (2002). *ICAP reports 4 (Revised): Drinking age limits.* Washington, DC: Author.

International Center for Alcohol Policies (ICAP). (2003a). *ICAP reports 13: Alcohol and the workplace.* Washington, DC: Author.

International Center for Alcohol Policies (ICAP). (2003b). *ICAP reports 14: International drinking guidelines.* Washington, DC: Author.

International Center for Alcohol Policies (ICAP). (2004). *What drives underage drinking? An international analysis.* Washington, DC: Author.

Jessor, R. (Ed.). (1998). *New perspectives on adolescent risk behavior.* Cambridge, United Kingdom: Cambridge University Press.

Johannessen, K., & Glider, P. (2003). University of Arizona's campus health social norms media campaign. In H.W. Perkins (Ed.), *Social norms approach to preventing school and college age substance abuse: A handbook for educators, counselors, and clinicians* (pp. 65–82). San Francisco: Jossey-Bass.

Kaner, E.F.S., Wutzke, S., Saunders, J.B., Powell, A., Morawski, J., & Bouix, J.C. (2001). Impact of alcohol education and training on general practitioners' diagnostic and management skills: Findings from a World Health Organization collaborative study. *Journal of Studies on Alcohol, 62*(5), 621–627.

Kanof, M.E. (2003). *Youth illicit drug use prevention: DARE long-term evaluations and federal efforts to identify effective programs.* Washington, DC: General Accounting Office (GAO).

Kaskutas, L.A., & Greenfield, T.K. (1997). Behavior change: The role of health consciousness in predicting attention to health warning messages. *American Journal of Health Promotion, 11*(3), 183–193.

Kesmodel, U., & Kesmodel, P.S. (2002). Drinking during pregnancy: Attitudes and knowledge among pregnant Danish women, 1998. *Alcoholism: Clinical and Experimental Research, 26*(10), 1553–1560.

Kumpfer, K.L., Alvarado, R., Tait, C., & Turner, C. (2002). Effectiveness of school-based family and children's skills training for substance abuse prevention among 6–8-year-old rural children. *Psychology of Addictive Behaviors, 16*(4S), S65-S71.

Kumpfer, K.L., Alvarado, R., & Whiteside, H.O. (2003). Family-based interventions for substance use and misuse prevention. *Substance Use and Misuse, 38*(11–13), 1759–1787.

Kypri, K., McGee, R., Saunders, J.B., Langley, J.D., & Dean, J.I. (2002). Interpretation of items in the AUDIT questionnaire. *Alcohol and Alcoholism, 37*(5), 465–467.

Kypri, K., Langley, J.D., McGee, R., Saunders, J.B., & Williams, S. (2002). High prevalence, persistent hazardous drinking among New Zealand tertiary students. *Alcohol and Alcoholism, 37*(5), 457–464.

Lapham, S.C., Gregory, C., & McMillan, G. (2003). Impact of an alcohol misuse intervention for health care workers. 1: Frequency of binge drinking and desire to reduce alcohol use. *Alcohol and Alcoholism, 38*(2), 176–182.

Lilja, J., Larsson, S., Wilhelmsen, B.U., & Hamilton, D. (2003). Perspectives on preventing adolescent substance use and misuse. *Substance Use and Misuse, 38*(10), 1491–1530.

Lindberg, L.D., Boggess, S., Porter, L., & Williams, S. (2000). *Teen risk-taking: Statistical portrait.* Washington, DC: Urban Institute.

Lloyd, C., Joyce, R., Hurry, J., & Ashton, M. (2000). Effectiveness of primary school drug education. *Drugs: Education, Prevention and Policy, 7*(2), 109–126.

Loop, K.Q., & Nettleman, M.D. (2002). Obstetrical textbooks: Recommendations about drinking during pregnancy. *American Journal of Preventive Medicine, 23*(2), 136–138.

MacKinnon, D.P., Nohre, L., Cheong, J., Stacy, A.W., & Pentz, M.A. (2001). Longitudinal relationship between the alcohol warning label and alcohol consumption. *Journal of Studies on Alcohol, 62*(2), 221–227.

Marlatt, G.A. (Ed.). (1998). *Harm reduction: Pragmatic strategies for managing high-risk behaviors.* New York: The Guilford Press.

Marlatt, G.A., Larimer, M.E., Mail, P.D., Hawkins, E.H., Cummins, L.H., Blume, A.W. *et al.* (2003). Journeys of the circle: A culturally congruent life skills intervention for adolescent Indian drinking. *Alcoholism: Clinical and Experimental Research, 27*(8), 1327–1329.

Mattern, J.L., & Neighbors, C. (2004). Social norms campaigns: Examining the relationship between changes in perceived norms and changes in drinking levels. *Journal of Studies on Alcohol, 65*(4), 489–493.

McBride, N., Farrington, F., & Midford, R. (2000). What harms do young Australians experience in alcohol use situations. *Australian and New Zealand Journal of Public Health, 24*(1), 54–59.

McBride, N., Farringdon, F., Midford, R., Meuleners, L., & Phillips, M. (2003). Early unsupervised drinking: Reducing the risks. The School Health and Alcohol Harm Reduction Project. *Drug and Alcohol Review, 22*(3), 263–276.

McBride, N., Farringdon, F., Midford, R., Meuleners, L., & Phillips, M. (2004). Harm minimization in school drug education: Final results of the School Health and Alcohol Harm Reduction Project. *Addiction, 99*(3), 278–291.

McCammon, K. (2001). Alcohol-related motor vehicle crashes: Deterrence and Intervention. *Annals of Emergency Medicine, 38*(4), 415–422.

Midford, R., & McBride, N. (2001). Alcohol education in schools. In N. Heather, T.J. Peters, & T. Stockwell (Eds.), *International handbook of alcohol dependence and problems.* Chichester, United Kingdom: John Wiley and Sons Ltd.

Milgram, G. (2001). Alcohol influences: The role of family and peers. In E. Houghton & A. Roche (Eds.), *Learning about drinking* (pp. 85–101). Philadelphia: Brunner-Routledge.

Miller, E.T., Kilmer, J.R., Kim, E.L., Weingardt, K.R., & Marlatt, G.A. (2001). Alcohol skills training for college students. In P.M. Monti, S.M. Colby, & T.A. O'Leary (Eds.), *Adolescents, alcohol, and substance abuse: Reaching teens through brief interventions* (pp. 183–215). New York: Guilford Publications, Inc.

Miller, P., & Plant, M. (2003). Family, peer influences and substance use: Findings from a study of UK teenagers. *Journal of Substance Use, 8*(1), 19–26.

Moran, J., & Reaman, J.A. (2002). Critical issues for substance abuse prevention targeting American Indian youth. *Journal of Primary Prevention, 22*(3), 201–233.

Morrison, D.S., Petticrew, M. & Thomson, H. (2003). What are the most effective ways of improving population health through transport interventions? Evidence from systematic reviews. *Journal of Epidemiology and Community Health, 57*(5), 327–333.

Murphy, J.G., Duchnick, J.J., Vuchinich, R.E., Davison, J.W., Karg, R.S., Olson, A.M., *et al.* (2001). Relative efficacy of a brief motivational intervention for college student drinkers. *Psychology of Addictive Behaviors, 15*(4), 373–379.

National Resource Center on Native American Aging (2001). *Motor vehicle crashes involving rural Native American elders.* Grand Forks, ND: National Resource Center on Native American Aging at the University of North Dakota.

Okamoto, S.K., Hurdle, D.E., & Marsiglia, F.F. (2001). Exploring culturally-based drug resistance strategies used by American Indian adolescents of the Southwest. *Journal of Alcohol and Drug Education, 47*(1), 45–59.

Paglia, A., & Room, R. (1999). Preventing substance use problems among youth: A literature review and recommendations. *Journal of Primary Prevention, 20*(1), 3–50.

Patton, R., & Touquet, R. (2003). General practitioner screening for excessive alcohol use: Brief screening tools should be used in general practice. *BMJ: British Medical Journal, 326*(7384), 337.

Perkins, H.W. (Ed.). (2003). *Social norms approach to preventing school and college age substance abuse: A handbook for educators, counselors, and clinicians.* San Francisco: Jossey-Bass.

Perkins, H.W., & Craig, D.W. (2002). *A multifaceted social norms approach to high-risk drinking: Lessons from Hobart and William Smith Colleges.* Newton, MA: Higher Education Center for Alcohol and Other Drug Prevention.

Perry, C.L., Williams, C.L., Forster, J.L., Wolfson, M., Wagenaar, A.C., Finnegan, J.R. et al. (1993). Background, conceptualization and design of a community-wide research program on adolescent alcohol use: Project Northland. *Health Education Research: Theory and Practice, 8*(1), 125–136.

Perry, C.L., Williams, C.L., Komro, K.A., Veblen-Mortenson, S., Stigler, M.H., Munson, K.A. et al. (2002). Project Northland: Long-term outcomes of community action to reduce adolescent alcohol use. *Health Education Research, 17*(1), 117–132.

Perry, C.L., Williams, C.L., Veblen-Mortenson, S., Toomey, T.L., Komro, K.A., Anstine, P.S. et al. (1996). Project Northland: Outcomes of a communitywide alcohol use prevention program during early adolescence. *American Journal of Public Health, 86*(7), 956–965.

Pinkleton, B.E, Austin, E.W., & Fujioka, Y. (2001). The relationship of perceived beer ad and PSA quality to high school students, alcohol-related beliefs and behaviors. *Journal of Broadcasting and Electronic Media, 45*(4), 575–597.

Plant, M. (2001). Learning by experiment. In E. Houghton & A.M. Roche (Eds.), *Learning about drinking* (pp.129–146). Philadelphia: Brunner-Routledge.

Plant, M., & Plant, M. (1997). Alcohol education and harm minimization. In M. Plant, E. Single & T. Stockwell (Eds.), *Alcohol: Minimising the harm. What works?* (pp. 193–210). New York: Free Association Books Ltd.

Plant, M., & Plant, M. (1999). Primary prevention for young children: A comment on the UK government's 10 year drug strategy. *International Journal of Drug Policy, 10*(5), 385–401.

Reis, J., & Riley, W. (2002). Assessment of a computer-supported alcohol education intervention program. *Health Education, 102*(3), 124–132.

Saffer, H. (2002). Alcohol advertising and youth. *Journal of Studies on Alcohol,* (Suppl. 14), 173–181.

Sanchez-Sosa, J.J., & Poldrugo, F. (2001). Family and cultural influences on alcohol and young people. In E. Houghton & A.M. Roche (Eds.), *Learning about drinking* (pp.57–83). Philadelphia: Brunner-Routledge.

Schaps, E., DiBartolo, R., & Moskowitz, J. (1981). Review of 127 drug abuse prevention program evaluations. *Journal of Drug Issues, 11*, 17–43.

Seppa, K. (2003). Development of country-wide strategies for implementing Early Identification and Brief Alcohol Intervention (EIBI) in primary health care. *Nordisk Alkohol- & Narkotikatidskrift (Nordic Studies on Alcohol and Drugs), 20* (English Suppl.), 91–96.

Sheehan, M., Schonfeld, C., Hindson, E., & Ballard, R. (1995). Alcohol education in an indigenous community school in Queensland, Australia. *Drugs: Education, Prevention and Policy*, *2*(3), 259–273.

Slater, M.D. (1999). Drinking and driving PSA's: A content analysis of behavioral influence strategies. *JADE: Journal of Alcohol and Drug Education*, *44*(3), 68–81.

Smart, R.G., & Ogborne, A.C. (2000). Drug use and drinking among students in 36 countries. *Addictive Behaviors*, *25*(3), 455–460.

Somers, J.M. (1996). Harm reduction and the prevention of alcohol problems among secondary school students. *Dissertation Abstracts International*, *56*(12), 7056B.

Spoth, R.L., Guyll, M., & Day, S.X. (2002). Universal family-focused interventions in alcohol-use disorder prevention: Cost-effectiveness and cost-benefit analyses of two interventions. *Journal of Studies on Alcohol*, *63*(2), 219–228.

Spoth, R.L., Redmond, C., & Lepper, H. (1999). Alcohol initiation outcomes of universal family-focused preventive interventions: One- and two-year follow-ups of a controlled study. *Journal of Studies on Alcohol*, *13*(Suppl.), 103–111.

Sroufe, L.A., Cooper, R.G., & DeHart, G.B. (1996). *Child development: Its nature and course*. New York: McGraw-Hill.

Stockley, C.S. (2001). Effectiveness of strategies such as health warning labels to reduce alcohol-related harms: An Australian perspective. *International Journal of Drug Policy*, *12*(2), 153–166.

Stockwell, T. (1997). Regulation of the licensed drinking environment: A major opportunity for crime prevention. In R. Homel (Ed.), *Crime prevention studies: Vol. 7. Policing for prevention: Reducing crime, public intoxication and injury* (pp. 7–33). Monsey, NY: Criminal Justice Press.

Stockwell, T. (2001). Harm reduction, drinking patterns and the NHMRC drinking guidelines. *Drug and Alcohol Review*, *20*(1), 121–129.

Stockwell, T., & Lemmens, P. (1994). Would standard drink labelling results in more accurate self-reports of alcohol consumption? *Addiction*, *89*(12), 1703–1706.

Stockwell, T., & Single, E. (1997). Standard unit labelling of alcohol containers. In M. Plant, E. Single, & T. Stockwell (Eds.), *Alcohol: Minimising the harm. What works?* (pp. 85–104) New York: Free Association Books Ltd.

Wagenaar, A.C., Murray, D.M., & Toomey, T.L. (2000). Communities Mobilizing for Change on Alcohol (CMCA): Effects of a randomized trial on arrests and traffic crashes. *Addiction*, *95*(2), 209–217.

Wald, H.P., Flaherty, M.T., & Pringle, J.L. (1999). Prevention in prisons. In R.T. Ammerman, P.J. Ott, & R.E. Tarter (Eds.), *Prevention and societal impact of drug and alcohol abuse* (pp. 369–381). Mahwah, NJ: Lawrence Erlbaum Associates.

Wechsler, H., Nelson, T.F., Lee, J.E., Seibring, M., Lewis, C., & Keeling, R.P. (2003). Perception and reality: A national evaluation of social norms marketing interventions to reduce college students' heavy alcohol use. *Journal of Studies on Alcohol*, *64*(4), 484–494.

Weintraub, T.A., Saitz, R., & Samet, J.H. (2003). Education of preventive medicine residents: Alcohol, tobacco, and other drug abuse. *American Journal of Preventive Medicine*, *24*(1), 101–105.

Westphal, L.L. (2000). Prenatal alcohol use among urban American Indians/Alaska Native women. *American Indian and Alaska Native Mental Health Research*, *9*(3), 38–48.

White, D., & Pitts, M. (1998). Educating young people about drugs: A systematic review. *Addiction*, *93*(10), 1475–1487.

Williams, C.L. & Perry, C.L. (1998). Lessons from Project Northland: Preventing alcohol problems during adolescence. *Alcohol Health and Research World, 22*(2), 107–116.

Williams, C.L., Perry, C.L., Farbakhsh, K., & Veblen-Mortenson, S. (1999). Project Northland: Comprehensive alcohol use prevention for young adolescents, their parents, schools, peers and communities. *Journal of Studies on Alcohol, 13*(Suppl.), 112–124.

Williams, R.J., & Gloster, S.P. (1999). Knowledge of fetal alcohol syndrome (FAS) among natives in northern Manitoba. *Journal of Studies on Alcohol, 60*(6), 833–836.

Worldwide Brewing Alliance (2003). *Global social responsibility initiatives*. London: Author.

Ziemelis, A., Bucknam, R.B., & Elfessi, A.M. (2002). Prevention efforts underlying decreases in binge drinking at institutions of higher education. *Journal of American College Health, 50*(5), 238–252.

Chapter 16

Report on the Framework for Responsibility

Eleni Houghton, Gaye Pedlow, and Adrian Botha

CORPORATE RESPONSIBILITY IN CONTEXT

The beverage alcohol industry's social responsibility activities can best be described in two parts. First, there are activities that pertain to alcohol itself. Alcohol beverages, when consumed responsibly, can be part of a balanced, healthy lifestyle, but when consumed inappropriately have the potential for harm. This has led leading members of the beverage alcohol industry, especially within the past decade, to form separate organizations—social aspects organizations (SAOs)—whose function is to promote responsible alcohol use.

Over the years, industry members have funded innovative campaigns especially to deter drink driving and underage drinking. They have also supported peer-reviewed alcohol research that increases the understanding of alcohol's positive and negative consequences.

The impact of such initiatives has been sustained over time. Over the past 12 years, significant decreases in drink driving fatalities are evident in Australasia, Europe, and the United States. Major producers also have or subscribe to company advertising codes and support self-regulatory and independent mechanisms to attempt to ensure that advertising is directed to the target market—legal drinking age consumers—and that it does not appear to condone inappropriate drinking behavior. Although other factors beyond industry initiatives are clearly significant in helping to reduce drink driving problems, the industry's contribution is noteworthy and significant.

The second part of the industry's corporate responsibility activities relates to the bigger picture. The beverage alcohol industry recognizes that good corporate citizenship is more than ensuring that alcohol beverages are used safely and responsibly across the community. It also entails balancing the needs of its employees for a safe and rewarding job, and improving the environments in which they work and the wider culture in which they engage in business with the needs of shareholders for a fair return on their investment.

In practice, this means that most major alcohol producers comply with or exceed governmental requirements and international norms governing the environmental impact of the products they produce through improvements in the use of water, packaging, greenhouse gases, energy, solid waste, air emissions, hazardous substances, and transport. High standards are set regarding their business conduct and those of the partners with whom they work, and they support a host of cultural and educational activities in the communities where they operate.

Although these efforts are supported in mature and emerging markets, at the local, national, and international levels and in partnership with a variety of stakeholders from the public and private sectors, efforts in emerging markets, especially in developing countries, have sometimes been uneven. In part, this was because it takes a company time to have a sufficient corporate presence to affect change and because developing countries sometimes pose unique challenges in terms of social responsibility efforts.

FOCUS ON THE DEVELOPING WORLD AND EMERGING MARKETS

When the International Center for Alcohol Policies (ICAP)[1] was founded in 1995, one of its primary responsibilities was to increase the understanding of alcohol policy issues in emerging markets, located primarily in developing countries, by bringing public health researchers, government, and the beverage alcohol industry together to address alcohol issues of common concern.

This commitment resulted in the publication of a major book on the subject, *Alcohol and Emerging Markets: Patterns, Problems, and Responses* (Grant, 1998). The book presented the most current research on alcohol in developing countries and emerging markets. It included reports on sub-Saharan Africa,

---

[1] ICAP's current sponsors are: Allied Domecq, Asahi Breweries, Bacardi-Martini, Brown-Forman Corporation, Coors Brewing Company, Diageo, Foster's Brewing Group, Heineken, Molson Breweries, and SABMiller.

Asia, Southeast Asia, China, India, Central and Eastern Europe, Russia, Latin America, and Mexico. It also contained chapters that delved more deeply into some of the common themes from these reports, exploring issues from economic, anthropological, epidemiological, and industry perspectives.

The chapter "Alcohol in Emerging Markets: Identifying the Most Appropriate Role for the Alcohol Beverage Industry," written by Gaye Pedlow (1998) in collaboration with her colleagues on the ICAP board of directors, identified the challenges and opportunities confronting the sponsor companies of ICAP. One of the practical contributions to this chapter was the development of the Framework for Responsibility. The framework is a list of activities that the ICAP sponsors pledged to undertake in developing countries in an effort to demonstrate how seriously they take the issue of corporate responsibility wherever they are active in the world. The level of activity would be dependent on the size of their corporate or collective presence in a given country, and they pledged to report back on progress within 5 years.

This chapter is a report on that progress for the period 1999–2003. Although the framework's aim was to focus industry attention specifically on alcohol issues, the chapter also touches on the more general corporate social responsibility (CSR) issues ICAP sponsors were engaged in during the reporting period.

THE DEVELOPMENT OF THE FRAMEWORK

The framework was developed and agreed to by the ICAP board of directors in 1998. It was reviewed and revised in light of comments by public health researchers in the developed and developing world and is viewed by ICAP sponsors as a work in progress.

The framework is divided into three sections:

* understanding perceptions of alcohol and patterns of consumption;
* responsible promotional and advertising practices; and
* alcohol education and initiatives to promote sensible drinking.

A checklist of framework activities undertaken during the reporting period is presented in Appendix 1 to this chapter. Under each of the three main sections listed above is a list of related activities in the order of their degree of difficulty. A company with an active presence in a given market might undertake the activities toward the end of the list, while those with a small local presence would be more likely to choose activities in the beginning of the list. What follows is a report on activities undertaken in each of the three sections.

UNDERSTANDING PERCEPTIONS OF ALCOHOL AND PATTERNS OF CONSUMPTION

This section focuses on research and has two broad objectives. It seeks to encourage where possible:

- efforts to collect data on patterns of alcohol consumption and any associated problems in developing countries and emerging markets;
- research projects that will provide or supplement such data in situations where they do not exist or are incomplete.

Most of ICAP's sponsors monitor social or political developments that might impact the levels of consumption. Depending on the size of the company, reports regarding health and social issues related to alcohol consumption are also monitored. This is increasingly true in Eastern Europe and the Asia-Pacific region.

In terms of marketing, one company has begun to include questions relating to social issues and perceptions of alcohol-related problems in market research studies. Several companies monitor consumption levels of locally (licit or illicit) produced alcohol and associated problems as a part of this research. This has occurred in the Seychelles, East and West Africa, Zambia, and Mexico. All ICAP sponsors have supported a cross-national study of the patterns of nonindustrial beverage alcohol consumption in Brazil, India, Mexico, Russia, Tanzania, and Zambia. The results of these studies were published in a book titled *Moonshine Markets: Issues in Unrecorded Alcohol Beverage Production and Consumption* (Haworth & Simpson, 2004). This book also looks at some of the wider implications of these country studies, including economic, anthropological, and health issues.

ICAP's sponsors have also commissioned research to supplement data on consumption levels. In India, for example, the local SAO, the Society for Alcohol and Social Policy Initiative (SASPI),[2] commissioned a study in 1999–2000 to analyze consumption patterns in Goa, in partnership with the Sangath Society for Child Development and Family Guidance. A workshop involving government, researchers, nongovernmental organizations, and the private sector was held to present the results and discuss their implications.

In South Africa, the Industry Association for Responsible Alcohol Use (ARA) established and continues to support the Foundation for Alcohol Related Research (FARR) at the University of Cape Town. FARR works in partnership with several respected research centers and is conducting ground-

---

[2] SASPI ceased operating in 2003. It has been replaced by the individual company efforts of four international beverage alcohol companies.

breaking studies, especially in the area of fetal alcohol syndrome (FAS) (see Case Study 1 for more information).

CASE STUDY 1: ADDRESSING CRITICAL RESEARCH NEEDS

Professor Dennis Viljoen is a leading South African human geneticist and ranks among the world's top authorities on FAS. During his visits to clinics in what are now the Western Cape and Eastern Cape provinces of South Africa, he noticed what he believed to be an alarming number of FAS cases. Wanting to investigate this scientifically, he approached government and research institutions for funding but without success. Finally, he approached the ARA. After careful consideration, the ARA agreed to provide seed money to establish FARR in 1996.

FARR's mission is to facilitate scientific research on alcohol-related issues. It hopes to identify factors that predispose individuals to alcohol-related harm and initiate preventive programs to reduce such harm. Since its inception, FARR has undertaken studies on FAS in five provinces in South Africa with the support of ARA and other collaborators including: the U.S. National Institute on Alcohol Abuse and Alcoholism (NIAAA), the U.S. Centers for Disease Control and Prevention (CDC), the University of New Mexico, the South African Institute for Medical Research, University of Cape Town Medical School, the South African Directorate for Mental Health and Substance Abuse, the Department of Health of South Africa, and provincial departments of health. The research undertaken by FARR in collaboration with these partners, and with additional support from ARA, includes studies on ultrasound, neurodevelopment, and alcohol metabolism.

ARA's involvement in FARR has been a continuing one. It funds the foundation's administrative costs. It also funds a postgraduate fellowship with the aim of building capacity in alcohol-related research, especially among previously disadvantaged groups in the community. This arrangement of funding administration but not research projects is intended by FARR to protect the integrity of the foundation's research agenda.

In partnership with government, the beverage alcohol industry, and the research community, FARR broadens our understanding of alcohol issues in South Africa and their implications for other countries, while addressing critical areas of research.

ICAP's sponsors also supported the publication of noted Brown University Professor Dwight Heath's (2000) book, *Drinking Occasions: Comparative Perspectives on Alcohol and Culture*, which explores when, where, how, and why people drink alcohol. Many examples are drawn from developing countries. The book was published as a part of the ICAP Series on Alcohol in Society.

RESPONSIBLE PROMOTIONAL AND ADVERTISING PRACTICES

As with the other two sections of the framework, the section on responsible promotional and advertising practices has several broad objectives. The four objectives are to encourage where possible:

- strict industry compliance with all existing legislation or self-regulatory codes of practice;
- initiatives aimed at establishing self-regulatory codes in countries where they do not exist;
- efforts to ensure that such codes of practice adequately reflect local culture and values;
- the development of appropriate enforcement mechanisms to ensure that such codes are adhered to.

The list of related activities ranges from ensuring compliance with all existing codes of practice to publishing the findings of self-regulatory review bodies.

Establishment of Self-Regulatory Mechanisms

Codes of practice that include alcohol beverages within their framework, either as stand-alone self-regulatory systems or as part of a combination of statutory and self-regulatory controls, exist in a growing number of emerging markets, including Argentina, Brazil, Chile, Hong Kong, Mexico, Nigeria, the Philippines, Singapore, South Africa, and Uruguay. During the review period, brewers in the Czech Republic established a self-regulatory code, steps were taken to establish a self-regulatory organization in Thailand, and one of the codes cited above was strengthened. In addition, an ICAP self-regulation tool kit was produced. Several of these developments are described below.

The ARA in South Africa set up a self-regulatory code in 1989 that regulates advertising, packaging, and promotional activity. Since 1989, the code has been amended three times. In 1996, the Advertising Standards Authority of South Africa accepted all the advertising clauses of the ARA code as its own, thus making the ARA code applicable to nonmembers of the ARA as well. In 2000, the ARA developed a code of practice that applied specifically to practices in the licensed trade, including the need to avoid sales to minors and to discourage excessive or irresponsible consumption. The ARA code is therefore more stringent than the code of the Advertising Standards Authority and includes provision for an external ombudsman who settles code disputes. In 2003, the code was updated again to include further advertising restrictions.

In 2002, ICAP published a self-regulation tool kit for emerging markets and the developing world (International Center for Alcohol Policies, 2002). The tool kit, which was prepared by Gaye Pedlow on behalf of the ICAP board, is intended to give an overview of self-regulation, including all the elements that make up the most effective self-regulatory system. It is aimed especially at those countries where there are no self-regulatory mechanisms in place, but also may be useful to self-regulatory bodies wishing to modify their codes. References and a model code of practice for the marketing and promotion of alcohol beverages are also included. Culture plays a very important role in determining provisions in any code, and thus the model code in the tool kit should be seen as only a guide. It has, however, now been used as the basis for self-regulatory codes in both Mexico and Thailand.

The tool kit has been printed and circulated to governments, the beverage alcohol industry, and associated organizations, as well as others interested in self-regulation. The kit is also available on ICAP's website.[3]

Company and Industry Codes of Practice

One of the activities listed in this section of the framework calls for parent company guidance on minimum standards of conduct in countries where no codes or regulations exist. Six of ICAP's 10 sponsors have their own company codes of practice governing advertising and promotion of alcohol beverages internationally.

The specific provisions of each of these codes are listed in Appendix 2 of this chapter. The principles common to all of these companies' codes are:

- compliance with all existing codes of practice/advertising regulations;
- where no codes exist, ensuring that the parent company gives guidance regarding minimum standards;
- ensuring that advertising and promotional activities are consistent with local culture;
- no encouragement of immoderate or excessive drinking;
- no targeting of illegal underage consumers;
- no placement at events where the majority of the audience are underage;
- no subjects in advertisements are aged under 25;
- no implication of enhanced physical, sexual, or social ability;
- no depiction of unsafe conditions;
- no depiction of intoxication;
- no claims of unsubstantiated and/or therapeutic benefits; and
- no emphasis on high alcohol content.

---

[3] For the full text of the tool kit, visit ICAP's website at www.icap.org.

Most of the codes also contain provisions against association with violence, association with illegal activity, depiction of religious symbols, and negative portrayal of abstinence.

Five companies have set up processes to ensure that joint venture partners, advertising agencies, and other local partners know of the company's commitment to responsible marketing practices and are aware of the company code of practice.

Effectiveness and Enforcement

All ICAP sponsors or their operating companies have internal review mechanisms to attempt to ensure that advertising and other promotional activity are in keeping with the spirit of responsible consumption. Most sponsors review their codes on a regular basis.

In 2001, one company commissioned a worldwide independent audit of its marketing code. The results of that audit have been reflected in a revised and strengthened company code of marketing practice (see Case Study 2).

CASE STUDY 2: COMPLIANCE

Below are examples of two ICAP sponsors taking action to ensure that words reflect the actions of all operating companies.

In 2001, Heineken created the Responsibility Management Program for Heineken companies. The program was established to create greater consistency and clarity, both to further communicate Heineken's identity and to enable Heineken to evaluate and, where necessary, reinforce its policy. Since 2002, local company management teams have been initiating dialogue with employees and local external parties as a basis for translating the Heineken Values and Principles into procedures and activities that are consistent with the culture of local communities. Pilot projects based on this approach were launched in Ghana, Indonesia, Poland, and Rwanda.

In 2001, Diageo appointed an independent auditor to report on its compliance with the Diageo Code of Marketing Practice. The auditor looked at advertising for 27 brands in 47 countries, reviewing approximately 1,000 advertisements. He also reviewed internal code compliance processes and made some suggestions on ways those processes could be improved.

Diageo then sent out the marketing code for review by a range of alcohol policy experts, regulators, governments, and intergovernmental organizations. This included bodies such as Alcohol Concern and the Portman Group in the United Kingdom, the state and federal governments of Australia, and the liquor control boards in Canada. At the same time, a wide-ranging internal consultation process was carried out to collect the views of Diageo brand teams, marketing directors, and external affairs managers around the business. The code was updated during 2002, addressing all the issues raised during the internal and external reviews. A comprehensive training program was developed to help embed the standards of the code in the way Diageo carries out its business. All marketing teams have been trained in the use of the code. The training programs also cover external advertising and brand public relations agencies, and an e-learning tool has been developed to help reinforce the training workshops.

The model code in ICAP's self-regulation tool kit outlines the following key points in developing effective self-regulation:

• Prevention is better than cure: a good self-regulatory system will aim to preempt and resolve possible problems before they arise, for example, through advice on advertising copy and internal company compliance activities.
• Self-regulation needs to have teeth: compliance mechanisms and/or penalties and sanctions have to be meaningful.
• The credibility and overall effectiveness of any self-regulatory system may be enhanced by ensuring that there is independent representation on the complaints panel.
• Specific rules for alcohol beverages are preferable, where possible, to general principles applicable to all products. This enables specific issues to be addressed, in particular ensuring that alcohol beverages are only marketed to adults and that advertisements only promote responsible consumption.

ALCOHOL EDUCATION AND INITIATIVES TO PROMOTE SENSIBLE DRINKING

ICAP's sponsors have increased their participation in education activities in terms of the number of projects and their geographic reach. The main objectives of this section of the framework were to encourage:

• the researching and piloting of such initiatives in a selected number of developing countries and emerging markets;
• the sharing of "good practice" through identifying initiatives that have been successful elsewhere;
• dialogue with government, public health professionals, and other parties to explore possibilities for cooperation and partnership on specific issues or projects.

The activities supporting the objectives cited above can be divided into those that are concerned with education within the company and those that relate to the public.

In terms of educating company employees, seven ICAP sponsors have established companywide alcohol policies to educate employees about sensible drinking, and one is in the process of ensuring that the current policy applies to all markets. These written policies are communicated through the external affairs departments or via the company's Intranet, and have been established or strengthened since the publication of the framework. These same companies have also taken measures to ensure that company managers know the parent company's views on responsible drinking and related issues. This is accomplished through regular visits to parent company headquarters by country managers or visits to the field by corporate representatives. In the past several years, senior external affairs staff from at least two companies have increased their efforts to raise awareness of responsibility issues by traveling to the field to hold meetings and workshops specifically to impart this message.

Since the publication of the framework, there has been a concerted effort to increase the number of SAOs in developing countries or emerging markets. Three SAOs in developing countries existed in 1998 in India, Mexico, and South Africa. Efforts to establish SAOs are currently under way in Brazil, the Czech Republic, and Poland. One new SAO was established in Taiwan within the reporting period, and two more have since been established in Thailand and Hungary. In addition to SAOs, or when SAOs do not exist, ICAP sponsors often fund their own social responsibility programs. Seven ICAP sponsors either fund their own programs in developing countries or are members of SAOs that manage programs on their behalf.

Initiatives supported by ICAP sponsors since the framework was published include campaigns against drink driving (in Brazil, Cameroon, Ghana, Hungary, Kenya, India, Nigeria, South Africa, Taiwan, Thailand, and Venezuela), life skills education (in Botswana, Seychelles, and South Africa), fetal alcohol syndrome education (in South Africa), and general alcohol education (in India, Mexico, and South Africa).

Although not within the 1999–2003 review period, several ICAP sponsors supported the World Health Organization "Safe Roads" theme for World Health Day (WHD) in April 2004. A brief summary of the activities launched in association with WHD 2004 include:

- SABMiller: The South African Breweries is the sponsor of the driver-education campaign, launched in several South African communities, including Moloto Village, Thembisile Municipality, Mpumalanga Province. The sponsorship is part of the company's commitment to ensuring responsible alcohol consumption, and runs under the banner of "Drink Responsibly, Drive Responsibly, Live Responsibly." Furthermore, the campaign recognizes that road safety issues in South Africa go much further than just "drinking and driving" and therefore include messages about speeding, road worthiness, safety belts, visibility, and pedestrians. The long-term goal of the campaign is to encourage a cultural change among South African drivers to make a difference to the country's unacceptably high road accident statistics.

- Diageo: Diageo launched during 2004 over 30 local programs around the world covering countries in all six WHO regions, designed specifically around the WHD theme of Safe Roads. As part of its ongoing commitment to promote a shared understanding of responsible drinking and to combat alcohol misuse, Diageo has developed a range of programs reminding the public about the consequences of drink driving and being a safe road user.

- Allied Domecq: Allied Domecq featured WHD on its internal website that reaches its 12,000 employees worldwide. Included was the WHO fact sheet and a linked message to The Century Council's blood alcohol educator to encourage employees to test their knowledge about the effects of alcohol on driving.

- Coors Brewing Company: Coors supported the The Amsterdam Group (TAG) participation in the European Road Safety Charter, which entails concrete commitments over a 3-year period aimed at supporting the objective of the European Commission to reduce by 50% the number of road deaths by 2010.

ICAP sponsors understand that those who serve alcohol beverages to consumers have an opportunity to influence the way in which it is consumed. One ICAP sponsor has supported responsible server training in several countries, including Brazil, Kenya, Korea, Nigeria, Scotland, Seychelles, and Thailand, in which over 10,000 bartenders have participated.

These initiatives have often been supported in partnership with a number of different government bodies and NGOs. The ARA in South Africa, for example, has funded fetal alcohol syndrome prevention campaigns through FARR (see Case Study 1) and a range of national and international partners. In Mexico, the local SAO—FISAC—supports health promotion workshops that aim to spread knowledge about beverage alcohol consumption to health professionals, sociologists, anthropologists, teachers, parents, and community leaders. This is done in cooperation with the Mexican Ministry of Health, the Ministry of Education, the National Parents Association, NGOs, and public and private companies.

In India, SASPI, the local SAO, worked in partnership with the Bangalore Agenda Task Force, the Bangalore Police, the Global Road Safety Partnership (an initiative of the World Bank and the Federation of Red Cross and Red Crescent Societies to support safer roads in developing countries), the National Institute of Mental Health and Neurosciences (NIMHANS), and ICAP to research, develop, implement, and evaluate a campaign against drink driving (see Case Study 3 for more details).

CASE STUDY 3: PARTNERSHIP TO PREVENT DRINKING AND DRIVING

Drinking and driving is a major problem in Bangalore, India. A study of road accident victims conducted by the Bangalore-based NIMHANS in 2001 revealed that 21% of casualties were under the influence of alcohol and the majority of them were males between the ages of 18 and 35 years.

The Bangalore Agenda Task Force, a group that has been charged with making Bangalore the most livable city in India, joined forces with the Bangalore police and the Global Road Safety Partnership, an international organization initiated by the World Bank and the International Federation of Red Cross and Red Crescent Societies, to address road safety issues in Bangalore. Given the high incidence of drinking and driving cited above, a project to educate the citizens of Bangalore about the dangers of drinking and driving was developed under the road safety theme. SASPI, the local Indian SAO, and ICAP joined the partnership to advise on alcohol-related issues and to help develop the publicity campaign by providing international examples from other countries. NIMHANS also joined the partnership with responsibility for the precampaign surveys and the project evaluation.

The approach undertaken by this partnership involves a baseline survey, an intensive publicity campaign to educate citizens about the laws governing drinking and driving, followed by strict enforcement of those laws by the police, and an evaluation. Under the banner, "Don't drink and drive. Your family needs you!" the project aims to build awareness about the risks of drinking and driving and to inform young people about responsible drinking.

The partnership launched the publicity campaign in December 2002 and conducted an evaluation in 2004. It is expected that lessons learned can be applied to drink driving campaigns in other parts of India, in addition to other countries. This international public-private partnership also proved to be a useful model, in which all partners brought their specific expertise to an important issue.

Although there is still a need for proper evaluation of industry initiatives, some of the projects within the framework period have been evaluated. As a part of the drink driving campaign in Bangalore, India, NIMHANS carried out a precampaign survey commissioned by the police. NIMHANS also conducted the project evaluation when the drink driving campaign was completed in 2003 (see Case Study 3). The life skills education programs in Botswana and South Africa were also independently evaluated, and the results were published by ICAP (International Center for Alcohol Policies, 2000).

SUMMARY OF THE FRAMEWORK

ICAP sponsors view the progress on the framework as an important beginning. In terms of research, the FARR in South Africa is a partnership of international reputation, and the publication of *Moonshine Markets* has shed new light on a neglected but important area of alcohol research in developing countries (Haworth & Simpson, 2004). More research is certainly needed, in spite of the two-edged sword industry sponsorship represents—the industry can be criticized for funding research because of vested interests but also criticized for not doing enough in this regard.

In the area of responsible promotion and advertising practices, seven companies have developed their own minimum standards for promotional and advertising activities in all markets in which they operate. Several companies make their company guidelines known to joint venture partners, advertising agencies, and other local partners. A toolkit on self-regulation has been produced by ICAP to guide interested parties through the establishment of self-regulatory mechanisms (International Center for Alcohol Policies, 2002). The model code it contains sets high standards for regulating advertising and promo-tion in all markets. Areas to focus on in the future will include developing more codes of practice in developing countries and mechanisms for enforcing those codes.

The alcohol education section has received the most extensive reporting since the framework was written. It illustrates that ICAP sponsors are responding to some of the main problems that involve alcohol in developing countries—drink driving issues, server training, and alcohol awareness—though much remains to be done. Observing behavior change in alcohol education efforts over time is a challenge for the industry as well as the public health community. With an increased emphasis on evaluation within industry-sponsored programs, the knowledge base on how to effectively manage programs in developing countries can only increase. From the framework experience, partnerships among a variety of sectors hold the greatest promise for education efforts.

Building partnerships between the beverage alcohol industry and public health institutions is a relatively new concept, even in North America and Europe. As a starting point, consensus must be built across the different sectors within the local industry in order to pursue programs to promote responsible drinking. In addition, there may be differing views on the importance of social aspects between domestic and international producers. Against a backdrop of challenging socioeconomic conditions prevalent in many developing countries, this means that the process of building partnerships and making progress on many of these activities can be slow.

NON-ALCOHOL-RELATED ACTIVITIES

As ICAP sponsors have increased their activities on alcohol-related issues in developing countries and emerging markets, they have also been working on corporate responsibility efforts within the company and the communities where they are active.

As with the framework, the breadth of activities internationally is to a certain extent determined by company size and depth of commercial activity in a given market. Almost all ICAP sponsors have set environmental standards for their companies. Half have had those policies externally audited, and many have won awards relating to environmental performance. One company allows governments and NGOs to review its policies as well.

Almost all ICAP sponsors support charities and make contributions to the communities in which they are active. Such support ranges from contributing financially or through employee involvement in the arts, sporting events, community revitalization, literacy programs, and job training to disaster relief, health causes, and international humanitarian efforts. Four sponsors earmark a percentage of their pretax profit to support their CSR efforts.

Most sponsors have a written set of core values and business codes of conduct that govern their activity in the marketplace. More than half of them have developed independent environmental and employee policies that, once established, are merged into a health, safety, and environment segment of the company either at the level of the board of directors or at the executive level. Such policies are binding in all markets.

A few sponsors have joined other joint international corporate efforts to address societal issues, such as improving the environment or fighting HIV/AIDS. Two sponsors and one subsidiary of a sponsor are members of the United Nations Global Compact, an initiative set up by the secretary general of the United Nations, Kofi Annan, to challenge corporations to develop sound policies and programs in the areas of labor, the environment, and human rights.

Finally, several sponsors have completed detailed annual social reports, which are public documents outlining a broad range of environmental, community, and social areas in which they are taking action. These generally report on a global basis, for example, reports by Allied Domecq, Diageo, and SABMiller, but also on a national or regional basis, for example, reports by Coors in the United Kingdom and Diageo in at least four markets.

CONCLUSION

ICAP was founded on the premise that meaningful change is possible when all relevant stakeholders come together to solve a problem. The Framework for Responsibility, an initiative of the ICAP sponsors, represents a start to what is possible when partnerships emerge in developing countries and demonstrates how an industry can challenge itself to do more for its employees, its communities, and its consumers.

APPENDIX 1: FRAMEWORK FOR RESPONSIBILITY CHECKLIST

1. Understanding Perceptions of Alcohol and Patterns of Consumption

ICAP sponsors will encourage where possible:

- Efforts to collect data on patterns of alcohol consumption and any associated problems in developing countries and emerging markets.
- Research projects that will provide or supplement such data in situations where they do not exist or are incomplete.

Related Activities

1.1 Monitoring social or political developments that might have an impact on levels or patterns of alcohol consumption. For example:
- Allied Domecq monitors social and political developments via national and international pan-industry organizations.
- All Bacardi companies monitor on a permanent basis social/ political developments that might have an impact on levels of consumption.
- Brown-Forman affiliates monitor these developments.
- Diageo monitors social/political developments in all markets.
- Foster's Group monitors social and political developments via national and international agencies and pan-industry organizations.

1.2 Requiring a local agency, manager, or distributor to monitor and report to the parent company on health and social issues related to alcohol consumption. For example:
- Diageo national external affairs managers worldwide report on such issues (it is not a requirement for smaller markets unless the issue has a broader regional impact).
- Brown-Forman regional managers are expected to report on such issues and their impact.
- Executives from Allied Domecq in Eastern Europe and Asia-Pacific are increasing involvement in such activities.
- Bacardi country managers and external affairs managers and local management of its distributors report on such issues as part of the regular updates on market situations.
- Many ICAP sponsors monitor such activities through the Centre for Information on Beverage Alcohol, based in London.

1.3 Including questions relating to social issues, perceptions of alcohol-related problems and so on, in market research studies. For example:
- All Diageo in-market companies are required to analyze relevant social issues and incorporate the key findings and priorities in their strategic plans.
- Various local SAOs supported by ICAP sponsors also regularly carry out such research.

1.4 Monitoring consumption levels of local alcohols and associated problems as part of company/industry market research. For example:
- Diageo Seychelles and Diageo East Africa have undertaken research into local alcohols, in an effort to inform public policy on the issue of local alcohols in both regions.
- South African Breweries, part of SABMiller, supported research regarding patterns of drinking among brewery workers in Zambia.
- Allied Domecq, Bacardi, Diageo, and Molson supported a study on local alcohol in Brazil.
- FISAC,[4] a local SAO, monitors such activities in Mexico.
- Bacardi country managers, external affairs managers, and local management of its distributors report on such issues as part of regular updates on market situations.

---

[4] FISAC is supported by the following ICAP sponsors: Allied Domecq, Bacardi-Martini, and Diageo.

1.5 Commissioning research to provide or supplement data on consumption levels and misuse. For example:

- Diageo supports this type of research through its active membership of national and international SAOs where appropriate. Directly commissioned research by Diageo is uncommon but has been carried out where SAO resources are sparse or where its resources are best placed, as in India and the Seychelles.

- ARA, South Africa,[5] supports epidemiological studies on fetal alcohol syndrome (FAS). Such studies have been conducted in South Africa's Western Cape province and are currently under way in the provinces of Gauteng, Northern Cape, and Eastern Cape. The Foundation for Alcohol Related Research (FARR) has undertaken these studies in collaboration with the NIAAA, the U.S. Centers for Disease Control, the University of New Mexico, USA, the South African Institute for Medical Research, University of Cape Town (UCT) Medical School, Witwatersrand University Medical School, Directorate for Mental Health and Substance Abuse, the Department of Health of South Africa, and the South African provincial departments of health.

- Additional studies undertaken by FARR and supported by ARA include: (1) An alcohol metabolism study in collaboration with the NIAAA, University of Cape Town (UCT) Medical School, and Indiana University School of Medicine, Indiana, USA. (2) An ultrasound study in collaboration with the NIAAA and UCT Medical School. (3) Neurodevelopment studies in collaboration with the NIAAA, UCT Medical School, and Wayne State University, Michigan, USA.

- ARA has also supported a second research fellow at FARR and the completion of FAS studies in two more provinces of South Africa, cosponsored the purchase of a gene analyzer to assist FARR in its research, cosponsored a conference on birth defects, and supported a cost-benefit analysis study on alcohol.

- ICAP supported a cross-national study of patterns of nonindustrial beverage alcohol consumption in Brazil, India, Mexico, Russia, Tanzania, and Zambia. The results of these studies were published in a book titled *Moonshine Markets: Issues in Unrecorded Alcohol Beverage Production and Consumption* (Haworth & Simpson, 2004). The book is part of the ICAP Series on Alcohol in Society.

---

[5] ARA is supported principally by SABMiller. Of ICAP's sponsors, Diageo also contributes to ARA projects.

- Also as part of its Series on Alcohol in Society, ICAP commissioned a book called *Drinking Occasions: Comparative Perspectives on Alcohol and Culture*, which explores when, where, how, and why people drink alcohol (Heath, 2000). Many examples are drawn from developing countries.
- ICAP sponsors support such research through their membership in SAOs.

1.6 Sharing results with the local public health community and arranging for publication as appropriate. For example:
- Diageo and Allied Domecq have an active stakeholder dialogue policy, which means sharing information and promoting discussion with stakeholders in the alcohol policy environment.
- ICAP widely disseminates all its project results and publications to public health professionals, researchers, governments, and the alcohol beverage industry.

2. Responsible Promotional and Advertising Practices

ICAP sponsors will encourage where possible:

- Strict industry compliance with all existing legislation or self-regulatory codes of practice.
- Initiatives aimed at establishing self-regulatory codes in countries where they do not exist.
- Efforts to ensure that such codes of practice adequately reflect local culture and values.
- The development of appropriate enforcement mechanisms to ensure that such codes are adhered to.

Related Activities

2.1 Ensuring compliance with all existing codes of practice/advertising regulations. For example:
- All marketing activities relating to Diageo brands must be in keeping with both the spirit and the letter of all applicable national laws, local advertising codes, and self-regulatory codes of practice. Compliance with the above is mandatory, as is compliance with the Diageo Code of Marketing Practice.
- This is a requirement of Foster's Group Limited's "Alcohol in the Community: Responsible Marketing Guidelines."
- This is a requirement of the Coors Global Commitment.

- This is a requirement of Brown-Forman's Responsible Marketing and Advertising Guidelines ("Brown-Forman's Guidelines").
- This is a requirement of Allied Domecq's company and advertising code.
- This is a requirement of Miller Brewing Company's International Market Code.
- This is a requirement of Heineken's Alcohol Policy.
- This is a requirement of all Bacardi company advertising policies.

2.2 Where no codes and regulations exist, ensuring that the parent company gives guidance regarding minimum standards. For example:
  - The Diageo Code of Marketing Practice sets out global standards for markets where local regulations may not exist, or may exist only in basic form. Code training for all those involved in marketing Diageo's brands and for its agencies is mandatory.
  - ARA has developed an advertising, packaging, and promotions code and media rules.
  - In 1997, Coors adopted a Global Commitment including sales and marketing guidelines for all international markets.
  - Brown-Forman's Guidelines contain minimum standards that apply to all international markets, even in the absence of local laws or regulations.
  - Foster's Group Limited's "Alcohol in the Community: Responsible Marketing Guidelines" are minimum standards set by the company and applicable to all international markets.
  - Allied Domecq has a Global Marketing Code to which all its employees must adhere. The code sets out global standards for markets where local regulations may not exist, or may exist only in basic form.
  - Heineken Rules and Guidelines for Commercial Communication have a section on "Training & Advice: Corporate Affairs and the Heineken Intranet."
  - Bacardi legal and external affairs managers give training and advice on Bacardi advertising codes where appropriate.

2.3 Developing advertising and promotional activities that are in keeping with local culture, religion, and traditions. For example:
  - The Diageo Code of Marketing Practice specifically warns of the need for sensitivity to cultural variations, and the company expects its marketing staff to be aware of the possibility of inadvertent cultural offense.
  - ARA developed a human resources policy framework for members and a code of business practice for all industry participants. It was

appointed to a panel drafting alcohol policy and legislation in Western Cape province, South Africa.
• This is a requirement of Brown-Forman's Guidelines.
• All ICAP sponsors supported the development of a "how-to" kit for self-regulation for countries where no codes and self-regulatory mechanisms exist (International Center for Alcohol Policies, 2002).
• This is a requirement of Bacardi's advertising codes.

2.4 Establishing processes to ensure that joint venture partners, advertising agencies, and other local partners know of the company's commitment to responsible marketing practices. For example:
• The Diageo Code of Marketing Practice specifically requires business partners to abide by the provisions of the code, and places responsibility with its marketing staff to ensure that agencies and other partners are provided with the code.
• All Coors employees and international business partners must comply with existing legislation, regulations, and self-regulatory codes of practice that are consistent with the company's Global Commitment.
• Brown-Forman's Guidelines are applicable to Brown-Forman's employees and agents.
• Allied Domecq's codes are applicable to all employees and agents. Specific training has been given to the company's marketing agency on the spirit and letter of the global marketing code.
• Compliance with Bacardi's advertising codes is applicable to all parties involved in marketing practices, including third-party distributors of its products.

2.5 Responding promptly to criticisms of advertising and promotional activities, making changes where necessary. For example:
• It is a specific requirement of the Diageo code that any criticism of marketing activities should be reported to senior management immediately. If a self-regulatory body rules against an advert for a Diageo brand, the advertising is immediately withdrawn.
• This is a requirement of Allied Domecq's Global Marketing Code.
• Brown-Forman's Guidelines require change to any activities that are not consistent with local requirements or its own minimum standards.
• Miller Brewing Company takes seriously and responds to criticisms of advertising and promotional activities.
• Bacardi takes seriously and responds promptly to criticisms of its advertising and promotional activities. Its close links with many

national SAOs and self-regulatory associations allow it to react quickly and make appropriate changes where necessary.
* Foster's Group takes seriously and responds to criticisms of its marketing activities.

2.6 Working with international and local companies to establish industry trade associations with responsibility for enforcing self-regulation. For example:
* Diageo actively supports self-regulatory organizations and trade association work globally, in addition to promoting the principles and benefits of self-regulation via membership and support of international and national trade associations.
* The SAO in Taiwan, Taiwan Beverage Alcohol Forum (TBAF),[6] includes such activities in its work plan.
* Brown-Forman's Guidelines require support of efforts to develop local industry codes where they do not exist.
* Through its involvement in major global and regional industry associations, Bacardi supports the establishment of industry associations and codes where necessary and appropriate.

2.7 Improving the effectiveness of codes through regular reviews, updating, and amendment as necessary. For example:
* An independent "compliance" audit of the Diageo Code of Marketing Practice was carried out on global marketing activities in 2001, sampling advertising for 27 brands across 47 countries, liaising with five international advertising agencies and approximately 50 of Diageo's in-market staff around the world. Both internal and external stakeholders were consulted. The new code, published in December 2002, takes into account all issues raised during this audit.
* Allied Domecq, in 2003, appointed an independent advertising review board as part of its ongoing efforts to improve industry standards in advertising and promotion for alcohol beverages. The board, consisting of three external experts and four internal senior members of staff, will meet quarterly to review and approve all company advertising and promotional materials globally across all the company brands.
* Brown-Forman's Global Guidelines are in the process of being revised. An updated version is to be released in 2005.
* ARA is a member of the Advertising Standards Authority's Advertising Standards Committee for alcohol products.

---

[6] ICAP sponsors supporting TBAF are: Allied Domecq, Diageo, and Heineken.

- Issue 9 of ICAP Reports was devoted to self-regulation practices around the world (International Center for Alcohol Policies, 2001).
- Heineken's Company Alcohol Policy and Rules and Guidelines are regularly reviewed.
- Foster's Group Limited's "Alcohol in the Community: Responsible Marketing Guidelines" are regularly reviewed, as are sponsorship and promotional protocols used by its businesses.
- Miller's advertising policies are reviewed and updated on a regular basis.
- Bacardi's advertising codes are regularly reviewed and updated.

2.8 Involving nonindustry organizations (broadcasting authorities, media owners, advertising standards authorities, consumer organizations, etc.) in self-regulatory bodies where this is appropriate/practical. For example:

- Several SAOs and all self-regulation organizations (SROs) involve nonindustry representation in the self-regulatory system.
- Allied Domecq, in 2003, appointed an independent advertising review board as part of its ongoing efforts to improve industry standards in advertising and promotion for alcohol beverages. The board, consisting of three external experts and four internal senior members of staff, will meet quarterly to review and approve all company advertising and promotional materials globally across all the company brands.

2.9 Publishing the findings of self-regulatory review bodies if appropriate. For example:

- Several SAOs and SROs publish the findings of their complaints panels.
- Allied Domecq has decided to make the Advertising Review Board process as transparent as commercially possible to ensure that a summary of meeting discussion of the review board can be shared with interested parties, including competitors, so that it can catalyze a general improvement in industry standards. Excerpts of the proceedings of the board will be posted on the company website.

3. Alcohol Education and Initiatives to Promote Sensible Drinking

ICAP sponsors will encourage:

- The researching and piloting of such initiatives in a selected number of developing countries and emerging markets.

- The sharing of "good practice" through identifying initiatives that have been successful elsewhere.
- Dialogue with government, public health professionals, and other parties to explore possibilities for cooperation and partnership on specific issues or projects.

Related Activities

3.1 Taking steps to establish a companywide alcohol policy, educating employees about sensible drinking. For example:
   - *Diageo Employee Alcohol Policy: A Guide for Employees* forms part of the induction pack for all new employees. The policy document is displayed on company premises and embedded in staff-event promotional literature.
   - FMBLI[7] in Malaysia has produced an alcohol policy for member companies, covering alcohol and the workplace issues, drink driving, and education for employees about responsible drinking.
   - Coors employee orientation includes information on responsible alcohol consumption, and Coors employees are required to make responsible decisions about their drinking.
   - Brown-Forman's Guidelines as well as related employee policies are circulated to all employees worldwide. Brown-Forman has a written policy on responsible consumption that is distributed to all management employees, *Brown-Forman's Management Policy.*
   - Foster's Group Limited's employee orientation includes information on the company's drug and alcohol policy as well as responsible alcohol consumption. Employees are required to make responsible decisions about their drinking. Guidelines for employee participation in company-sponsored receptions or promotional activities are increasingly used and promoted.
   - Allied Domecq promotes a set of minimum standards for all employees worldwide. Its national companies can produce policies to reflect their own needs as long as the basic elements are covered. All employees also receive a booklet "Alcohol and You," which gives both health advice and the company position on a range of social issues.
   - Heineken's Alcohol and Work project has introduced the basics of alcohol policy in operating companies. The Alcohol and Work project has been reinforced through the organization of five regional conferences and a worldwide conference to convey these policies.

---

[7] ICAP sponsors supporting FMBLI are: Allied Domecq, Diageo, and Heineken.

- Miller regularly issues guidelines for employee participation in company-sponsored receptions or promotional activities.
- Bacardi companies regularly educate employees on sensible drinking. Many Bacardi companies have specific policies regarding the responsible consumption of beverage alcohol.
- ICAP, through a process of wide consultation, has created tools that will help governments develop effective alcohol policies and will assist researchers, governments, and others with ethical issues governing alcohol research. These tools include The Geneva Partnership: Towards a Global Charter, Building Blocks and the Dublin Principles.

3.2 Ensuring that operating company country managers know of their parent company's views on responsible drinking and related issues such as drink driving. For example:
- Ensuring adherence to Diageo policies on responsible drinking and marketing code compliance is the responsibility of general managers and marketing directors of each country in which Diageo operate. Policies are shared via company Intranet and by proactive workshop training.
- All Coors international staff have been trained on corporate commitments to responsible sales and marketing under its Global Commitment.
- Brown-Forman's country managers are aware of the company's views through its Guidelines, Management Policy, and other related communications.
- Allied Domecq managers are fully aware of company views on responsible drinking and related issues. In 2004, Allied Domecq produced its first Social Report that looks directly into these issues, along with many more. This report has been communicated to all country managers.
- Presentations at company conferences are part of Heineken's in-house training. Alcohol policy is an important pillar of the Heineken responsibility management program.
- All relevant Miller employees receive training in responsible advertising, including SABMiller's views on the subject.
- Bacardi employee training programs include training devoted to responsible drinking and drink driving issues.

3.3 Identifying priority issues for a given country. For example:
- Diageo has a program that encourages alcohol education initiatives to be put in place by the company in every country where it has an operational base.

- ARA supports the Horizon Life Skills education project, reaching approximately 100,000 students per year. It also funded Phase I of a major project to educate parents on how to support the life skills teachings their children receive.
- ARA lobbied local governments to incorporate life skills education in the normal school curriculum; the objective was achieved in that tenders were awarded for curriculum development.
- ARA is supporting the development of a licensee training program in collaboration with state bodies and standards and qualifications authorities.
- Campaigns against drink driving have been carried out in Thailand and Hong Kong with the support of Allied Domecq, Diageo, and Heineken.
- Allied Domecq Mexico and partner National Council on Addictions (CONADIC) have introduced an education project in order to prevent alcoholism in the native Indian population. The project has been developed in the following states of the republic: Chiapas, Jalisco, Mexico, Nayarit, Puebla, Queretaro, San Luis Potosi, Tamaulipas and Veracruz.
- Brown-Forman participates locally in South Africa in the "Stop the Violence" campaign, which includes an element to combat alcohol abuse.
- The Heineken Company Alcohol Policy advocates a dialogue with government and health organizations to work together in preventing abuse.
- Through intensive participation in national SAOs, Bacardi secures proper attention, focus, and support for priorities in markets. Furthermore, Bacardi participates with and educates employees accordingly about issues raised by industry trade associations.

3.4 Identifying possible partners for initiatives. For example:
- The vast majority of Diageo-supported alcohol education initiatives are based on partnerships. For example, a responsible server training project initiated in São Paulo, Brazil, was carried out in partnership with the national training agency (SEAC) and restaurant trade organizations. Other partners have included police forces, educational establishments, and road safety organizations.
- ARA sponsors a postgraduate research fellowship at FARR to build capacity in the field of alcohol research and prevention.
- ICAP's work is always in partnership with the beverage alcohol industry and public health researchers. In addition, it often includes other actors such as governments or NGOs interested in alcohol issues.

• In 1999, ICAP hosted a meeting in Washington, DC, between the beverage alcohol industry and public health researchers from developing countries to help identify meaningful ways for both to collaborate in developing countries. As a result of this meeting, two projects were identified and funded: one regarding alcohol legislation and its enforcement, and the other on noncommercial alcohol (outcome since published—see 1.5).
• In some national markets, Bacardi is encouraging initiatives with NGOs in the field of alcohol education.

3.5 Researching and piloting responsible drinking initiatives in such markets, with appropriate local partners.

Projects Run by SAOs/Industry Associations

ARA, South Africa

• Sponsoring research undertaken by the Institute for Health Training and Development, South Africa, to establish needs of parents for life skills education. Cosponsored a training workshop run by the Centre of National and Provincial Personnel from the Departments of Health and Social Development.
• Sponsoring workshops for the African National Congress Youth League in its efforts to develop policies and programs for substance abuse prevention.
• Developing a training program for the retail and hospitality industry.
• "Buddy" programs on university and technikon campuses promoting responsible alcohol consumption and behavior.
• Cosponsoring, with the Department of Transport, such initiatives as Arrive Alive campaigns aimed at reducing alcohol-associated road accidents.
• Sponsoring community interventions—for example, in the Lebanon farming community in the Western Cape—in the areas of education, rehabilitation, and prevention.
• Supporting FAS prevention campaigns through FARR with the collaboration of the Department of Health, the Directorate of Mental Health and Substance Abuse, and provincial departments of health.
• Conducting a national campaign to prevent illegal underage drinking.

TBAF, Taiwan

• Runs anti-drink driving initiatives in Taipei.

FISAC, Mexico

- Administers a middle and high school education/responsibility campaign.
- Publishes a newsletter about preventing addiction and promoting a healthy lifestyle.
- Supports responsible alcohol consumption workshops aimed at different professional disciplines, in collaboration with the Mexican Ministry of Health, Ministry of Education, National Parents Association, and public and private companies.

SASPI, India[8]

- Developed an alcohol quiz.
- Created a guide for employers on how to create a company alcohol policy, which was distributed to over 500 companies in India.
- Supported and helped to create a pilot drink-drive campaign in Bangalore in partnership with ICAP, the Bangalore Agenda Task Force, the National Institute for Mental Health and Neurosciences and the Global Road Safety Partnership.

Projects Undertaken by ICAP Sponsors on Their Own (with appropriate local partners, but no other drinks companies involved)

Diageo

- Diageo South Africa supports anti-drink driving programs during holiday seasons plus a special campaign to prevent pedestrian deaths as part of the government-run Arrive Alive campaign.
- In 1999–2003, Diageo companies ran anti-drink driving campaigns in Brazil, Cameroon, Kenya, Nigeria, South Africa, Thailand, and Venezuela. Since then, Diageo has supported "Safe Roads," the World Health Organization theme for World Health Day 2004, by running over 35 such initiatives worldwide, many of them in emerging markets. Further information is available on www.diageo.com.
- Diageo currently chairs the Global Road Safety Partnership in Ghana and in Nigeria has received recognition for its commitment and contribution

---

[8] SASPI was supported in part by the following ICAP sponsors: Allied Domecq, Bacardi, and Diageo. SASPI ceased operating in 2003 and has been replaced by the individual company efforts of four international beverage alcohol companies.

to anti-drink-drive education in the form of honorary membership of the Federal Road Safety Corps.

- Diageo Brazil runs the Bartender Project in São Paulo. The project aims to provide unemployed young people with the skills they need to find work in the hospitality and tourist trades, combined with a robust alcohol server responsibility module. Bartender training projects have also been established in Kenya, Korea, Nigeria, Thailand, Uruguay, and Venezuela, training over 10,000 bartenders.
- Diageo has signed up to the United Nations Global Compact, becoming the largest drinks company to commit to United Nations' principles in the areas of human rights, labor standards, and the environment.

Allied Domecq

- Supports project in Thailand where university students are sponsored to design marketing plans to curb drink driving.
- Allied Domecq Mexico and partner National Council on Addictions (CONADIC) have introduced an education project in order to prevent alcoholism in the native Indian population. The project has been developed in the following states of the republic: Chiapas, Jalisco, Mexico, Nayarit, Puebla, Queretaro, San Luis Potosi, Tamaulipas, and Veracruz.

Foster's Group Limited

- Foster's has leveraged major sporting sponsorships to raise awareness about responsible drinking and driving especially in connection with such major events, e.g., Foster's international link with Grand Prix auto racing. Ongoing dialogue by Foster's Group executives with government organizations involved in anti-drink-drive programs has assisted the company to produce responsible consumption messages in line with and reinforcing official government messages.

South African Breweries

- Sponsors a major "Think, Before You Drink, Before You Drive" advertising campaign over the Easter holiday period and over the festive season. The campaign supports the government-run Arrive Alive campaign and SAB has also donated funds directly to the government for the campaign.

- Provided seed capital for the establishment of the only Alcohol and Drug Abuse Prevention, Rehabilitation and Research Centre in Bloemfontein, Free State province.
- Provided seed capital for the establishment of the Institute for Health Training and Development in Bedfordview, Gauteng province, an organization that offers training programs for those dealing with substance abuse.
- Sponsors programs run by the South African National Council on Alcoholism and Drug Dependence, which include peer-counseling and primary prevention education for young people through stories.
- Sponsored the development of life skills education in North-West and Gauteng provinces under the leadership of Dr. van der Merwe.

Heineken

- Initiating self-regulation of commercial communication in St. Lucia and Ghana.

Miller

- Miller distributes responsible drinking advice for parents in English and Spanish called Parent Guide. Miller also sponsors server training and campus abuse prevention programs.

ICAP

- ICAP supported an early identification and lifestyle counseling project for problem drinking in Chile. Partners included the Ministry of Health in Chile, the Faculty of Pharmaceutical Sciences, University of Chile, and the International University Exchange in Washington, D.C.
- ICAP commissioned five papers on how young people learn about alcohol in southern Africa, Latin America, Europe, Australasia, and China. These papers formed the basis for ICAP's book, *Learning About Drinking,* which addresses the main influences that come to bear on a young person's decision to drink alcohol (Houghton & Roche, 2001).
- ICAP supported a pilot life skills project in South Africa and Botswana for primary school children. Its aim was to assist young people in making responsible lifestyle choices. The project received technical support from the Program on Mental Health at the WHO.
- ICAP supports the World Bank/International Federation of Red Cross and Red Crescent Societies' Global Road Safety Partnership (GRSP), which

is a broadly based initiative involving public and private sectors in efforts to reduce road traffic casualties, with special emphasis on developing countries. In 2003, ICAP's president served as chairman of GRSP.

3.6 Ensuring that examples of successful initiatives are shared through ICAP across the industry for possible application elsewhere.
- The Corporate Citizenship section of Diageo's website www. diageo.com was revised, refreshed, and updated to aid successful sharing of best practice.

APPENDIX 2: ICAP SPONSORS: THE SCOPE OF COMPANY CODES OF PRACTICE

Provisions Against	Allied Domecq	Brown-Forman	Coors	Diageo	Foster's	Heineken	SABMiller
Encouragement of Immoderate/ Excessive Drinking	y	y	y	y	y	y	y
Targeting of Minors	y	y	y	y	y	y	y
Placement at Events Where Audience Majority is Underage	y	y	y	y		y	y
Subjects in Adverts Being Under 25	y	y	y	y	y	y	y
Implication of Enhanced Ability (Physical)	y	y	y	y	y	y	y
Implication of Enhanced Ability (Sexual)	y	y	y	y	y	y	y
Implication of Enhanced Ability (Social)	y	y	y	y	y	y	y
Depiction of Unsafe Conditions (Driving)	y	y	y	y	y	y	y
Depiction of Intoxication	y	y	y	y	y	y	y
Association with Violence	y	y	y	y	y	y	y
Association with Illegal Activity/Drugs	y	y	y	y	y	y	y
Claim Unsubstantiated Medical and/or Therapeutic Benefits	y	y	y	y	y	y	y
Depiction of Religious Symbols	y	y	y	y			
Emphasis of High Alcohol Content	y	y	y	y	y	y	y
Negative Portrayal of Abstinence	y		y	y	y	y	y

Companies have also enacted the following specific advertising prohibitions.

Allied Domecq

- Use of symbols that are culturally offensive to ethnic and gender groups.

Brown-Forman

- Use of any symbol, language, gesture, cartoon, animated character, or child's toy intended to appeal to minors.

- Use of sexual slang, situations, or depictions that offend local standards of decency.
- Use of symbols likely to offend a particular ethnic group.
- Use of product name or logo on clothing, toys, game equipment, or other items intended for minors.

Coors

- Use of imagery considered demeaning to any individual or group.
- Use of imagery considered offensive to the local culture.
- Depiction of littering or inappropriate disposal of beer containers.
- Promotion of product through boycotts of ethnic, religious, or national groups.

Diageo

- Use of symbols, images, or figures that are likely to offend or demean any ethnic, cultural, or minority group.
- Use of brand names, logos, or trademarks on children's clothing, toys, games, or other materials intended for use primarily by persons under the legal purchasing age.

Foster's Group Limited

- Use of brand names, logos, or trademarks for use on children's clothing, toys, games, or other materials intended for use primarily by persons under the legal purchasing age.
- Depiction of littering or other improper disposal of beer containers.
- Has in place a promotional protocol that covers and enforces the responsible representation of its brands in:
  - Product placement/seeding in broadcast/telecast
  - Competitions/promotions by external partners that intend to feature its brands
  - In-house competitions/promotions managed by the company or in collaboration with third party
  - Fundraising directly by the company or other agencies that intend to use its brands by agreement
  - Product donations made by the company to external parties, e.g., charities, to ensure that they are promoted in a responsible context
- Has in place sponsorship guidelines that detail the responsibility requirements of company sponsorships

Heineken

- Relation of brand to sports linked with aggression or violence.
- Sponsorship of individual sports teams or motor vehicle events, or use of athletes in advertising.

SABMiller

SABMiller has developed an Alcohol Manifesto specifying that the following apply to all group companies:

- In addition to complying with existing national legislation, statutory regulations and industry self-regulatory codes, group companies adhere to the SABMiller plc Code of Commercial Communication.
- Internal compliance committees monitor and review commercial communications and ensure that these comply with the letter and the spirit of the code.
- Wherever appropriate, SABMiller plc group companies include responsible messages in commercial communication.

In addition to the provisions noted in the list above, the SABMiller Code of Commercial Communications includes the following provisions:

- Commercial communication must:
  - be legal, decent, honest and truthful, and conform to accepted principles of fair competition and good business practice
  - be in keeping with local cultural values
  - be prepared with a due sense of social responsibility and be based on principles of fairness and good faith
  - comply with all regulatory requirements
  - not be unethical or otherwise impugn human dignity or integrity
  - be mindful of sensitivities relating to culture, gender, race, and religion
  - not employ themes, images, symbols or figures, which are likely to be considered offensive, derogatory or demeaning
- Commercial communication may not depict or include pregnant women.

REFERENCES

Grant, M. (Ed.). (1998). *Alcohol and emerging markets: Patterns, problems, and responses.* Philadelphia: Brunner/Mazel.
Haworth, A., & Simpson, R. (Eds.). (2004). *Moonshine markets: Issues in unrecorded alcohol beverage production and consumption.* Philadelphia: Brunner-Routledge.

Heath, D. (2000). *Drinking occasions: Comparative perspectives on alcohol and culture.* Philadelphia: Brunner/Mazel.

Houghton, E., & Roche, A. M. (Eds.). (2001). *Learning about drinking.* Philadelphia: Brunner-Routledge.

International Center for Alcohol Policies (ICAP). (2000). *Life skills education in South Africa and Botswana.* Washington, DC: Author.

International Center for Alcohol Policies (ICAP). (2001). *Self-regulation of beverage alcohol advertising.* ICAP Reports 9. Washington, DC: Author.

International Center for Alcohol Policies (ICAP). (2002). *Self-regulation and alcohol: A toolkit for emerging markets and the developing world.* Washington, DC: Author.

Pedlow, G. (1998). Alcohol in emerging markets: Identifying the most appropriate role for the alcohol beverage industry. In M. Grant (Ed.), *Alcohol and emerging markets: Patterns, problems, and responses* (pp. 333–351). Philadelphia: Brunner/Mazel.

Chapter 17

Conclusion

Hurst Hannum

Although alcohol beverages provide considerable personal pleasure and social benefit, they can also cause serious personal and social harm if consumed irresponsibly. If one accepts that it is possible to have a healthy community in which alcohol is consumed, then one needs to examine the conditions in which this can occur. This will also require that the government, the alcohol industry, and individuals sacrifice certain self-interests for the common good. Each must act in a manner that does not undermine the public good, exercising social responsibility. Although each player has his or her own role, all should work in collaboration as far as possible.

Many areas of agreement are evident from the various contributions to this volume. These include the nature and goals of alcohol policies, the meaning of social responsibility, and the role of partnerships.

THE NATURE AND GOALS OF ALCOHOL POLICIES

Although it seems obvious, it is worth repeating that developing an appropriate alcohol policy involves complex health, privacy, revenue, and cultural issues. There are no simple solutions or formulas, and neither unfettered, unregulated alcohol consumption nor complete prohibition is feasible or desirable. Although we can identify some general ethical principles that should be followed—such as honesty and transparency—alcohol policies also must reflect the specific cultural, social, and political realities of different societies. It is because of this complexity that there can be no one-size-fits-all model of reasonable alcohol policy. That, however, does not detract from the fact that alcohol policies should be based on broad stakeholder agreement as articulated, for example, in the Dublin Principles (International Center for Alcohol Policies and National College of Ireland, 1997) and the Geneva Partnership document (International Center for Alcohol Policies, 2000).

The minimum goal of any appropriate alcohol policy is to reduce alcohol-related harm, but there remains a great deal of disagreement as to whether this should be the only goal. For example, is decreasing overall consumption of alcohol also a legitimate goal? Or encouraging moderate drinking? Or protecting young people from the sort of risky behavior in which young people have always engaged?

One cannot identify goals without identifying more specifically the target group for the policy. Different groups require different policies, and attempting to lump them all together is likely to create unnecessary tension or lead proponents of various policies to act at cross-purposes. In particular, policies need to address at least three categories of drinkers separately: children (those below the legal drinking age), young adults (who may drink legally but are still considered immature), and mature adults.

Dealing with children is relatively easy, since all agree that illegal drinking should be reduced to the absolute minimum possible. Although there may be some disagreement as to who should be considered "a child," there is no disagreement that there should be a minimum age for consuming alcohol and that at least unsupervised drinking below that age should be combated through education, persuasion, and penal sanctions where necessary.

There also seems to be considerable consensus as to the freedom of mature adults to drink responsibly, as they see fit, subject only to reasonable restrictions on alcohol availability. Abuse of alcohol that leads to harm (e.g., driving while under the influence of alcohol or behaving violently against others) could be dealt with through after-the-fact sanctions in the same way that other harmful or criminal behavior is punished. Thus, one's behavior in driving recklessly or being disorderly in public would be punished, as opposed to one's status as having legally consumed alcohol.

"Young people," on the other hand, present a much more problematic case. It does not seem sufficient to lump together 14- to 25-year-olds and consider them all as "young people at risk." Common sense suggests that at least the extremes of this age range must be treated very differently, and the age at which it is legal to drink is certainly relevant. Of course, education is important, but we must recognize that young people often conduct themselves unwisely; they engage in risky behavior, defy authority, and assert their independence in a variety of ways. One should also not confuse alcohol abuse as a *symptom* of rebellion with alcohol use as a *cause* of young people's problems. Both descriptions are no doubt true in part, but different responses must be developed to each set of problems.

Although some may not like the analogy, there are certainly similarities between the way young people drive automobiles and the way they use alcohol. Young people are not familiar with the potential dangers of either activity, whether it is driving too fast and recklessly or drinking too much, too quickly.

It would be possible for society to develop a totally safe car by imposing higher standards on automobile manufacturing or to significantly decrease traffic deaths by drastically reducing the legal speed limit; however, neither approach has been adopted. As should be the case with alcohol, the safety and public health consequences of dangerous driving are balanced against the social utility (including pleasure) that is derived from driving. Although the balance need not always be struck in the same way in every country, perhaps the debate over alcohol policy would be clearer if stakeholders discussed more transparently whether they see alcohol as a social good (like automobiles) or whether their view of alcohol policy is tinged with a degree of moral disapproval that often tilts the balance toward "protecting" young people from themselves when they drink. A neutral approach would be more consistent with the way young people are treated in other situations, such as driving, where they engage in risky behavior. Once they have acquired licenses, young drivers are no longer "protected" in any formal way, even though evidence clearly shows that they are at greater risk for accidents than are those with more experience.

THE MEANING OF SOCIAL RESPONSIBILITY

Everyone has social responsibility. Individuals are responsible to themselves and others for their behavior, but they need information and guidance to help them define the appropriate extent of that responsibility.

Education is clearly a necessary, but not sufficient, component in any program to promote the responsible use of alcohol. It should not be limited to schools or other formal educational systems, nor should education be limited to children. Family and community are responsible for facilitating the development of their children and increasing the welfare of all their members. Schools have an important responsibility in educating their charges, but parents and peer groups are among the most important educators when it comes to drinking. In fact, a number of formal alcohol education programs in schools appear to be rather ineffective. Education normally includes the provision of accurate information, as well as the inculcation of social values, and alcohol education should follow the same pattern. But we also must recognize the limits of formal education—it does not automatically lead to more responsible behavior, whether with regard to alcohol, sex, or corporate standards of honesty.

Scientists and public health professionals are responsible for providing good science, free of their own ideological or moral biases. Neither public health nor science provides direct answers to most of the policy questions addressed in this volume; however, each is responsible for providing accurate information that will enable the development of sound strategies to achieve the goals decided on by other sectors of society.

The alcohol industry must accept that it has a social responsibility over and above that of meeting shareholders' short-term needs. The beverage alcohol industry should be responsible to its consumers and the public at large, both because responsible behavior is ethical and because, in the long run, it is self-serving. If alcohol is seen as a dangerous product whose abuse causes widespread social damage, the consequent public, media, and public health backlash will be damaging and sales will suffer. Therefore, the alcohol industry is obliged to regulate itself in order to maintain market share and consumer goodwill. Moreover, if the industry regulates itself, it may achieve agreed-upon goals more successfully than if governments force regulation upon it.

The theme of this book has been that it is not imperative for the beverage alcohol industry to chase higher annual shareholder dividends at the expense of the public good. Indeed, the exercise of responsibility by encouraging their consumers to drink sensibly is in the long-term interest of the companies. There will always be rogue enterprises that will not follow such principles, but the sponsors of the International Center for Alcohol Policies and many other multinational players in this field appear determined to follow the route of responsible corporate citizenship. These efforts should be supported until they become the industry norm.

As has been made clear, the beverage alcohol industry undertakes specific activities directed at promoting more responsible consumption. These have been outlined in chapter 10 and include promoting education programs, fostering alternatives to drinking and driving, regulating advertising and marketing, training servers, and sponsoring research. Chapter 16 describes the industry's efforts in emerging markets and developing countries in the field of data collection and research, promotional and advertising practices, alcohol education, and initiatives to promote sensible drinking. In addition, companies sponsor social projects, which are not directly aimed at countering possible harms from drinking, such as Diageo's Water of Life project in 34 countries and SABMiller's collaboration with the South African Department of Water Affairs and Forestry to supply potable water to rural areas in that country.

Whatever the roles of other actors, governments retain the power to define, regulate, and enforce ethical or "appropriate" behavior, and a democratic government is ultimately responsible for balancing all of the different interests identified in this volume, keeping in mind the basic rights of individuals and the need to protect society. Government provides the context in which many alcohol policies are developed, and it should arrive at its decisions in a manner that is transparent and responsive to all of its constituents, not just to those who are noisy or powerful. Any reduction in the amount of irresponsible drinking, however, is unlikely to occur until individuals see merit in adopting attitudes and behaviors that contribute to the greater good, rather than acting purely selfishly. This means that people need to accept that the government has a right to intervene where an individual's drinking causes harm to him- or herself or others, or where it imposes unreasonable social or financial costs on the community. In such circumstances, industry also has a duty to support appropriate government interventions.

THE ROLE OF PARTNERSHIPS

Partnerships among the industry, the public health and scientific communities, government, and consumer advocates are both possible and necessary in order to achieve the goals of developing and implementing an appropriate and effective alcohol policy. Of course, some unilateral measures by various sectors are also needed: government regulates the terms under which alcohol is made and consumed; industry self-regulation need not wait for partners; and consumer and other nongovernmental campaigns of persuasion can be undertaken by such groups on their own. But an effective alcohol policy—like most other social policies—is likely to depend on cooperation and coordination among all those concerned, not simply on the unilateral imposition of norms.

A basic tenet of conflict resolution is to try to achieve a "win-win" solution. Such a solution may not be immediately obvious, and achieving it is largely about identifying and accommodating diverse interests, as opposed to merely defending positions. It is too simplistic to suggest that one is either part of the problem or part of the solution, whether the subject is the war against terrorism or responsible alcohol policy.

Effective partnerships may be the best way to ensure that the interests of all of the relevant stakeholders can be articulated and discussed openly. Being ethical and acting responsibly means being honest, transparent, consistent, and tolerant of those with different values. Only with such tolerance can there be mutual respect among those with different viewpoints. That respect can, in turn, lead to ethical partnerships and to the ultimate goal of a sound, effective alcohol policy that balances the interests of all concerned to the greatest extent possible.

Experience shows that, with goodwill and effort, it is possible for key stakeholders to work together to prevent and reduce alcohol-related harm, without abandoning their individual objectives (International Center for Alcohol Policies, 2000). Adversarial relationships between the stakeholders only serve to weaken initiatives. While acknowledging differences, those involved need to show mutual respect, trust, and transparency for fruitful partnerships to be formed.

REFERENCES

International Center for Alcohol Policies (ICAP). (2000). *The Geneva partnership on alcohol: Towards a global charter.* Washington, DC: Author.

International Center for Alcohol Policies (ICAP) and National College of Ireland. (1997). *The Dublin principles of cooperation among the beverage alcohol industry, governments, scientific researchers, and the public health community.* Washington, DC: Authors.

Index

Corporate Social Responsibility and Alcohol: The Need and Potential for Partnership

By Grant, M., & O'Connor, J. (Eds.). (2005).
New York: Routledge.
[Hardback; ISBN# 0-415-94948-3]

Book Review by Manoj Sharma, University of Cincinnati

These days the corporate companies are continually being held accountable for being active and contributing meaningfully to the communities in which they exist, besides achieving their financial worth and goals. This is known as corporate social responsibility (CSR). The issues involving CSR and alcohol are complex and are the focus of this book. The International Center for Alcohol Policies (ICAP), which is a not-for-profit international organization funded by 10 international alcohol beverage companies, has commissioned this book. Most of the contributions in the book are from presenters at the "Alcohol, Ethics, and Society" international conference held in Dublin in October 2002.

The first chapter in the book is an introduction by the editors that presents the background of the book and how it has been conceptualized. The second chapter defines CSR, its history and issues. The three major components of CSR have been identified as (1) the basic values, ethics, policies and practices of the company's business; (2) the voluntary contributions made by a company to community development; and (3) management of social and environmental issues by the company and its business partners involving the acquisition of raw products, staff welfare, product sale, use or disposal. The third chapter deals with the issue of product safety where a company's products have the potential to do harm. The chapter discusses the chemical industry, tobacco industry, breast-milk substitutes, automobile industry, and pharmacological industry. The fourth chapter focuses on different partnership perspectives for CSR in beverage alcohol industry. Partnerships with government, intergovernmental organizations, private sector, non-governmental organizations, and the research community are discussed.

The fifth chapter talks about the role of partnerships in alcohol policy development. The chapter discusses the results of the survey done in 2002 covering 48 countries in which perspectives on various issues relating to alcohol policy were discussed (Babor & Xuan, 2004). It was interesting to note that the opinion regarding the role of the alcohol industry was equally divided with half of the nations viewing the alcohol industry as a viable partner and half did not. The chapter also discusses the issue of conflict of interest, which is of paramount importance with regard to the role of the alcohol industry. However, this section could have been expanded and some parallels regarding conflict of interest and tobacco industry also included (Bero, 2005).

The sixth chapter is titled, "Drinking education: Negatives or optimizing potential." This chapter discusses the pleasures of alcohol and how public health groups place the harms of alcohol foremost. It also discusses the trends of drinking in youth and educational programs for youth. The role of theory in designing such educational programs (Sharma, 2005) could have been stressed more in this chapter. The seventh chapter focuses on findings on issues pertaining to marketing and promotion of alcohol to youth. The findings of the World Health Organization's meeting held in May 2002 in Valencia, Spain on this topic are presented. The eighth chapter presents a perspective from New Zealand on governmental regulation, CSR, and rights and responsibilities of the individual.

The ninth chapter is about CSR and its role on alcohol policies. A case study of Coors Brewing Company has been presented in this chapter. The tenth chapter presents practice issues with regard to CSR within the beverage alcohol industry. A number of alcohol beverage companies have made efforts to promote responsible drinking and have formed what are known as social aspects organizations (SAO). There are over 30 social aspects organizations in North America, Europe, Australasia, and Africa. Issues of brand marketing, advertising, self-regulation by the industry and research are also discussed. The eleventh chapter discusses the issues of responsible drinking promotion programs. This is a very well written chapter that discusses contextual factors which have an impact on alcohol advertising, product innovations in marketing, internet sales, television, film, and music video advertisements, print media advertisements, and general principles of good alcohol advertising. The twelfth chapter is a brief account written by a person who has been involved with alcohol advertising for over 20 years and discusses various aspects of alcohol advertisements.

Chapter thirteen is about setting standards when it comes to marketing beverage alcohol. The chapter emphasizes the need for the alcohol industry to take responsibility with regard to advertising and marketing its products responsibly. Chapter fourteen discusses the issue of abusive drinking on college campuses. Binge drinking and drinking and driving are important problems on college campuses (Knight, Wechsler, Kuo, Seibring, Weitzman, & Schukit, 2002). In this context a three-way partnership between campus, community, and industry can prove to be very useful. Research-based strategies have been underscored in this regard, which is praiseworthy. Chapter fifteen is about alcohol education. The importance of behavior change with regard to harmful drinking behaviors has been underscored. Alcohol education programs for the general public and for "at-risk" populations have been presented. Interventions in school, university, community, and worksite settings have been discussed. Interventions that are targeted as opposed to being broad, having clear and measurable objectives, and those utilizing multiple approaches have been generally found to be more effective.

Chapter sixteen presents a framework for CSR. The framework was developed by the International Center for Alcohol Policies (ICAP) Board of Directors in 1998. The framework includes three sections, namely, understanding perceptions of alcohol and patterns of consumption, responsible promotional and advertising practices, and alcohol education and initiatives to promote sensible drinking. Three case studies, the first one pertaining to critical research needs, the second one pertaining to compliance, and the third one pertaining to partnerships are also presented in the chapter. The final, concluding chapter re-emphasizes the role of CSR and partnerships in addressing the issue of alcohol.

The book is a very good compilation of chapters that bring in issues of ethics, business and health. This would be a good book for graduate students and other scholars interested in understanding the issues related to CSR and partnerships between college campuses, communities, and the alcohol industry. The book would also be relevant for administrators in academic and community settings who are looking for collaborations with the alcohol industry.

References

Babor, T. & Xuan, Z. (2004). Alcohol policy research and grey literature. *Nordisk Alcohol & Narkotikatidskrift, 21 (English Supplement)*, 125-127.

Bero, L. A. (2005). Tobacco industry manipulation of research. *Public Health Reports, 120*, 200-208.

Knight, J. R., Wechsler, H., Kuo, M., Seibring, M., Weitzman, E. R., & Schuckit, M. A. (2002). Alcohol abuse and dependence among U.S. college students. *Journal of Studies on Alcohol, 63*, 263-270.

Sharma, M. (2005). Improving interventions for prevention and control of alcohol use in college students. [Editorial]. *Journal of Alcohol and Drug Education, 49 (2)*, 3-6.